Literacy Programs for Adults With Developmental Disabilities

One day with a great teacher is better than a thousand
days of intense study.
—*Japanese Proverb*

Literacy Programs for Adults With Developmental Disabilities

Gerard Giordano, Ph.D.

New Mexico State University—Las Cruces

SINGULAR PUBLISHING GROUP, INC.
SAN DIEGO · LONDON

Singular Publishing Group, Inc.
4284 41st Street
San Diego, California 92105-1197

19 Compton Terrace
London, N1 2UN, UK

© 1996 by Singular Publishing Group, Inc.

Typeset in 10/12 Cheltenham Book by So Cal Graphics
Printed in the United States of America by McNaughton & Gunn

Library of Congress Cataloging-in-Publication Data

Giordano, Gerard
  Literacy programs for adults with developmental disabilities/
Giordano, Gerard
    p. cm.
  Includes bibliographical references and index.
  ISBN 1-56593-629-9
  1. Learning disabled—Education—United States—Language arts.
2. Handicapped—Education—United States—Language arts. 3. Adult education—United States. 4. Literacy programs—United States.
I. Title.
LC4818.5.G56   1996   95–43149
374'.012—dc20   CIP

Contents

Preface

For years I had been running everyday at lunch time. But a change in my schedule obstructed this routine. I had to run in the early morning instead. I planned a new route, across several miles of rural, southwestern villages and chili fields. My bones, muscles, and joints protested against the unaccustomed jarring of morning exercise. But there were no cars. The sunrises were marvelous. And the odors of breakfasts and the glimpses of families awakening altered common occurrences into poetic encounters. I ran along the same route that Don Juan de Oñate, the Spanish Conquistador, traveled 400 years earlier. I felt genuinely privileged. Had it not been for Lucifer, I would have grown to love running at dawn.

Lucifer was the largest, most muscular, and most aggressive dog I had ever observed. He was confined in a wire fence yard, adjacent to a deteriorating hacienda with turquoise trim. As I ran by that fence each day, Lucifer would throw himself angrily at me, biting and clawing at the thin metal separating us. He would pursue me along the fence, leaving glistening trails of saliva at the points where he had smashed into the wire.

As weeks passed, I became less startled by Lucifer's ferocious antics. I would approach his yard cautiously, but with the confidence that he could not break through the restraining wire. This was my attitude on a spring morning just before dawn. For several hundred yards I had been looking ahead at the house, the yard, and the fence. In the marginal light of the not yet risen sun, I could discern the still, poised shape of Lucifer. Following the predictable script of our daily ritual, he would wait until I was parallel with him before exhibiting his predatory rage. Habituated to this schedule, I came closer and closer, never interrupting the rhythm of my running stride. Consequently, it was not until I was within ten yards that I realized that Lucifer was outside the fence.

The dog, completely still, seemed to register my sudden terror. I slowed my pace, searching for a tree to climb or a place to retreat. But there was no place. So I looked about for any object with which to defend myself. To my side was a thin, bent branch from a pecan tree. Dried leaves were still fixed to it. The branch was brittle, able to be snapped with a single hand. As I lunged for the fragile twig, Lucifer attacked.

Grasping the branch in one hand, I clutched dust and gravel from the roadside with the other. When I had raised myself with these weapons, Lucifer was so close that I could smell his breath. I simultaneously poked his eyes with the branch while hurling dirt at them.

The dog was stunned.

I retreated several steps and grabbed another handful of dirt. Lucifer recovered and lunged. Again, I poked with the stick and threw the gravel. But Lucifer was more cautious. Anticipating my attack, he dodged away from it. Along the length of Lucifer's property, I stepped backwards, poking his eyes and throwing dirt. And eventually, poking and throwing, I escaped.

On the following day, I resolved to run along my usual route. I attempted to assure myself that Lucifer would not be loose. He had always been confined prior to the previous day, and logic convinced me that he would be confined again. I would not be intimidated from running my usual course. And if he were loose, I would change my path well before he could attack.

I spoke to myself in this manner as I approached the turquoise trimmed hacienda. As I had predicted, Lucifer was confined on that day. And he was confined on the subsequent days on which I ran past that animal's yard. Lucifer remained as aggressive as ever. And I maintained my routine, running along the identical route that I'd run before that terrifying incident.

But my attitude had changed. A casual observer wouldn't have discerned the change. I never again passed by Lucifer without first assuring myself that he was secure within the fence. And as I passed each time, I rehearsed tactics for evading him or defending myself, should he escape.

Inverted Priorities?

A decision about how to survive an encounter with an enraged animal is likely to be expedient—one will focus one's decision on the best thing to do at the time. To ensure that the choices one makes are correct, one would hope that the decision is "scientific," reflecting the careful assessment of factual information relevant to the incident at hand.

Though encounters with enraged animals are likely to be expedient, there will be encounters in other areas of one's life where the course that should be followed can be equally difficult to predict. In the case of teaching reading to adults with disabilities, should instructors be prepared to make decisions that are expedient or scientific? Before this question can be answered, one must anticipate the type of situation likely to be encountered in adult reading instruction.

Some instructors think that the teaching of reading is comparable to instruction in chemistry or engineering—fields based on scientifically devised facts that can be circumscribed, counted, and weighed. When taught with an emphasis on phonics, vocabulary drills, and word patterns, reading education may seem similar to such fields.

But science teachers don't characterize science education as an encyclopedic compilation of facts. These teachers view it as the development of methods of inquiry. Similarly, social studies educators argue that their field is only incidentally concerned with records and archives. Like the physical sciences, disciplines within the social studies such as history, anthropology, political science, sociology, or geography are investigative techniques that comprise opportunities to train students about solving problems. The process of inquiry rather than the compilation of minutia is the focus of learning in social studies education as well as science education.

The widespread availability of instructional materials organized into problem-solving approaches is evidence that these views are popular not only in science and social studies education but in English composition, foreign language, literature, mathematics, health science, and other areas of learning. There may have been a tradition among some teachers that identified the internalization of facts as the goal of learning. But instructors in many academic disciplines are inverting this tradition, transforming learning into a dynamic process of communication, inquiry, and problem solving.

Could there also be an opportunity to invert the traditional literacy curriculum for adults with disabilities? Place yourself in the position of a teacher instructing adults who are illiterate. Suppose some learners in your program have mastered the fundamental rules for pronouncing printed words. The learners in this group have systematically completed drills that reflect all of the competencies within a structured skills-based program. However, these learners have never developed the most elementary notions about reading functionally. Are you at all distressed about this group?

Suppose there are other learners who have not mastered any academic skills. They cannot even name the letters of the alphabet. Nonetheless, they are able to use contextual clues to understand some print in their environment. Does this group or the group with phonetic skills have the best chance for learning to read successfully?

Some instructors would select the first group as the one in which they have more confidence. For these instructors would feel they can work most productively with learners who have already demonstrated academic success. But other teachers would predict that prospects for future learning would be better with those persons who had developed rudimentary functional reading skills.

The logic of teachers attempting to make a decision of this sort can be analogous to that of building contractors forced to choose between making renovations to distinct types of houses. Should they choose houses filled with amenities but flawed in design? Or should they choose structurally sound homes with limited amenities? Which choice will result in houses that best meet the needs of their clients? As would be the case with builders, all instructors would designate programs with structural integrity as the optimal programs. However, what are the criteria of optimal literacy programs?

No matter how carefully one evaluates an adult learner with a disability, physical, cognitive, social, or emotional factors may remain undetected. And even those factors that are detected may not have been reduced to the most refined levels of specificity. Consequently, one reason that models for instructing individual adults are always expedient is that the assessment linked to those models, no matter how detailed, is always incomplete.

Because assessment is tentative, optimal literacy instruction for adults is expedient—it is the best thing to do at the time. Instructors in literacy programs for adults with disabilities build on the interests and backgrounds of learners and are sensitive to the distinctive constraints of working with adults. These constraints may originate with precise disabilities such as visual impairment or lack of mobility. But the constraints may also be associated with gender, culture, or language. And there are constraints associated with the predictable stages of development through which all adult learners progress.

Other constraints that influence optimal instruction include the skills of instructors, the availability of resources, the number of learners in the program, and the objectives of the program. Even if practical limitations limit one from adapting instruction on the basis of these constraints, the mere awareness of these constraints may enhance the effectiveness of instruction.

Cautious and Calculated Vantages

This book is a systematic exploration of the factors on the basis of which instructional programs should be adapted. Six popular programs that lend themselves to adaptation are discussed and illustrated.

- Computer-Assisted Programs
- Skills-Based Programs
- Whole Language Programs

- Psychoeducational Programs
- Programs that Employ Children's Materials
- Functional Literacy Programs

Model activities, complementary assessment strategies, and auxiliary resources are highlighted. Research linked to these programs is reviewed, synthesized, and critiqued. Special issues, such as transition, multicultural programs, and programs for persons with severe disabilities, are discussed in detail.

Do programs for adults with disabilities need to be radically different from the extensive and popular children's literacy programs? When looked at casually, teaching literacy to adults may seem indistinct from teaching reading to children. Just as an encounter with a vicious dog does not always have to result in an altered route, does adult reading instruction have to be a search for alternative programs? For some persons respond to threatening encounters by changing their attitudes rather than their routes. Keeping this in mind, should instructors be searching for cautious and calculated vantages from which to anticipate, observe, and react to learning problems?

Readers of this book can answer these questions for themselves as they identify optimal instructional practices in literacy programs for adults with disabilities. Analogous to the behaviors they might have displayed after an unnerving encounter, some readers may adopt more careful attitudes as they continue to implement programs in which they remain confident. Other readers may change their programmatic routes, adapting materials and methods within programs. And still others may adopt whole new programs. If any of these response are elicited from readers, the goal of this book will certainly have been achieved.

Contributors

Bruno J. D'Alonzo, Ph.D.
New Mexico State University

Jozi DeLeon, Ph.D.
New Mexico State University

Linda Leeper, Ph.D.
New Mexico State University

Robert Ortiz, Ph.D.
New Mexico State University

Michael Shaughnessy, Ph.D.
Eastern New Mexico University

Janna Siegel, Ph.D.
Eastern New Mexico University

Nile Stanley, Ph.D.
Eastern New Mexico University

Sheela Stuart, Ph.D.
New Mexico State University

Dedication

To my family — Karen, Gabe, Kara, and Peter

CHAPTER

1

Issues in Adult Literacy

How many adults with disabilities are illiterate? Because definitions of literacy are so varied, this question cannot be answered precisely. Functional literacy has been defined as the ability to employ reading and writing to understand and use the printed material one normally encounters in work, leisure, and citizenship (Stedman & Kaestle, 1991). The number of adults who are functionally illiterate in the United States has been estimated as ranging between 20 million to 30 million (Chisman, 1990b; Jacobson, 1993). After an extensive review of functional literacy tests administered during the past two decades, Stedman and Kaestle (1991) concluded that, "a substantial portion of the population, from 20 to 30 percent, has difficulty coping with common reading tasks and materials" (p. 128).

But the definition of illiteracy can be expanded to include critical reading tasks. Examples of critical reading tasks would be differentiating fact from opinion, drawing conclusions, establishing cause and effect, evaluating authors' attitudes, or problem solving with printed information. If one includes individuals who lack critical reading skills among persons who are illiterate, that estimate might increase by as many as 35 million more adults (Kozol, 1985). And if literacy is expanded to include oral communication and mathematics (Chisman, 1990a; Hunter & Harman, 1985), an estimate of 55 million illiterate Americans is certainly inadequate.

In the same way that scientific literacy, art literacy, and cultural literacy are used as figures of speech, computer literacy can be employed as figurative term indicating a person's knowledge of technical information. However, interaction with computers can be viewed as types of reading, writing, and problem solving that are characteristically distinct from other types of literacy (Tuman, 1992). If one adopts this view, it may be necessary to change the way that literacy instruction is designed and implemented (Landow, 1992; Schwartz, 1992). As opportunities to interact with computers have increased, the potential inclusion of computer abilities as an essential component of traditional literacy has become a critical question (Tuman, 1992).

A survey of literacy skills among more than 26,000 adults was sponsored by the U.S. Department of Education (Kirsch, Jungeblut, Jenkins, & Kolstad, 1993). In this survey, literacy was defined as the use of "printed and written information to function in society, to achieve one's goals, and to develop one's knowledge and potential" (p. 2). The authors of this survey emphasized that literacy was not a univocal skill but rather an ordered set of skills "called into play to accomplish diverse types of tasks" (p. 3). As part of the assessment, they developed three literacy scales that could be applied to prose (e.g., newspaper stories, editorials, or fiction), documents (e.g., job applications, schedules, or graphs), and quantitative tasks (e.g., balancing a checkbook, determining a tip, or completing an order form). Using five levels to classify the performance of the adults in the survey, the researchers concluded that 21 to 23% of respondents, representative of more than 40 million persons in this country, "demonstrated skills in the lowest level of prose, document, and quantitative proficiencies" (p. xiv).

Although individual critics have charged that reports about literacy problems have been overstated (Aronowitz, 1981; Hunter & Harman, 1985), there has been a consensus among educators, scholars, and policy makers for more than 15 years that adult illiteracy is a significant, complex, and widespread problem (Holcomb, 1981; Kirsch et al., 1993; Monteith, 1980; Negrin & Drugler, 1980; Skagen, 1986; Stedman & Kaestle, 1991). Figure 1–1 illustrates several types of illiteracy that have been proposed and roughly estimates the proportions of adults affected by each type of illiteracy.

The complexity of the illiteracy problem is illustrated by statistics about illiterate workers. As many as 15 million adult workers lack the literacy skills to be effective at their jobs (National Advisory Council on Adult Literacy, 1986). Increasing numbers of illiterate adolescents will eventually join the work force and exacerbate this problem (Davidson & Koppenhaver, 1993). As a result of the passage of the Americans with Disabilities Act of 1990 (P.L. 101-336), persons with disabilities have an

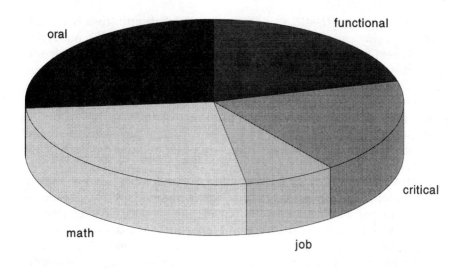

Figure 1-1. Although more than 20 million persons are estimated as functionally illiterate, other types of illiteracy can characterize adults.

unprecedented opportunity to become employed and remain members of the work force (Parry, 1993). The security of persons with disabilities as workers is further ensured by the emergence of alternative models for employment. These models raise the probability that workers with disabilities will be successful at job sites where they will be integrated with workers without disabilities (Chadsey-Rusch & O'Reilly, 1992; Hughes & Wehman, 1992; Wehman, 1992, 1993; Wehman, Sale, & Parent, 1992).

The problem of illiterate adult workers is compounded by projections that workers will be employed for progressively longer spans and then experience longer retirements (Rice & Feldman, 1983). The percentage of older persons in western countries, which presently averages more than 12% of the population, should double over the next 25 years (Anderson, 1993). Eighty percent of all current deaths occur among persons who are at least sixty years old (Bengtson & Schaie, 1989), and, as a result of more efficient social and medical services, this proportion is likely to continue increasing (Anderson, 1993; Thurman, 1986). Age expectancy in the United States and Britain has nearly doubled since 1900 (Laslett, 1991).

These projections extend to persons with disabilities as well as to persons without disabilities (Anderson, 1993; Blake, 1981; Lubin & Kiely, 1985; Simpson, 1990). More than 85% of all children born with disabilities during the 1990s will survive at least until their twentieth birthdays (National Center for Youth with Disabilities, 1993). Anderson (1993) reviewed research studies indicating that, though their life expectancy remained below that of their peers without disabilities, persons with mental retardation were likely to live into their senior years. Even among institutionalized clients with profound and serious disabilities, mortality rates have declined dramatically over the past two decades. This extension in life expectancy is remarkable because of the increasing number of persons with serious disabilities who are being identified each year.

Attempting to divide the life span into predictable periods, Laslett (1991) identified four ages. The first age is one of dependence, socialization, immaturity, and education, while the second age is characterized by independence, responsibility, earning, and accumulation of possessions. He argued that the third age, in which one retires from a career and reduces the responsibilities for children, is a period with great opportunities for personal growth and fulfillment. The fourth age is one of dependence and decrepitude. In the case of persons with disabilities, the separation between the third and fourth ages is not as precise as it can be among individuals without disabilities.

As the degree of mental disabilities decreases, the likelihood that the disabilities will influence age expectancy decreases as well (Eyman, Grossman, Tarjan, & Miller, 1987). Among persons with moderate disabilities, the probability of an extended life increases progressively if mobility is not restricted and if there is access to community living, employment, and leisure activities (Walz, Harper, & Wilson, 1986).

Questions about the extent of illiteracy among adults and older adults with disabilities are difficult to resolve because there is no universally agreed upon definition for literacy. However, neither are there universally accepted definitions of disability, adulthood, or old age. The concept of *developmental disability* was introduced officially into legislation in 1970 in The Developmental Disabilities Services and Facilities Construction Act of 1970 (P.L. 91-717). The term has been defined in several more recent pieces of legislation, including the Developmental Disabilities Assistance and Bill of Rights Act of 1990. According to the 1990 Act, developmental disabilities can be physical or mental impairments that are manifest before the age of 22, likely to persist, require special types of intervention, and result in functional limitations. The functional limitations can be in areas such as self-care, language, learning, mobility, self-direction, independent living, and employment. Examples of developmental disabilities would certainly include severe mental retardation, autism, and cerebral palsy. However, developmental disabilities can be interpreted broadly to include mild mental retardation, learning disabilities, sensory impairments, communication disorders, emotional impairments, and learning disabilities that impact on three or more functional life activities (Wolfe, 1992).

When discussing adults with developmental disabilities, even the specification of the ages that distinguish adulthood and old age are controversial. Different businesses and government agencies have defined adulthood as commencing at the age of 18, the age of 21, or some age between these. When does old age begin? It has been stipulated as beginning at 55, 60, 65, or at retirement. Because the age expectancy of persons with disabilities is approximately 10 years less than that of their peers without disabilities, Thurman (1986) suggested that the age limits associated with adult developmental milestones be reduced by 10 years for persons with disabilities. If this position were accepted, persons with disabilities would become eligible for retirement at 55 in businesses where 65 was the established retirement age for individuals without disabilities.

It is somewhat arbitrary to estimate developmental ages for persons with disabilities by extrapolating statistics from populations without disabilities. The characteristics of aging to which adult stages can be linked can be physical, cognitive, social, and emotional (Older Americans Act Amendments, 1989). Consequently, it may be more appropriate to define adult stages descriptively, referencing classifications of individuals' ages to the abilities that they exhibit and the amount of support that they require (Thurman, 1986).

Varying definitions of literacy, adulthood, and old age contribute to the difficulty of answering questions about the extent of illiteracy among adults and older adults with disabilities. Nonetheless, there can be no dispute that the rate of prevalence for illiteracy among adults with disabilities is unacceptably high. Earlier in this chapter, there was a reference to the 1993 survey about the literacy of more than 26,000 adults. In that survey, "Twelve percent of the respondents reported having a physical, mental, or other health condition that kept them from participating fully in work or other activities" (Kirsch et al., 1993, p. xvii). These individuals demonstrated literacy skills at levels that were lower than those of any other persons surveyed.

Adults who are illiterate are present in the work force, will remain in that work force for extended periods, and, after retirement, will live to ages that are becoming progressively longer. Demographic data confirm that this pattern characterizes adults with disabilities as well as those without disabilities. Additionally, there will be opportunities to interact with adult learners as a result of a trend within society to encourage adult learning throughout all stages of adulthood. This trend has been referred to under various headings, the most popular of which may be lifelong learning (Van Fleet, 1990).

Other Issues That Impact on Literacy Learning

Learning that is developmentally restricted can influence the acquisition of literacy by adults with disabilities. For example, *postformal operations*, a stage through which adults may pass, is characterized by an increase in those cognitive abilities that depend on experiential memory. At the same time, there may be a diminution of other intellectual traits, such as the ability to solve timed, spatial problems. Optimal literacy instruction is sensitive to the profiles of cognitive strengths and weakness that adult learners exhibit. These profiles can be influenced both by learners' disabilities as well as by the developmental stages through which they are progressing.

With regard to optimal instruction, there are six popular approaches for developing the literacy of adults with disabilities. The approaches include skills-based programs, computer-assisted programs, whole language programs, psychoeducational programs, children's materials programs, and functional literacy programs. The most widely used programs are those that are skills-based.

In skills-based programs, learners are instructed so that they acquire reading strategies in an orderly manner. Although there are variations among programs, phonetics is the most commonly employed foundation for learning. Skills like phonetics can enable learners to become independent readers who can decipher words that they do not recognize visually.

Though skills-based programs dominate adult literacy instruction, there has been an unprecedented interest in whole language programs over the past two decades. These programs, which employ materials that the learners themselves have created, build on learners' oral language abilities and background experiences. Instruction is presented in a communicative context so that the learners can see the purposeful rationale for each activity. Because of an instructional format and philosophy that are dramatically distinct from those associated with skills-based programs, whole language programs have been referred to as the "new literacy" (Willinsky, 1990).

The degree to which the skills developed in programs transfer to real world situations is a critical feature on the basis of which literacy programs can be evaluated. Skills transfer when learners generalize the information that they acquire in literacy programs to nonacademic contexts. For example, if learners could complete workbook activities, that learning would be successful only when they could apply those workbook skills to the situations that they encountered in their day to day lives. Even if they were able to fill out simulated job applications as part of workbook activities, that learning would be mastered completely only if those skills generalized to actual vocational situations. Analogously, learners who were able to read simulated financial statements during instructional activities would have to generalize that learning to their actual credit card statements for the learning to be completely successful.

Other features on the basis of which literacy programs can be differentiated include opportunities for immediate and sustained reinforcement of learning, the prospects for the long term continuity of instruction, the likelihood that adults will be motivated by the materials and the learning procedures, cost effectiveness, and the probability that programs can meet the distinctive needs of individual learners with disabilities.

Because there can be great variance in personalities as well as disabilities, personality traits of adults with disabilities can significantly influence their responses to instructional programs. Persons intrigued by technology will respond differently to computer-assisted instruction than persons intimidated by technology. Persons who are driven to participate in the planning of their instruction and the selection of their instructional materials will not respond well to programs where materials and instructional activities are predetermined.

Not only personality factors but learners' cognitive styles can predispose them towards instructional approaches that emphasize or suppress information that is visual, auditory, or kinesthetic. *Cognitive style* refers to the preferences, attitudes, and predispositions that characterize learners as they acquire knowledge, communicate, and solve problems. Although some aspects of cognitive style can to some extent be modified (Gerber & Reiff, 1994), such as decision making, planning, and memorizing, other dimensions resist adaptation. Jarvis (1983) reviewed the literature on cognitive style and identified nine frequently cited examples of learners with contrasting cognitive styles:

active learners—passive learners

assimilators—accommodators

concrete learners—abstract learners

convergent learners—divergent learners

field dependent learners—field independent learners

focusing learners—scanning learners

holistic learners—serial learners

reflective learners—impulsive learners

rigid learners—flexible learners

As an example of the impact that cognitive style can have on learning to read, persons with visually dominated cognitive styles might learn most effectively after personally reading passages. In contrast, learners with auditory cognitive styles might learn best after listening to passages as these were read. And learners with kinesthetically dominated cognitive styles might learn most effectively after writing words or after typing them at keyboards. Masters, Mori, and Mori (1993) reviewed research studies indicating that learning can be improved when it was channeled through learners' primary modalities. Situational factors influencing the responses of learners included the behaviors of the instructors, the format of the learning materials, and environmental circumstances such as furniture, lighting, and background distractions. They recommended that instruction of learners with mild learning and behavioral problems be built on flexible environments, response to acoustic preferences, reduction of visual distractions, and the characteristic processing strengths of the individual learners.

In addition to the examples that have been cited, multiple other factors can influence learning. Environment, culture, type of disability, and severity of disability could predispose learners toward success or failure in instructional programs. The instructional needs of learners and their preparation for learning could influence success or failure in literacy programs. And the preparedness of teachers to be instructors would certainly influence successful learning by adults.

Multicultural Issues

As society has become progressively multicultural, the importance of multicultural learning within instructional programs has increased proportionately. Multicultural learning programs adapt literacy instruction so that persons from minority groups can be successful and so that they can form insights about the abilities, needs, viewpoints, values, and goals of individuals from other groups (Anderson, 1988; Banks, 1994; Gollnick & Chinn, 1987; Pai, 1990; Tesconi, 1990).

Multiculturalism may seem linked inextricably to race. For example, "On all measures of literacy, at all points during the last century, white Americans have been more literate than black Americans" (Stedman & Kaestle, 1991). Though these data can hardly be contested, nonracial characteristics of learners, such as social class, age, or exceptionality, may be the causative elements for this profile of performance (Banks, 1994; Traustadottir, Lutfiyya, & Shoultz, 1994). And because of pervasive poverty among ethnic minority groups, poverty itself can be a plausible explanation for the achievement of multicultural learners (Traustadottir et al., 1994). The link between poverty and education may be especially relevant to issues of adult literacy since a significant number of illiterate adults live in poverty (Kirsch et al., 1993). Access to literacy instruction can be a political tool that can reduce or increase poverty as well as other social differences (Eggington, 1992; Friere & Macedo, 1988; Hooks, 1990; Mohanty, Russo, & Torres, 1991; Welch & Freebody, 1993).

But irrespective of whether one views multiculturalism from a narrow or broad perspective, culture and language are predictable obstacles for learners in a multicultural society (Dubin & Kuhlman, 1992; Graham & Cookson, 1990). These two factors by themselves may explain why there are significantly lower rates of literacy among adults from minority groups than among persons who are not from minority groups (Kirsch et al., 1993; Stedman & Kaestle, 1991).

The rates for certain disabilities among persons from minority groups have been unusually high. These high rates underscore the need for services and education to individuals with disabilities from minority groups. However, programs that should respond to this need have only been somewhat successful. The distinctive views and values of persons from minority groups can restrict the impact of service models that were developed with nonminority populations (Christensen, 1989; Collier & Hoover, 1987; Joe & Malach, 1992; Levine, 1987; Rogler, Cortes, & Malady, 1991). Consequently, optimal models for delivering services and education may be ones that are sensitive to the social, psychological, and philosophical values of minority groups.

Competition is another factor that can influence responses to educational models by learners from different cultures. Competition can be positive for some learners and negative for others. When adult learners respond productively, competition can be employed. In cases where competition has a detrimental effect on learning, small groups, cooperative learning, or shared responsibility for completing assignments can be remedies.

Similar to the different responses from learners to competition, there can be different reactions to the ways of grouping for instruction. For example, some persons may learn best when they are isolated whereas others prefer group learning activities. Persons from certain cultures may respond best to learning tasks that reflect the patterns of day to day social interactions within those cultures (Baca & Cervantes, 1989; Bloome, 1987; Castaneda, 1976; Chan & Rueda, 1979; Field & Aebersold, 1990; Fillmore, 1981).

Language may be the most significant learning barrier encountered by persons who speak English as a second language. Literacy curricula that are sensitive to learners' languages as well as their backgrounds, values, and goals can be critical to helping them pass beyond this barrier (Schaafsma, 1993). The relevance of literacy curricula can be further enhanced if learners themselves participate in the selection of materials, instructional techniques, and scheduling (Riggs & Allen, 1989).

Perez and Torres-Guzman (1992) recommended that Spanish-English bilingual learners be taught with instructional approaches that discouraged competition and that reflected the environments of the learners. They cited the whole language approach to literacy instruction as a program that had these characteristics. Their enthusiasm about the benefits of whole language programs for bilingual and nonnative speakers of English has been shared by other experts in education (Flores, Garcia, Gonzalez, Hidalgo, Kaczmarek, & Romero, 1985; Green, 1989; Heald-Taylor, 1986; Montero Sieburth, 1990; Peyton & Reed, 1990; Riggs & Allen, 1989; Smallwood, 1991). Whole language approaches have the additional benefit of promoting retention by allowing learners to associate instructional materials with referents from their daily lives (Allen, 1986; Enright & McCloskey, 1985).

Adults with disabilities are not addressed specifically in much of the extensive literature about the education of culturally and linguistically diverse learners. Nonetheless, many of the insights that have been developed have implications for the instruction of adults with disabilities. Two themes that run through the literature on literacy programs for bilingual and nonnative speakers of English concern the need to incorporate learners' native language abilities and their distinctive background experiences. These themes are restated within the field of special education in the literature about multicultural education (Ada, 1986; Baca & Cervantes, 1989; Cardenas, 1986; Castaneda, 1976; Cummins, 1984; Ford & Jones, 1990; Ramirez, 1988; Salend, 1990).

Culture and language are factors that differentiate diverse learners with disabilities. Programs that respond effectively to the needs of diverse learners encourage them to view themselves as successful and enable them to learn to their full potential. Additionally, effective programs help participants develop sensitivity to persons from other groups.

Combining Literacy Instruction With Transition

Transition is the process that enables persons with disabilities who are dependent to become independent, employed, and capable of interacting within the mainstream of society. Preparing persons for this transition can be a lifelong process that may begin before school and continue into the adult years (Halpern, 1994).

Although legislation and litigation preceded the 1984 introduction of transition in federal legislation (Amendments to the Education of the Handicapped Act, P.L. 98-199), it was in these 1984 Amendments that the scope of transition was specified to include high school programs and post high school support programs for adolescents and adults with disabilities. The legislation attempted to encourage cooperative planning between schools and service agencies in communities.

The legislation was precipitated by reports that the majority of adults with disabilities who had exited the schools were segregated within their communities, unemployed, and not achieving their full potential (Halloran, 1993). Estimates of the percentage of adults with disabilities who are unemployed have ranged between 50 and 75% (Wehman, 1992). Peraino (1992) extensively reviewed follow-up and longitudinal studies of adults who had formerly been students in special education programs. He concluded that "youth with disabilities do not fare as well as their counterparts with disabilities in any aspect of adult status soon after high school. In many cases, they never fare as well" (p. 69).

On the basis of this analysis, Peraino identified characteristics of learners which, if present, raised the probability that those learners would be employed. Some of these characteristics, such as severity of disabilities, were beyond the control of educators. However, other characteristics could be influenced by educators. A key example of a learner characteristic that increases the probability of employment and that can be influenced by instructors would be graduation from high school. Other instructor-influenced characteristics that raise the probability of employment would be appropriate social skills and job-related skills. These skills have been referred to as *life skills* (Clark, Field, Patton, Brolin, & Sitlington, 1994), *functional skills* (Clark, 1994), *adaptability skills* (Mithaug, Martin, & Agran, 1987), *major life demands* (Cronin & Patton, 1993), and *life-centered career education competencies*

(Brolin, 1995). In each case, the skills designated by these diverse terms were intended to enable individuals with disabilities to function as family members, neighbors, citizens, and workers who participated in their communities (Clark et al., 1994).

Transition programs that encompass the full range of learners' lives are referred to as *life-span transition programs*. Life-span transition programs emphasize that learning activities can be taught in functional and natural settings. Such functional formats for learning can enhance the acquisition of skills, the generalization of skills, and retention. Transition programs can prepare adult learners for employment while simultaneously developing communication skills and academic skills. Literacy skills, which can be viewed as both academic and communicative, can be taught with varied and motivating strategies that complement instruction about diverse careers. Additionally, learning functional skills in natural settings can be a pathway to independent living. This pathway becomes apparent when functional learning provides opportunities for adults with disabilities to interact with persons without disabilities.

Although persons with developmental disabilities who are maintaining or seeking employment can be successful while living in various residential settings, independent living and other residential models that encourage unrestricted access to communities have the greatest potential for developing traits such as community competence, family cooperation, functional independence, and personal empowerment. These are traits that complement the learning objectives of both transition programs and adult literacy programs.

Bates (1990) identified 12 quality indicators to be used to gauge the effectiveness of transition to community programs. The initial four quality indicators concerned involvement by parents (or guardians), by learners, by a variety of school staff, and by personnel from nonschool agencies. These four quality indicators complement interdisciplinary approaches to transition in which career and vocational skills are critical components. For example, Clark and Kolstoe developed a popular model of transition (1994) that included the learning of occupational skills as well as daily living skills, human relationship skills, values, attitudes, and positive habits. Models of adult literacy that complement literacy have this same character, being built on an eclectic foundation of technical, emotional, cognitive, physical, and linguistic skills.

Assessment of Adult Literacy

Assessment of adult literacy is a complex process. For example, seven major assessments of functional literacy among adults were conducted from 1970 through 1985. The rates of literacy among the groups tested ranged between 3 and 54% (Stedman & Kaestle, 1991). Stedman and Kaestle conjectured that the wide range in literacy rates in these studies resulted from the use of different tests and different criteria for passing those tests.

Tests and the assessment process may seem to be linked inextricably. Though the usefulness of tests as part of assessment is obvious, tests may contain biases that can limit or even invalidate their results. Examples of biases that can affect performance of individuals during tests would be competition, limited time, culture, gender, dialect, and ambiguity of test items

Some biases may be specific to items within a test. For example, the type of information assessed in a question might be handled better through another type of question. Other biases could result if the format of questions was inappropriate for the skills being measured, if the language used in the test items was unclear, or if the response alternatives were overlapping. The biases that have been listed could affect the performance of all learners, irrespective of whether they had disabilities.

However, some testing biases may have a disproportionate impact on adults with disabilities. For example, tests can be presented in a fashion that restricts the performance of persons with sensory or communicative impairments. As another example, adults with disabilities may have been exposed to extremely specialized instructional programs that could limit their performance on tests with a format and content distinct from that used in the instruction.

Tests that are not biased against adult learners with disabilities can be difficult to locate. Nonetheless, testing is attractive because it provides a common experience among learners that can be generalized. And, irrespective of questions one may raise about validity, tests can be required by agencies, school systems, or states. Rather than searching for elusive, nonbiased tests of literacy, instructors may decide to assemble batteries of tests. Though all of the tests in a battery may contain flaws, that battery can be assembled so that the tests do not replicate the identical faults with reference to the same trait.

For example, there might be three tests in a battery attempting to measure reading comprehension. One of the tests might be extremely useful. Or that particular test might be required by an external agency. However, suppose that test contained a gender bias that could penalize females. Ideally instructors would wish all three tests to be free of this bias. However, if they could not designate three neutral tests, the instructors could validate the results of the biased test by comparing performance on it with performance on two measures of reading comprehension that did not contain a gender bias. By selecting batteries of tests in this complementary manner, the validity of those tests could be increased.

However, the results of even a carefully designed battery of formal tests should be refined and validated with supplementary assessment data. Examples of supplementary data that can be useful to instructors include analyses of oral reading errors, inventories of functional reading skills, observations by instructors, samples of work completed by learners in groups, responses to attitude inventories, samples of workbook activities, data about time on task by learners during different instructional activities, records of visits to instructional centers, and samples of creative work.

Literacy for Persons With Severe Disabilities

Some literacy programs for nonreading adults are similar to programs intended for beginning readers. Because programs for beginning readers are designed to facilitate a transition from illiteracy to academic reading, such programs are unsuitable for adults with severe disabilities when there is no short-range expectation that these learners will develop the academic skills to which the preparatory activities are linked.

In contrast, alternative reading activities can substitute for traditional literacy instruction. Though distinct from typical reading instruction, these alternative literacy activities are aimed at the same general goals and, to a limited extent, resemble the traditional reading instruction for which they substitute. These activities can be especially appropriate for learners with severe disabilities. Hess (1992) defined learners with severe disabilities as individuals who

- require a greater number of instructional trials
- can learn a relatively limited number of skills
- can learn skills of relatively limited complexity
- have difficulty retaining information
- have difficulty generalizing
- have difficulty transferring learning to novel contexts
- have difficulty synthesizing information

The range of alternative activities for learners with severe disabilities can include rudimentary learning tasks, such as the exhibition of overt readinglike behaviors. Other activities, such as picture reading, require progressively more refined degrees of attention. Alternative activities can develop generalization skills by directing learners' attention to the illustrations in books, magazines, or manuals, to global features of printed material, to print in the environment, or to items in learners' environments that have been selected and labeled for individuals. Augmentative or alternative communication devices can further increase the accessibility of these approaches to persons with severe disabilities.

The literacy programs that can be adapted for adult learners with severe problems can be based on pictorial cues, global features of printed materials, print in the environment, labeling, or rebus symbols. These programs can be viewed progressively as a ladder of literacy opportunities for persons with severe disabilities. This ladder may culminate in the development of actual reading skills.

With the exception of the rebus approach, these programs do not assume that adult learners have extensive language development. As such, the programs can be appropriate for many adults with severe and profound learning disabilities who would be unsuccessful in more complex literacy programs.

The activities in these programs do not require extremely structured drills or restrictive materials. Consequently, the programs can be implemented in the context of functional, on-site, field-based instruction, relying on stimuli that surround learners in their community environments. As such, the activities are compatible with an emerging paradigm of community living for persons with severe disabilities. Knoll and Racino (1994) called attention to this paradigm when they wrote that "there are no community based alternatives, the only alternative is the community; and . . . service systems should not develop homelike environments . . . rather they should figure out how to support individuals in their own houses" (p. 301).

Summary

If functional literacy is the ability to solve day to day problems with print, how many adults with disabilities are functionally illiterate? Because we lack objective techniques for assessing functional literacy, this question is difficult to answer. And the question becomes still more complicated if definitions of illiteracy are expanded to include critical reading, mathematics, oral language, or computer skills. Questions about the extent of illiteracy among adults with disabilities further compound this problem because the aptitude of specific individuals with disabilities to develop literacy skills may not always be clear.

There are six popular approaches for developing the literacy of adults with disabilities. The approaches include computer-assisted programs, skills-based programs, whole language programs, psychoeducational programs, children's materials programs, and functional literacy programs. A critical feature on the basis of which these programs can be differentiated is the degree to which each program promotes the transfer of skills to real world situations. Factors influencing transfer of skills could include the distinctive experiences and environments of learners, their personalities, and their problem-solving traits. Additional factors that affect instruction of adult learners with disabilities would include the nature and severity of their disabilities.

Adult literacy instruction can be combined with other components of adult learning as part of a comprehensive adult learning program. Transition, assessment, and multiculturalism are examples of other components of a comprehensive program that complement literacy instruction.

CHAPTER
2

The Developmental Basis for Adult Literacy Education

During the past several decades, developmental theories of psychology have become increasingly popular. Birren and Schaie (1990), reviewing the history of developmental psychology from the early part of this century to the present, noted that developmental theories have highlighted predictable stages of biological, psychological, social, and cognitive change through which persons progress. For example, Erickson (1968) depicted individuals as wrestling with conflicting alternatives during eight stages of their lives. During the initial five stages, which were experienced prior to the age of 20, individuals wrestled with problems of self-identity. However, the three stages that culminated this progression focused on commitment to others and confidence in society. Erickson viewed passage through stages as preparation for the final stage, one characterized by the wisdom necessary to maintain a strong self-identity as one's body, and possibly one's mind, became progressively less responsive. (Incidentally, persons with disabilities are at a disadvantage because they do not have a lifetime of preparatory experiences with which to steel themselves for this deterioration.)

Observing the development of adult males over a 25-year period, Vaillant (1977) confirmed opportunities to pass through the stages identified by Erikson. He cautioned that all persons were not successful in dealing with the predictable anxieties that could emerge at the different stages and that had the potential to restrict their progress through those stages.

Vaillant identified four types of strategies that adults employed to deal with these anxieties: psychotic, immature, neurotic, and mature strategies. Whereas psychotic strategies might lead persons to deny patently true but personally threatening information, neurotic strategies could result in the repression of that information. Similar to neurotic strategies, the use of immature strategies could result in escapism or personal inertia as a demonstration of one's resistance. Vaillant noted that such strategies were used by normally developing and psychologically healthy adults. However, overreliance on psychotic, neurotic, and immature strategies could be an indication of an aberrant personality. Dependence on neurotic, psychotic, and immature strategies was also correlated with an inability to achieve the final stages on Erikson's developmental ladder. Persons who dealt with anxiety by employing mature mechanisms had the highest probability of achieving full maturation. Mature adaptive techniques, unlike the other three strategies, were characterized by humor, unselfishness, and altruism.

Havighurst (1961) identified developmental tasks that challenge persons at predictable stages of their lives. He illustrated how developmental tasks can lead to personal happiness and societal approval. Additionally, successful responses to these tasks incorporate learning that is required for success with subsequent developmental tasks. Adult developmental tasks are linked to milestones such as choosing a career, finding a mate, setting up a home, and becoming a parent. During the later years, developmental tasks are associated with predictable events such as retirement, failing health, and the death of a spouse. Multiple issues that affect finances, social status, independence, personal relationships, security, and identity can be associated with each developmental task (Sheehy, 1976; Troll, 1982).

Levinson and his associates (Levinson, Darrow, Klein, Levinson, & McKee, 1978) conducted an intensive, longitudinal study of 40 men from different social, educational, and economic backgrounds. On the basis of observed stages through which all of the participants passed, they postulated that there were universal milestones that characterized the aging of males from adolescence through their late forties. The milestones included transition to adulthood, entry into the world of work, development of a more serious commitment to work and family, development of an independent adult identity, transition to mid-life, and the emergence of a new identity during middle adulthood.

Gould (1978) identified periods of adult development that encompassed the following transitions: departure from the family, occupational choice, initial confusion about adult roles and choices, intensified confusion about adult roles and choices, discontent, introspection, and reconciliation to one's mortality. Although Gould concluded that adult stages were age-dependent, social circumstances and events such as marriage, divorce, job promotions, career changes, or deaths of family members could restrict or precipitate movement from one stage to another.

Critics have questioned whether popular theories of adult development such as those of Gould, Erikson, and Havighurst are not biased because of an exclusive observation of males (Gilligan, 1982; Loevinger, 1976). Gilligan argued that initial, discrete stages of development in Erikson's model should be collapsed in the cases of maturing adult females. Loevinger criticized Erikson's model because it was based on culturally derived stereotypes of males. She suggested that females as well as males passed through psychologically complex developmental stages that can not be encapsulated within such a simple model.

Although numerous scholars are responsible for the popularity of developmental theories of cognition, Jean Piaget, the European psychologist, may have had the greatest impact on education. Piaget argued that there were four stage through which all persons passed—sensorimotor, preoperations, concrete operations, and formal operations. In the initial stages, learners' thoughts depended heavily on characteristics of the external objects with which they were interacting. As learners aged, they exhibited progressive cognitive independence.

Piaget (1970; 1972) concluded that cognitive independence reached its peak in the fourth stage, formal operations, when persons developed the ability to think in genuinely abstract fashions. Piaget indicated that this last stage of cognitive development was achieved by most learners during early adolescence. Having made this qualitative step, learners continued to accumulate additional experiences, but they did not develop novel, cognitive structures. As such, adult learning was viewed as a time when, at best, learners could remain on a cognitive plateau until the inevitable period of decline when their senses, nervous system, memory, language, and skills would ebb.

Postformal Cognition

Researchers have raised questions about Piaget's characterization of adult learning. And even without consulting the research, adults do not accept Piaget's depiction of themselves as unable to advance cognitively beyond the stage of formal operations. After all, society accords respect to adults by describing them as *wise* and *insightful*, terms applied infrequently to adolescents who have entered the formal operations stage. Could there be an additional stage of cognitive development through which adults progress?

This fifth stage of cognitive development has been referred to predictably as the postformal stage of reasoning. Psychologists have analyzed data in an attempt to describe the characteristics of postformal thought (Dittmann-Kohli & Baltes, 1986; Kramer, 1983; Rybash, Hoyer, & Roodin, 1986). There is consensus that persons who have progressed to the stage of postformal thought exhibit attributes of the following types:

- Focus on the context for problems
- Concentration on practical aspects of problems
- Respect for first-hand experience
- Tolerance for unexpected or contradictory responses
- A view that solutions to problems can be expedient, dynamic, and evolutionary
- Realization that knowledge is not absolute

It is not difficult to locate examples of adults who do not exhibit postformal responses to problems—religious zealots convinced that members of other religions are in error, politicians who genuinely believe in the certainty of economic policies, nationalists who irrationally support their country's interests, or researchers who search for single, correct answers to behavioral questions.

Just as one can easily adduce examples of persons who have not progressed to postformal cognitive operations, there are plentiful examples of postformal problem solving. Sherlock Holmes, as well as the many pundits who are the protagonists in detective novels, certainly exhibit postformal cognitive skills.

Or consider the story of Mary Magdalen. According to the New Testament of the Bible, Judaic leaders brought to Jesus a woman accused of adultery. They asked whether she should be stoned, which was the explicit sentence required by Judaic law. On the other hand, the Roman law, under the jurisdiction of which they had been placed, forbade such stonings. The leaders asked Jesus about the course he recommended. Superficially, it might have seemed that there was no escape from the dilemma that confronted him—a choice between exhibiting his lack of confidence in the Judaic law or the secular law. Jesus' response to the question is famous. He encouraged those who had never sinned against Judaic law to execute the punishment prescribed by Judaic law. And of course, when phrased in this relative fashion, no one could lift a stone.

When Piaget identified the four stages of cognition through which persons progressed, he assigned ages at which each stage was typically evident. The last stage, formal operations, had the greatest latitude—11 years to 16 years. However, the age at which postformal cognitive operations emerge cannot be identified with even a range as wide as this. Clearly, there are adults who never exhibit the characteristics of the postformal stage. And there are adults who exhibit the traits only during certain episodes or only with reference to a narrow category of issues.

The fact that we all have observed older persons who view social groups stereotypically might seem to be an example that would invalidate the hypothesis that postformal reasoning correlates with age. However, research has indicated that the probability of stereotyped views of social groups and situations may decrease with age (Rankin & Allen, 1991). In a classic study of the cognition that characterized undergraduate students in college, Perry (1968) documented that significant changes occurred in students' intellectual abilities as well as in their ethical traits. Fundamental changes in ethical and moral perspectives, though these may transpire during adolescence and early adulthood, often continue into the senior years (Gilligan, Murphy, & Tappan, 1990).

The postformal stage is somewhat different from the monolithic stage of adult intelligence that Piaget identified. Although males and females both move into the postformal stage of cognition, their experiences may be sufficiently distinct to differentiate their approaches to answering questions and solving problems during adulthood (Huyck, 1990). And while there is no evidence demonstrating that members of ethnic minorities exhibit eccentric postformal cognition, the social experiences of persons from these groups may be sufficiently different to influence and qualify cognition (Jackson, Antonucci, & Gibson, 1990; Montero-Sieburth, 1990; Morgan, 1990; Nakanishi, 1990; Tippeconnic; 1990).

Just as postformal cognition can be influenced by experiences associated with gender, culture, or ethnicity, the experiences of persons with disabilities can be remarkably distinct from those of persons without disabilities. In addition to being shaped by interactions with peers with disabilities, the abilities of persons with disabilities can be shaped by their interactions with persons without disabilities (Heumann, 1993; Higgins, 1992). Ferguson, Ferguson, and Taylor (1992) assembled ethnographic research accounts of individuals with disabilities to explore the complex and profound interaction between those disabilities and their success in life. Hawkins (1993) explored the degree of life satisfaction experienced by older persons with disabilities as a factor that influenced their attitudes and abilities. She highlighted access to a wide range of social activities and participation in leisure activities as critical factors influencing life satisfaction. Weisgerber (1991) extensively reviewed research on the quality of life for persons with disabilities, exploring changes in the factors that contributed to positive quality of life during four stages—early childhood, school, employment, and retirement.

Nutt and Malone (1992), employing a developmental viewpoint to review research on older persons with disabilities, identified adequate health care and access to community programs as factors required for continued learning and positive attitudes. The emergence of the term *developmental disability* and the widespread, multidisciplinary use of that term is an indication of a conviction among professionals that there are progressive stages through which adults with disabilities pass. Figure 2–1 identifies characteristics of the postformal stage of cognition that many researchers believe to characterize adult development.

The Birren Hypothesis

The first handbook on the psychology of aging was published in 1959 by James Birren. Readers cannot help but be struck by the relative currency with which a book on this important phase of adulthood was written. The portions of developmental psychology dealing with infancy, early childhood, and childhood had accumulated a robust literature. Though not as well developed, the literature on adolescent psychology was still impressive when compared to the literature on adult developmental psychology available in 1959.

In that initial book on the psychology of aging, Birren reviewed the empirical research he had designed throughout the 1940s and 1950s. Birren, like his colleagues, had noted that the responses of adults to a range of measures declined as they aged. The most prominent measure featured in this research was response to intelligence tests.

Birren & Birren (1990) reviewed early works that had contributed to the widespread view of aging as one in which organisms, as a result of physiological decline and illness, were progressively unable to meet

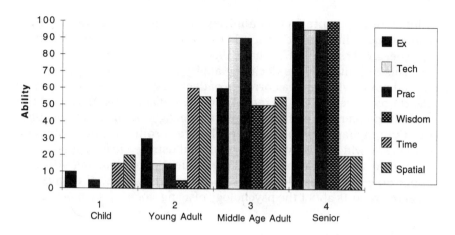

Figure 2-1.   Characteristics of postformal operations.

the challenges of intellectual tasks. Birren asked whether the ability to respond quickly to certain types of tasks should not be considered as an independent trait rather than as a consequence of physiological, psychological, and cognitive degeneration.

For example, 50-year-old athletes run predictably slower than 20-year-old athletes. However, 50-year-old athletes could still be in excellent physical shape; and, by virtue of other traits that they exhibited, they could perform specific tasks better than younger persons. Although it would be unlikely that 50-year-old runners would win a 100 meter sprint, the older persons might excel at an event that required endurance and strategy, such as a cross-country bicycle race. Birren (1966) himself explained this distinction eloquently.

> With maturation comes a great conceptual grasp so that we can size up the situation and then look at the relevant items in our store. This is what I call the race between the chunks and the bits. While younger people . . . can process more bits per second, the older person may process bigger chunks. The race may go to the tortoise because he is chunking, and not to the hare because he is just bitting along. (quoted by Butler, 1989, pp. 55–56)

Admittedly, there are cognitive tasks with which adults have predictable problems. Birren and Birren (1990) reviewed research indicating that adults do not respond well to memory tasks that involve time, that are based on an external regimen, that involve group competition, or that publicize the performance of adults on those mnemonic tasks. Several research studies have indicated a correlation between self-confidence in one's intellectual abilities and higher levels of cognitive achievement in later adulthood (Hultsch & Dixon, 1990; Lachman, Steinberg, & Trotter, 1987; Schaie, 1990).

This insight, that the declining ability to respond quickly to tasks should not be viewed as a correlate of declining ability, was enunciated clearly by Birren (1989; Birren, Woods, & Williams, 1980). One of Birren's students referred to this important insight as the *Birren hypothesis* (Cunningham, 1989). The hypothetical profile of developmental learning on which this hypothesis rests is illustrated in Figure 2–2.

Birren's research was extremely influential in changing attitudes about how aging was viewed and interpreted. In a set of essays and research reports about the psychology of aging, some of the most promi-

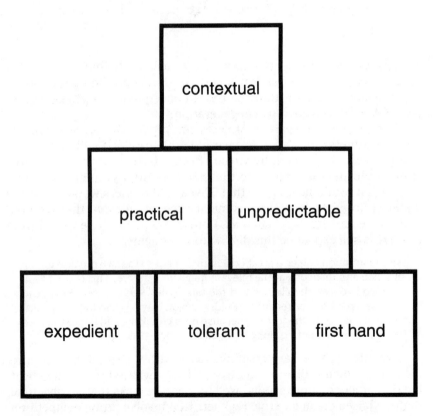

Figure 2–2.   Although ability to complete timed and spatial tasks diminishes with age, experience, technical expertise, practical knowledge, and wisdom do not necessarily diminish.

nent scholars in the field of adult psychology acknowledged the immense impact of Birren's work on their field (Bengtson & Schaie, 1989).

Horn and Donaldson (1976; 1980) conducted research that complemented that of Birren. Building on the work of Cattell (1971), they investigated two distinct types of intelligence. *Fluid intelligence* depends on visual and spatial abilities during timed responses. Items on tests measure fluid intelligence when they require persons to negotiate mazes, search for patterns among strings of letters, differentiate objects, or solve topographical analogies. Crystallized intelligence, on the other hand, represents the cumulative knowledge that persons gather about their society and culture. *Crystallized intelligence*, which would include verbal intelligence as well as contextual problem solving, could be measured by the general reasoning tasks on intelligence tests. However, because of the cultural, ethnic, linguistic, and gender biases inherent in the general reasoning portions of tests (Anastasi, 1982), the best measures of crystallized intelligence might be observations of persons as they solved functional, daily problems (Willis & Schaie, 1986).

Horn and Donaldson (1976, 1980) reviewed data confirming that fluid intelligence, similar to the physical reflexes of athletes, declined inevitably in old age. However, they were convinced that there was not an inevitable decline of crystallized intelligence and that there could even be a continual increase of this experiential type of intelligence over the initial 70 years of persons' lives.

Simonton (1988) developed a similar theory. He hypothesized that creativity develops through age related stages that are at first intuitive but that then become progressively analytical.

> Although some endeavors, such as lyric poetry, may demand a dominating proportion of enthusiasm, other endeavors, such as philosophy, history, and scholarship, may require the significant infusion of experience . . . [and] . . . contributions in these domains peak far later in life (Simonton, 1990, p. 326).

Differentiating technical expertise as a domain of knowledge distinct from that measured by psychometric tests, Salthouse (1990) observed that, in view of the decline in memory and perceptual motor performance, it is remarkable that technical knowledge can continue to grow during persons' senior years.

Educational Implications

Attempting to characterize the effects of aging, Birren and Birren (1990) disputed the often employed analogy of a clock unwinding. Rather, they suggested that an adult should be compared to a clock shop, in which some clocks are unwinding or wearing out but others continue to tick steadily, maybe even more steadily than during earlier days. If one adopts this developmental perspective then the problem of educating adults is very distinct from that of educating children. And the simple adaptation of instructional methods and materials designed for children is unlikely to have the greatest influence on adults.

Because much of the research on developmental adult psychology and the emergence of the very field itself is so recent, it is difficult to link instructionally best practices to precise pieces of research. Nonetheless, there has certainly been adequate interdisciplinary research to establish a developmental base for organizing adult instruction. And there has been adequate research within the field of developmental disabilities to warrant building on this instructional base. Viewed from this developmental perspective, the instruction that would be most successful for adults with disabilities could exhibit a cluster of the characteristics contained in the following list and highlighted in Figure 2–3.

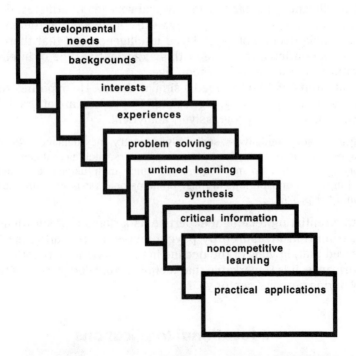

Figure 2–3.   Examples of factors that are the basis for optimal literacy programs for adults with developmental disabilities.

0284466

1. Instruction should build on the backgrounds, interests, and experiences of learners.
2. Instruction should be sensitive to the developmental needs of learners.
3. Instruction should not restrict persons with disabilities from exhibiting developmentally appropriate performance in areas not affected by their disabilities.
4. Instructors should display experiences relevant to the skills they are encouraging their students to develop.
5. Practical aspects of learning should be highlighted.
6. Problem solving should be emphasized.
7. Time constraints should be eliminated.
8. Competition should be discouraged.
9. Learners themselves should set the pace for learning.
10. Opportunities for synthesizing and critiquing information should be incorporated into instruction.

SUMMARY

During the past 40 years, developmental approaches have emerged and gained popularity in the general field of adult education as well as in specialized fields concerned with developmental disabilities. These developmental approaches have highlighted age-dependent stages that can influence instruction intended for adults.

Postformal operations, a stage through which adults may pass, is characterized by an increase in those cognitive abilities that depend on experiential memory. At the same time, there may be a diminution of other intellectual traits, such as the ability to solve timed, spatial problems. Effective instructors are sensitive to the profile of cognitive strengths and weakness that adult learners exhibit.

CHAPTER

3

Diagnosing Adult Literacy

The absence of a universally agreed upon definition of literacy is one of the factors preventing an accurate estimate of the number of adults with disabilities who are illiterate. However, this problem does not result solely from the absence of a common definition of literacy, for there are not agreed upon assessment procedures with which to differentiate literacy from illiteracy (Anders, 1981; Bishop, 1988; Cervero, 1985; Chisman, 1990b; Guthrie & Kirsch, 1984; Harman, 1986).

Academic achievement tests that have been designed for children in the elementary and secondary grades are used often to assess the literacy abilities of adults. Examples of such tests include the California Achievement Test: 5 (McGraw Hill, 1993), the Iowa Test of Basic Skills (Hoover, Hieronymous, Frisbie, & Dunbar, 1993), the Metropolitan Achievement Tests 7 (Balow, Farr, & Hogan, 1992), the SRA Achievement Series (Naslund, Thorpe, & Lefever, 1981), and the Stanford Achievement Test (Psychological Corporation, 1992a). Although these tests were not developed with adult populations, proponents of such tests can argue that the tests can be suited to the level of reading that may be exhibited by adults with literacy problems. The Test of Academic Skills (Psychological Corporation, 1992b) is distinct from these other achievement tests in that it is intended for persons exhibiting reading levels typical of ninth grade through community college students.

Some educators who have reservations about group administered achievement tests employ individually administered achievement tests. Examples of individually administered achievement tests are the Kaufman Test of Educational Achievement (American Guidance Service, 1985), the Peabody Individual Achievement Test—Revised (Markwardt, 1989), the Wide Range Achievement Test—3 (Wilkinson, 1993), or the Woodcock—Johnson Psychoeducational Battery—Revised (Woodcock & Johnson 1989). Because these tests are administered individually, examiners can build a rapport with test takers as well as observe adults' reactions to specific tasks on the tests. These opportunities are not available with tests administered to groups.

Instead of a group administered or individually administered achievement test, adults could respond to a specific reading test such as the Diagnostic Reading Scales (Spache, 1981), the Gray Oral Reading Tests (Wiederholt & Bryant, 1993), the Reading Comprehension Inventory (Giordano, 1988), the Stanford Diagnostic Reading Test (Karlsen & Gardner, 1985), the Test of Reading Comprehension Revised (Brown, Hammill, & Wiederholt, 1986), or the Woodcock Reading Mastery Tests—Revised (Woodcock, 1987). The Nelson–Denny Reading Test (Brown, Bennett, & Hanna, 1981) is a distinctive reading test designed specifically for adults who have graduated from high school.

Textbooks on assessment (Hoy & Gregg, 1994; Mehrens & Lehmann, 1987; Salvia & Ysseldyke, 1995; Sattler, 1988; Wallace, Larsen, & Elksnin, 1992) contain detailed lists of standardized tests as well as critiques of these tests. The authors of these textbooks, as well as the developers of the original tests, warn persons who employ those tests that the instruments cannot be used alone to evaluate academic achievement or literacy. The tests supplement a decision-making process in which observations by trained instructors are critical (Gutkin & Curtis, 1982).

Biases

Reading ability is not the sole factor that explains the performance of adult learners on tests. There are extraneous factors, referred to as *test biases*, that can influence test scores. Tests contain biases if they provide an assessment based on characteristics different from those designated explicitly for measurement in the tests (Brown, 1983; Salvia & Ysseldyke, 1995). Biases that hamper the performance of adult learners can originate from the content of questions on tests. Biases can be the result also of motivation, competition, membership in specific groups, or instructional methods.

Content Bias

The results of any test would be limited if its content did not include all of the key features of the target performance that the test was designed to measure. In the case of a reading test, adults answering questions on that test might have demonstrated only a portion of the literacy skills involved in reading. For example, they may have only identified vocabulary on a test that purported to be a reading test. But if identification of vocabulary was the sole task on the basis of which reading was assessed in a test, competent readers who exhibited other types of literacy skills (such as ability to comprehend words in context) could have been penalized (Farr & Carey, 1986). Based on format and content, Hammill, Brown, and Bryant (1992) reviewed and classified over 100 reading tests. Among the categories they identified to differentiate the tasks on tests were comprehension, word and letter recognition, word and phonic analysis, and reading rate. These categories indicate the wide range of tasks that can characterize tests purported to be reading tests.

Sometimes tests fail to employ appropriate tasks to measure the trait targeted for measurement (Hernstein, 1982). As an example, all adults might not respond correctly to a reading test passage such as the following one:

> Henrietta read the train schedule carefully. She noted that there were two trains approaching the station in which she was waiting. The trains were traveling from opposite directions at 100 mph each. Since it was noon and the remaining distance between the trains was 200 miles, she speculated about the time that the two trains would pass each other.

Some adults might not understand this passage because they had not read it accurately. But others might not understand the passage even though they had read it accurately. Persons from this latter group might not understand the passage because the task requires them to read and respond to an academic problem simultaneously. When persons do not score well on tests in which they must read and respond to academic problems, how can one determine if their failure originates from reading, from the academic problems, or from both?

Other Biases

Not all tasks on reading tests are motivating to adult learners. For example, reading tests on which adults identify words presented out-of-context, read aloud passages aimed at school-age children, verbalize nonsensical letter groupings, or differentiate letters may not be genuinely communicative to the participants. For similar reasons, writing tests on which adults must edit the errors made in passages that others have composed may not be genuinely communicative. And mathematical tests on which adult learners employ calculation procedures that are isolated from meaningful problems may not generalize to the functional situations in which the learners have developed their calculation skills. Consequently, the motivation to answer questions on such tests might be minimal.

Any test designed to be administered to groups can be biased against individual learners within those groups. But, if a test is given in a group, then there can be a competition bias as well. Adult learners can be motivated or inhibited by competitive pressure. Consequently, a competition bias, like many biases, may have either a positive or negative influence on different learners (Anastasi, 1982; Hopkins & Stanley, 1981).

Some adult learners who are inhibited by competition can become so stressed that they cannot effectively take a test. Similarly, when adult learners are aware that a test is limited by time, they can compete with the clock and show the same nervousness that they would when competing with other students (Anastasi, 1982). This bias becomes further accentuated if time limits have been introduced to facilitate the administration of a test and not because time is relevant to the skills or concepts being evaluated in that test.

American society has been represented as more test-oriented than other societies (Mitchell, 1992). Consequently, immigrant adult learners from societies that are not test-centered may be penalized for their lack of experience in taking tests. Learners who are members of select social groups can be penalized also if their backgrounds do not reflect the experiences highlighted in tests. For example, rural dwellers reading passages about urban issues could appear to be deficient readers when it is actually their inexperience that can be complicating an understanding of the passages. Persons from ethnic minorities could appear to be academically untalented if test items made assumptions about cultural information that was not within their experience (Langdon & Clark, 1993; Pipes, Westby, & Ingelbret, 1993; Wallace, 1993).

Because there may have been multiple instructional avenues along which different learners have approached the identical academic goal, instruction can be a bias that affects testing. If the tasks on a test are arranged in an instructional format distinct from that which adult learners encountered typically during their learning, this may cause problems that influence test scores (Anastasi, 1981). As an illustration, if the vocabulary portion of a reading test emphasized phonic rules for vocalizing unfamiliar words, adult learners not instructed in phonics would be at a disadvantage, irrespective of the degree to which they had developed reading vocabulary.

Multiple-choice questions, which are used extensively on many tests administered to adults, could be the basis for another potential test bias. Aiken (1985) noted that multiple-choice tests favor persons who respond rapidly. Conversely, these tests penalize individuals who don't respond quickly but who may be creative and thoughtful problem solvers. Such persons, who may read more into questions than the authors of tests intended, can be confused by the narrow scope of choices available in multiple-choice responses.

Biases Against Persons With Disabilities

Some biases affect adult learners with disabilities disproportionately or even exclusively. As an example of a test bias that may have a peculiar impact on learners with disabilities, the testing may be communicated through a sensory modality that is impaired (Alpern, 1967). Students with impaired hearing would be at a disadvantage if they were required to listen to directions for taking a test or listen to test questions. The impact of such a bias would be increased if the examiner lacked training in an appropriate compensatory strategy such as manual communication (Sullivan & Vernon, 1979).

Fuchs and Fuchs (1990) reviewed research indicating that when an unfamiliar examiner administered tests to students with language handicaps, the test performance of respondents declined. This bias did not interfere with the test performance of students without language handicaps. They concluded that "examiner error is source of systematic . . . bias in the assessment of language handicapped children" (p. 5). They speculated that this bias could affect learners with other handicapping conditions as well. Although this research did not examine adult learners, it is reasonable to assume that this bias could affect the testing of adults with language disabilities as well.

The manner in which students responded to questions could be another test bias. For example, testing by means of a computer could assume prerequisite skills, such as fine motor control, or prerequisite conditions, such as environmental access to the computer. Such prerequisite skills and conditions might not be readily apparent to the administrators of a test (Kramer & Mitchell, 1985). Depending on the restrictions present, tested individuals who exhibit disabilities such as visual impairment, a communicative disorder, or motor dysfunction can be penalized (Fox & Weaver, 1981; Gillespie & Lieberman, 1983; McKinney, 1983).

If persons with disabilities are penalized on tests because of such restrictions, it may require a sensitive and insightful instructor to differentiate the influence of those test biases from low achievement or negative attitudes by learners. Additionally, when tests are administered to students with disabilities that can range from mild to profound, the probability of erroneous assessment increases in proportion to the degree and the multiplicity of impairments (Brown, 1987; Dubose, 1978; Dubois, Langley, & Stass, 1977; Kierner & DuBose, 1974; Sparrow & Cicchetti, 1978).

Reducing the Impact of Test Biases

Metz (1989) reviewed traditional techniques for assessing adult literacy, potential biases associated with the techniques, and alternatives to traditional forms of assessment. Tests that contain biases are invalid if those biases significantly influence the scores on the tests. To estimate whether biases significantly influence scores, one could modify the tests to reduce the impact of the biases. A modified, instructor-made test or a modified, alternate version of a formal test can be administered to adults and compared with the results of the original, nonadapted test. The following types of modification could be appropriate for teacher-made tests:

- changes in printed format
- audio recordings of instructions and questions
- supplementary practice questions
- supplementary visual cues to highlight printed information
- photocopied enlargements of printed materials
- instructional assistants to aid in the recording of responses

In addition to supplementing formal tests with other tests modified to neutralize the impact of biases, one can supplement testing with less structured forms of assessment (Usher & Bryant, 1989). Less structured forms of assessment could include:

- analyses of errors made by learners
- self-assessment questionnaires completed by learners
- cumulative portfolios of learners' work
- journals in which adults comment upon instructional methods, topics, and materials
- learner-created tests
- responses to practical tasks using functional materials
- observations by instructors about learners

Such alternative assessment constitutes an antidote to biased tests. Because the curricula in adult educational programs are often individualized to suit the needs and abilities of learners, curriculum-based assessment can be used to evaluate learners' progress through the genuine curriculum to which they are exposed. These individualized but genuine curricula may depart significantly from the curricula that are the basis for standardized commercial tests.

Site-based, vocational assessment, employed frequently with adolescents and adults who exhibit disabilities, can be viewed as a specialized variation on curriculum-based assessment (Baumgart, 1990; McDonnell, Wilcox, & Hardman, 1991; Powell, Pancsofor, Steere, Butterworth, Itzkowitz, & Rainforth, 1991; Weisgerber, 1989). With this approach to assessment, evaluation is performed by a team of participants, which might include supervisory employment specialists, auxiliary professionals, employers, and the adult learners themselves. The assessment made by this team, which could involve literacy skills, is linked to explicit, vocational competencies that are required to acquire and maintain a job.

Before decisions are made about adult learners on the basis of test scores, one can critique the tests those learners have completed, possibly using the information in Table 3–1 as a guide. Because tests containing biases are not accurate, these inaccuracies can influence scores. However, one would still have to estimate the degree to which learners' scores were influenced by any biases that were detected.

Table 3–1   Questions That May Reveal Biases in Tests Administered to Adults

1.	Did the peculiar background experiences of the learners limit their ability to answer questions?
2.	Did differences between the content of the instruction to which learners had been exposed and the content of the tests limit the degree to which learners could answer questions?
3.	Was learning evaluated in an isolated or unnatural manner?
4.	Were several features of learning evaluated simultaneously?
5.	Could competition have affected performance?
6.	Were there warnings or cues about time limits?
7.	Were testing procedures explained in an accessible fashion?
8.	Were there sufficient practice items to familiarize learners with the testing procedures?
9.	Was the format of the test items familiar?
10.	If persons taking the tests recorded their own responses, was the answering technique familiar?
11.	Were the tasks on the tests motivating?

Note. From "How to Reduce Test Biases," by J. Cole, B. D'Alonzo, A. Gallegos, G. Giordano, and S. Stile, 1992, *Adult Learning, 4* (6), pp. 26–27, Copyright 1993 by American Association for Adult & Continuing Education. Reprinted with permission.

Biases can influence all adult learners irrespective of whether those
learners exhibit disabilities. Nonetheless, there are areas of assessment
that are likely to be biased in a peculiar way if disabilities are present.
Although Table 3–1 might reveal biases that could affect adult learners
with or without disabilities, Table 3–2 contains questions that highlight
the potential impact of disabilities as factors contributing to test bias.

If one concludes that test biases have been influential, or if one is
unsure whether test biases have been influential, one can gather distinct

Table 3–2   Questions About Tests That May Reveal Biases Against Persons With Disabilities

1.   Did sensory or communicative impairments make portions of the test inaccessible?
2.   Did sensory or communicative impairments limit students from responding to questions?
3.   Did the test or the method of responding limit students' physical access to test materials?
4.   Did the background experiences of the students limit their ability to respond to questions?
5.   Did the content of classroom instruction limit students from responding to questions?
6.   Were features of learning evaluated in an isolated and unnatural manner?
7.   Were several areas of learning evaluated simultaneously?
8.   If the test was administered to a group, did competition affect performance?
9.   If the test could have been halted because of unsuccessful responses, were students aware of this?
10.   Did the test materials contain instructions, warnings, or cues about time limits?
11.   Did the examiner provide instructions, warnings, or cues about time limits?
12.   Were students cognitively aroused during the test?
13.   Were students motivated during the test?
14.   If there were attempts to cognitively arouse or motivate students during the test, were these attempts like those with which students were familiar?
15.   Was the examiner familiar?
16.   Was the test administered in a setting that was familiar?
17.   Were instructions explained in a familiar fashion?
18.   Was the format of the questions familiar to students?
19.   If the students recorded their responses to questions, was the recording technique familiar?
20.   Was the editorial layout of the testing materials familiar?

Note. From "Test Biases that Hamper Learners with Disabilities" by J. Cole, B. D'Alonzo, A. Gallegos, G. Giordano, and S. Stile, 1992, *Diagnostique, 17,* pp. 209–225, Copyright 1992 by Council for Educational Diagnostic Services—a division of the Council for Exceptional Children. Reprinted with permission.

but complementary measures of abilities. The results of tests could be reconsidered in the light of these supplementary data. Although these procedures would not provide a definitive assessment of the impact of test biases, such procedures present opportunities to validate, repudiate, or qualify the scores on those tests. Additionally, because such procedures raise questions about the possibility that learners' test scores might have been influenced by biases, this awareness by itself can contribute to the objective assessment of adult learners.

Background Information

Irrespective of whether one assesses the literacy levels of adults with a formal test or with an informal measure, the accuracy of that assessment would be increased if it can be combined with supplementary information. Supplementary information might relate to the backgrounds or the learning experiences of adults with disabilities. Examples of supplementary information could include medical, academic, or psychological records.

Other information might be gathered from conversations or through surveys completed by learners, family members, or the associates of learners. Exhibit 3–1 is an example of a form that could be com-

---

Exhibit 3–1
Background Survey, Administered Orally or in Writing to an Adult Learner

Name_____

Date _____

1. The members of my family are _____

_____

2. Something I don't like about someone in my family is_____

_____

(continued)

Exhibit 3–1 *(continued)*

3. Someone in my family who I like is _____

_____

4. My job is _____

_____

5. A job I would never want is _____

_____

6. If I could have any job, I would choose_____

_____

7. My favorite foods are _____

_____

8. My worst foods are _____

_____

9. If I could read anything I chose, I would pick _____

_____

10. If I could read anything, I would never pick _____

_____

11. My favorite television programs are ones about _____

_____

12. My favorite music is_____

_____

13. My least favorite music is _____

_____

14. The persons I like to be around are _____

_____

(continued)

Exhibit 3–1 (continued)

15. The type of persons I don't like to be around are _____

_____

16. Something I like about my neighborhood is _____

_____

17. Something I don't like about my neighborhood is _____

_____

18. If I could live anywhere, I would choose _____

_____

19. If I could make one thing disappear, I would choose _____

_____

20. If I could have anything, I would choose _____

_____

21. My favorite hobby is _____

_____

22. I have the following pet(s) _____

_____

23. If I could have any pet, I would choose _____

_____

24. Something that I'm frightened about is _____

_____

25. A person I would feel safe with is _____

_____

pleted by adult learners. If persons were unable to complete the form independently, they might still be successful if assisted.

If background information were to be elicited through an oral interview, it could be more convenient to gather that information during an

informal conversation rather than by a structured survey such as
Exhibit 3–1. Exhibit 3–2 is a summary sheet for recording informally
gathered background information. Although the context for gathering
the background information would be informal, the summary sheet

---

Exhibit 3–2
**Background Survey, Recorded by an Interviewer After a
Conversation With an Adult Learner**

Name_____

Date _____

1. Family _____

_____

2. Job _____

_____

3. Foods _____

_____

4. Reading Interests _____

_____

5. Television Interests _____

_____

6. Musical Interests _____

_____

7. Friends _____

_____

8. Neighborhood _____

_____

(continued)

Exhibit 3-2 *(continued)*

9. Hobbies _____

_____

10. Fears _____

_____

11. Special Wishes _____

_____

12. Pets _____

_____

13. Special Caregivers _____

_____

14. Special Needs _____

_____

15. Personal Habits _____

_____

16. Social Activities _____

_____

17. Transportation _____

_____

18. Travel _____

_____

19. Languages _____

_____

20. Other Preferences _____

_____

directs the interviewer to categories of information that could help explain the origin of literacy problems. This information could also be useful for designing instructional approaches.

Exhibit 3–3 is another example of a form that could be used to gather background information. The form in Exhibit 3–3 is longer and

---

Exhibit 3–3
Background Record Form

Date of Record _____

Name _____

Social Security Number _____-_____-_____

Address _____

_____ Telephone Number _____

Date of Birth _____ Ethnic Group _____

Transportation _____

Schedule _____

1. Literacy Skills: _____

_____

2. Educational History: _____

_____

3. Current Employment: _____

_____

4. Employment History: _____

_____

5. Interest Areas: _____

_____

(continued)

Exhibit 3–3 *(continued)*

6. Learning Preferences (e.g., computers, one-to-one, small groups . . .) _____
_____

7. Disabilities: _____
_____

8. Health History: _____
_____

9. Special Assistance Services _____

    Technology: _____

    Health: _____

    Counseling: _____

    Mobility: _____

10. Financial Needs: _____
_____

11. Languages: _____
_____

12. Support from Social Service Agencies: _____
_____

13. Social Groups: _____
_____

14. Living Arrangements:_____
_____

15. Family: _____
_____

16. Family History: _____
_____

(continued)

Exhibit 3-3 *(continued)*

17. Goals_____

   Personal: _____

   Literacy: _____

   Career:_____

   Long Range:_____

18. Caregivers:_____

   _____

19. Entertainment: _____

   _____

20. Personal Preferences: _____

   _____

---

more comprehensive than the previous form. This form might be completed after a series of meetings, conversations, interviews, or lessons with an adult learner. A comprehensive summary of this sort could be especially useful in a program that attempted to build instruction on the interests and previous experiences of a learner, such as a psychoeducational program or a whole language program.

Error Analysis

Adults with literacy problems may have the ability to read passages orally. For adult learners who are completely illiterate, an extended period of instruction may be required before they can read orally. But once persons have developed the reading skills to verbalize passages, instructors can analyze the oral reading errors that these learners demonstrate.

Analysis of errors is based on the assumption that not all errors stem from a univocal source. Errors can be diverse, originating from different causes and requiring different instructional responses (Goodman, Goodman, & Hood, 1988).

The simplest procedure for analyzing errors is to make an audiorecording of an adult reading. While subsequently listening to that oral reading sample, an instructor can make notes on a transcript of the passage that the adult read. Figure 3–1 is an example of the types of notations that could be used to mark the passage. These notations enable instructors to create a record of oral reading that simplifies the analysis of errors and enables other evaluators to inspect the reading.

Figure 3–2 is an example of a printed passage that was read by an adult reader. The notations in Figure 3–1 have been used to indicate irregularities in the reading of that passage. If one were to make no further assessment, this annotated passage could comprise an analysis of the reading. For example, if different persons were to read this same passage, one could annotate their readings with this technique, spread those annotated reading transcriptions on a table top, and sort out readers who exhibited different profiles of reading.

Errors that adults make while reading orally can result from surface features. For example, readers might not be attentive to the visual pattern of a word or to the phonetic pattern of its letters. A reader who

Type of Error	Example
substitution	*brought* He bought a bowl of granola at the store.
omission	He bought a bowl of granola at the store.
insertion	*big* He bought a bowl of granola at the store.
repetition	3. 2. 1. He bought a bowl of granola at the store.
dialect or slang alteration	< dialect> *got* He bought a bowl of granola at the store.

Figure 3–1. Expanded list of notations for analyzing oral reading errors of adults. Handwritten notes indicate the passage as read. *(continued)*

Figure 3-1. *(continued)*

inarticulate utterance	He bought a bowl of granola at the store.

(annotation: *g — a* above "granola")

corrected error	He bought a bowl of granola at the store.

(annotation: crossed-out "the" above the sentence)

reversed letters or words	He saw a bowl of granola at the store.

(annotation: circles and reversal marks over "saw", "granola", "the store")

inappropriate pause	He bought a bowl of granola at the store.

(annotation: // between "bowl" and "of")

repeated word, phrase, or errors	He bought a bowl of granola at the store.

(annotation: *3. 2. 1. geraniums* above "granola")

inappropriate intonation	He bought a bowl of granola at the store.

(annotation: *?* and *∧* after "store")

---

1. *2. not*
It was a hot afternoon in July. The three men
3. store
came into the study with Cokes and set them on
4. hard   *5. cigarettes*
the wobbly card table. Two lit cigars and one
6. ate ⟨dialect⟩   *7.*
munched pretzels from a basket on a counter. A
8. rotting   *9. pushed*   *10. froth*
rotating fan on the floor purred back and forth
11. ground
across the group. Although they had all taken off

Figure 3-2. Passage indicating oral reading through expanded notations. *(continued)*

Figure 3–2. *(continued)*

¹². soaked

their jackets, their armpits were stained with

13 *sweat ⟨dialect⟩*   *14.*   *¹⁵. dealed ⟨dialect⟩*

perspiration. The tallest one dealt cards slowly to

16.

all three of them. There was no money on the

table, but the game was clearly important to them.

¹². beat

They bit their lips and bent the corners of their

¹⁸. watched

cards as they waited for the dealer to finish.

¹⁹. expecting   *20.* *21*   *²². drops*

Everyone was expectant, ignoring the droplets of

23.   *24*

sweat that were beading on their faces and

25 tickling

trickling onto soda cans, cigars, pretzels, and

cards.

said *rat* for *cat* in a sentence would be substituting a word that resembled the original word in the text visually and phonetically. In contrast,
a reader who said *giraffe* for *cat* would be substituting a word that did
not resemble the original word visually nor phonetically. Other areas
from which errors can originate are grammar and comprehension.
Table 3–3 explains and illustrates these three global areas from which
oral reading errors can develop.

Using the abbreviated notations indicated in Table 3–3 (underlin-
ing, diagonal lines, and circles) instructors can indicate errors originating from inattention to surface features, grammar, or comprehension.
An annotated transcription, such as that in Figure 3–2, can be supplemented with these abbreviated notations to facilitate the diagnostic
categorization of readers. Figure 3–3 is an example of this procedure
applied to the transcription in Figure 3–2.

Table 3–3   Abbreviated List of Annotations for Identifying the Source of Oral Reading Errors Made by Adults

Source of Error	Notation	Explanation
Surface	Underline	Surface errors do not affect grammar or comprehension. For example, persons who substitute synonyms such as *boat* for *ship* and *fruit* for *apples* would exhibit surface errors. Omitting the word *very* in the clause *he saw the very big balloon* would be a surface error.
Grammar	Diagonal Line	When persons make errors such as omissions or insertions, the sentences that result may be grammatically ill formed or grammatically well formed. The frame of reference for this decision is the entire altered sentence that the adult creates. For example, omitting the word *saw* in the following sentence would result in a spoken sentence that was grammatically ill formed: *He saw the very big balloon.* Omitting the word *very* in the same sentence would not create a grammatically ill formed sentence.
Comprehension	Circle	Comprehension errors are alterations that indicate a disruption of the message the author intended to convey in a passage. Omitting the word *very* in the following sentence would not disrupt the author's message: *He saw the very big balloon.* Omitting the word *very* in this sentence would most likely disrupt comprehension: *Although one poodle was big, the other was very big.* Omitting the word *poodle* would certainly disrupt comprehension.

It was a hot afternoon in July. The three men
came into the study with Cokes and set them on
the wobbly card table. Two lit cigars and one
munched pretzels from a basket on a counter. A
rotating fan on the floor purred back and forth
across the group. Although they had all taken off
their jackets, their armpits were stained with
perspiration. The tallest one dealt cards slowly to
all three of them. There was no money on the
table, but the game was clearly important to them.
They bit their lips and bent the corners of their
cards as they waited for the dealer to finish.
Everyone was expectant, ignoring the droplets of
sweat that were beading on their faces and
trickling onto soda cans, cigars, pretzels, and
cards.

Figure 3–3. Passage indicating oral reading through a combination of expanded and abbreviated notations.

When initially learning to use diagnostic notations, instructors may choose to use the expanded list of notations and then follow that analysis with the summary annotations, as illustrated in Figure 3–3. But as instructors become familiar with the abbreviated notations, they may choose to use these exclusively (Figure 3–4). Not only does the abbreviated procedure save time, the transcriptions that result are easier to interpret. Although long narrative passages may have to be analyzed in two stages, first with expanded notations and then later with abbreviated notations, short samples of functional reading are simple to analyze solely with abbreviated annotations (Figure 3–5).

It was a hot afternoon in July. The three men

came into the study with Cokes and set them on

the wobbly card table. Two lit cigars and one

munched pretzels from a basket on a counter. A

rotating fan on the floor purred back and forth

across the group. Although they had all taken off

their jackets, their armpits were stained with

perspiration. The tallest one dealt cards slowly to

all three of them. There was no money on the

table, but the game was clearly important to them.

They bit their lips and bent the corners of their

cards as they waited for the dealer to finish.

Everyone was expectant, ignoring the droplets of

sweat that were beading on their faces and

trickling onto soda cans, cigars, pretzels, and

cards.

Figure 3–4. Passage indicating oral reading through abbreviated notations exclusively.

(Measure) 2 scoops of detergent with the (measure)

that is (provided) Add the 2 scoops of detergent to

the load of laundry at the beginning of the wash

cycle. See the chart on the side of the box if you

are laundering a (partial) load.

Figure 3–5. Functional reading materials may be best suited for analysis with abbreviated annotations exclusively.

Abbreviated annotations allow instructors to assess three major areas from which oral reading errors may originate. However, the procedure is not without risk. After all, the requirement that adults read orally can be an unnatural and unfamiliar pretext which itself can cause the adult readers to exhibit eccentric reading behaviors. An estimate of reading aptitude based on an analysis of errors will not be valid if those errors are not representative of a person's typical reading.

Nonetheless, there are advantages as well as risks to error analysis. Oral reading gives instructors the opportunity to see the etiology of reading problems in a way that is not accessible during silent reading. One can think of the abbreviated annotations as a set of templates, respectively representing surface features (i.e., sound and appearance), grammar, and comprehension. These templates can be placed against oral reading errors to see if the errors reveal a deficiency in each area. With the aid of such diagnostic insights, instructors could designate the type of literacy program that would be most beneficial for adult learners. This concept is represented pictorially in Figure 3–6.

If the overlapping templates in Figure 3–6 are viewed as transparent, then there are clearly seven rather than three areas in which errors can originate. In addition to errors that originated exclusively with surface features, grammar, or comprehension, some errors might show that readers had been inattentive to two or three areas simultaneously. Figure 3–7 identifies the additional, overlapping areas as ones where there is dual inattention to surface features and grammar, comprehension

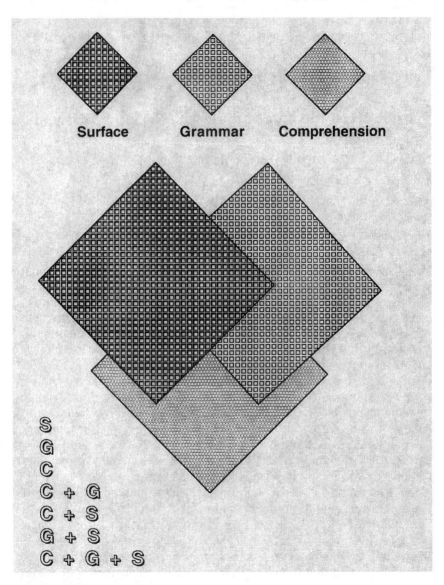

Figure 3-6. Graphic representation of the interaction between types of errors made by adult readers.

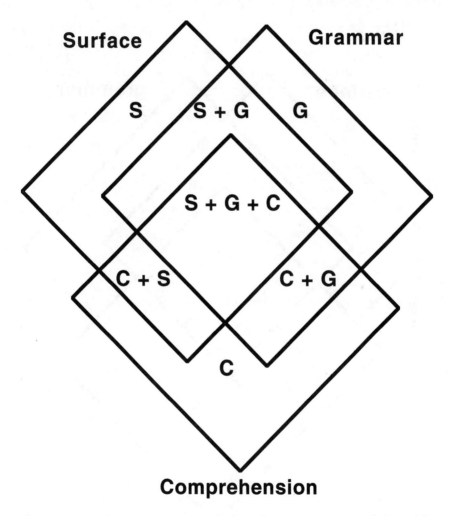

Figure 3-7. The seven areas in which oral reading errors made by adults can cluster.

and surface features, or comprehension and grammar. Finally, oral reading errors can exhibit inattention to all three areas simultaneously.

Figure 3–8 is an example of a template into which oral reading errors could be sorted. Figure 3–9 illustrates seven errors with corresponding notations. Each example of an error in Figure 3–9 corresponds to one of the seven areas of the template in Figure 3–8.

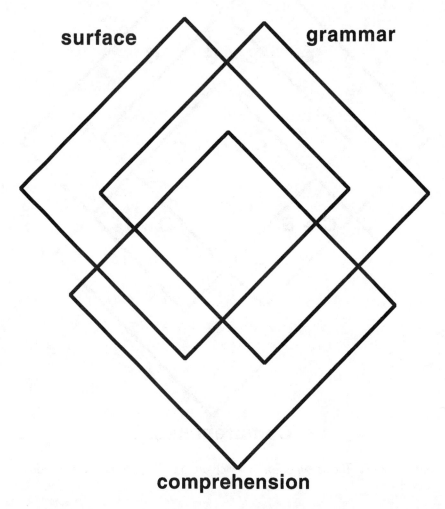

Figure 3–8. Template for sorting oral reading errors made by adults.

Surface:

a

He ate the bowl of linguini.

Grammar:

eat

He ate the bowl of linguini.

Comprehension:

ball

He ate the bowl of linguini.

Surface & Grammar:

eaten

He ate the bowl of linguini.

Surface & Comprehension:

cucumbers

He ate the bowl of linguini.

Grammar & Comprehension:

are

He ate the bowl of linguini.

Surface, Grammar, & Comprehension:

green

He ate the bowl of linguini.

Figure 3–9. Examples of oral reading errors that impact on surface, grammar, and comprehension.

The simplest method for sorting oral reading errors into an error analysis template would be to assign numbers to the errors in an annotated transcription. The numbers corresponding to the errors can then be entered into the template. Figure 3–10 uses this procedure to analyze the errors illustrated in Figure 3–4.

Twenty-five errors were analyzed and placed in the template in Figure 3–4. Sometimes all of the errors that a person exhibits cluster discreetly in a single area of the template, such as the comprehension area. More often, the errors range across several areas and the instructor has to discriminate the cluster. If a clear cluster is not discernible, the oral reading may genuinely exhibit a heterogeneous set of errors. In this case, instructors might decide to place additional errors in the template to validate this analysis.

In the case of Figure 3–10, a clear pattern does emerge. This reader made errors that rarely showed grammatical deviation. Occasional errors show an inattention to comprehension. However, when comprehension errors were committed, the reader was abandoning the surface features of the words in the text. (If this were not true, the comprehension errors would have clustered in the surface/comprehension area of the template.) The majority of oral reading errors clustered in the surface area of the template. In fact, the number of errors clustered in this area exceeded the combined number of errors from all the other areas of the template. Consequently, the type of literacy program that would be most beneficial for this individual would be quite distinct from that suitable for learners with a significant cluster of errors in the grammar or comprehension sections of the template.

Assessing Functional Reading

Persons can master academic reading tasks without being able to transfer academic skills to practical situations. Conversely, persons who do not excel at academic tasks may still develop functional literacy skills (Anders, 1981; Bishop, 1988; Cervero, 1985; Chisman, 1990a, 1990b; Guthrie & Kirsch, 1984; Harman, 1986). Consequently, tests of academic skills, by themselves, can present a biased view of persons' literacy abilities (Fox & Fingeret, 1984; Jones, 1981; Vacca & Sparks, 1981).

Functional reading skills can be an opportunity to escape from this impasse; they can be used to measure nonacademic reading skills that may be distinct from individuals' academic literacy skills. As such, the measurement of functional reading skills can provide a complementary but distinct perspective of persons' total literacy abilities.

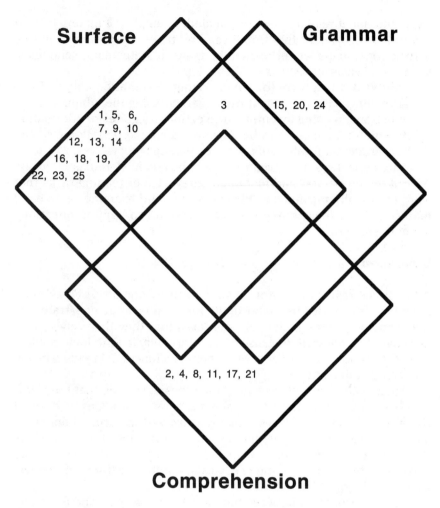

Figure 3-10. Analysis of the errors made by the reader of the passage in Figure 3-4.

Format of a Functional Reading Inventory

Functional reading is the ability to understand and use materials that the tested individuals themselves perceive as useful. Because there would be inevitable variability in the materials that readers viewed as useful, any reading task, such as the reading of road signs, might be viewed differently from one person to another. Because of this variability, a functional reading inventory includes samples of materials from several categories of functional reading tasks. Examples would be instructions, maps, advertisements, financial statements, schedules, forms, road signs, or recipes.

Exhibit 3–4 is a form for summarizing observations about functional reading skills that might be gathered during the administration of a functional reading inventory. The actual categories of information about which persons would be questioned should be tailored to the goals, attitudes, and values of the tested persons themselves.

A functional reading inventory would be administered individually. After a tested person had identified categories of reading tasks that were personally meaningful, that person would examine samples of materials from these categories and respond to applied questions about the materials.

Validation

A functional reading inventory is an informally administered achievement test. It provides the opportunity for persons to demonstrate that they can use printed materials from tasks that they themselves have designated as relevant. Because of its informality, a functional reading inventory is not standardized. Nonetheless, a functional reading inventory can be validated.

Adults can be asked to identify the types of reading that they view as most important in their nonacademic transactions. On the basis of these open-ended responses, reading tasks with correlated materials and questions can be developed. The appropriateness and accuracy of the materials and questions can be judged by experts who may include classroom teachers, learning specialists, adult educators, and educational psychologists.

As the correlation between functional reading skills and academic reading skills is not predictably positive, functional reading inventories cannot be validated by comparing the results of the inventories with the results of academic reading skills tests. On the basis of experimental administrations of a functional reading inventory, subsequent consultation with the persons who administered the inventory, and consultation with adult learners themselves about their own literacy expectations, the criterion level for passing a functional reading inventory could be established.

Appendix A contains examples of materials and questions that could be appropriate to assess the functional reading skills of some learners. There are two examples for each category of functional material in this appendix. Within each category, the first illustration is sim-

Exhibit 3-4
Form for Summarizing Responses of
Adults in a Functional Reading Inventory

Name_____

Date _____

FUNCTIONAL READING SKILLS SUMMARY

1. Recipes and Formulas _____

_____

2. Instructions (for example: toothpaste, packaged food, medicine, care of clothing tags, how to assemble and operate products) _____

_____

3. Maps (towns, buildings, weather, driving) _____

_____

4. Signs in the Environment (traffic, building, elevator) _____

_____

5. Graphic Information (tables, charts, sporting box scores)_____

_____

6. Schedules (bus, train, television, airplane) _____

_____

7. Contracts (book or record club, mail order catalogs, credit card agreements, purchase contracts)_____

_____

8. Advertisements _____

_____

9. Applications (jobs, clubs, insurance, driver's license, armed forces)_____

_____

10. Reports (credit card bill, utilities bill, bank account summary) _____

_____

pler than the second illustration. Consequently, Figure A–1, which is about following instructions, contains reading materials and a question about these materials that are less complex than the information and question in Figure A–2. The other categories of functional reading skills comprised in Appendix A include maps, advertisements, financial statements, schedules, forms, road signs, and recipes.

The materials in Appendix A could be administered to adult learners and the results could be summarized on the form in Exhibit 3–4. Ideally, one would choose personalized materials rather than the materials in Appendix A to assess functional skills. However, if one were faced with the choice of using the materials in the appendix or not assessing functional reading skills at all, the usefulness of these materials would be evident. Even under these circumstances, one would first have a dialogue with adults to be assessed and then use only those portions of the inventory relevant to them.

One would not use the materials in Appendix A if one could obtain comparable materials from an adult's own environment. Personalized materials and questions could be modeled after those in the appendix. For example, a map of an area familiar to a person being tested could be substituted for the map in Figure A–3. Or a schedule from a learner's community could be substituted for the bus schedule in Figure A–10. Correspondingly, the questions about those materials could be patterned after the questions in the appendix but edited so that these were appropriate to personalized assessment materials.

Cued Reading Inventory

Although employed frequently as a measure of functional writing, cued pictures can be used to assess functional literacy (Giordano, 1984). Pictorially cued inventories reflect the environmental contexts with which words, phrases, or printed items are associated. For example, the brand names of products may be associated with the packages into which those items are placed. One might alter a detergent package by covering the printed name of that detergent. If one presents an adult with a detergent package altered in this way, will he or she be able to determine the name of the product?

Altered packages and advertisements are opportunities for assessing functional reading. Similarly, illustrations or photographs of street signs, restaurants, stores, and familiar landmarks in the community present opportunities for developing the items that will constitute a cued writing inventory. Appendix B contains pictorial items associated with print in the environment. Note that the print has been removed. In response to such an inventory, adults could be asked to write the missing print or write any appropriate print.

An alternative format for administering a pictorially cued inventory would be the linking of pictorial cues with pairs of printed words. For example, the two words presented with a picture of a red, octagonal traffic sign could be *STOP* and *BANANA*. Using context, can adult learners select which of these words is appropriate?

As a third format for presenting the tasks in a pictorially cued inventory, learners can be asked to pair pictorial cues with appropriate items in a list of printed items. In this mode of administration, one creates a matching test in which learners draw lines connecting pictorial cues to appropriate words or phrases (Figure 3–11).

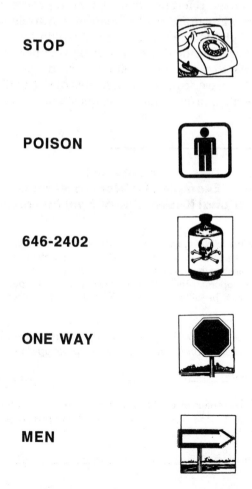

STOP

POISON

646-2402

ONE WAY

MEN

Figure 3–11. Example of a cued reading inventory in a matching format.

Global Knowledge of Print Inventory

Adult learners who cannot demonstrate rudimentary academic skills on achievement tests may have developed *global knowledge of print.* Global knowledge of print might be indicated through awareness of the parts of books, such as a table of contents, reference table, title, author, or index. It could include awareness of the functions of features of books such as illustrations, maps, page numbers, or captions for photographs. And it could include the discrimination of letters, numerals, and symbols, and pictorial illustrations.

Global knowledge of print can be assessed with schedules, menus, magazines, recipes, reference manuals, newspapers, instructions on products, or any functional reading materials. A straightforward way to begin a test of global knowledge of print would be to hand someone materials that are up-side down, observing whether that person reorients the material to the proper position for reading.

Exhibit 3–5 is a worksheet that indicates opportunities for assessing global knowledge of print. Some of the questions require that materials

---

Exhibit 3–5
Example of a Worksheet for a
Global Knowledge of Print Inventory

Directions: The following types of questions can be asked about materials that have been altered as indicated. After alterations, photocopy the materials so that the portions of the passage where there has been cutting, pasting, or taping are not apparent. The following questions are prototypes that could be adapted so as to be suitable for individual learners and individual materials.

1. One of the sentences is up-side down. Can you locate it? *(The sentence has been cut out and pasted back on the page up-side down.)*

   Response_____

2. One of the sentences contains a single word that is up-side down. Can you locate it? *(The word has been cut out and pasted back on the page up-side down.)*

   Response_____

(continued)

Exhibit 3–5 *(continued)*

3. One of the words contains a single letter that is up-side down. Can you locate it? *(The letter has been cut out and pasted back on the page up-side down.)*

Response_____

4. Can you locate a word that begins with the same letter as your name? *(The appropriate letter has been written in the margin.)*

Response_____

5. This word occurs more than once on this page. *(The word has been highlighted with a marker.)* Can you find another example of it?

Response_____

6. Which portions of the text correspond to this illustration? *(This question would be asked when there is an illustration with a caption.)*

Response_____

7. If I wished to locate something from the beginning *(of the book, schedule, manual . . .)*, where would I look?

Response_____

8. If I wished to locate something from the middle *(of the book, schedule, manual . . .)*, where would I look?

Response_____

9. If I wished to locate something from the end *(of the book, schedule, manual . . .)*, where would I look?

Response_____

10. Where is the title *(of this book, schedule, manual . . .)*?

Response_____

be altered. For example, some of the words on a bus schedule could be cut out and then pasted back. One of the words would be pasted back up-side down. Adult learners, who may not be able to read that word or any of the words in that schedule, can then be queried to see if their global knowledge of print enables them to recognize the inverted word.

Portfolio Assessment

Portfolios can be opportunities to assess learners, or portfolios can contain samples of learners' work that reflects their literacy skills. In a whole language program, where reading, writing, and oral language skills are taught in an integrated fashion, the portfolio could contain exhibits representative of all of these areas (Barrs, 1990; Baskwill & Whitman, 1988; De Fina, Anstendig, & De Lawter, 1991; Goodman, Goodman, & Hood, 1988; Paulson, Paulson, & Meyer, 1991). Although portfolio assessment has been documented extensively as a technique that can be appropriate for learners in the primary grades (Barrs, Ellis, Hester, & Thomas, 1990; Rhodes & Natehson-Mejia, 1992; Sharp, 1989; Simmons, 1990), portfolio assessment has been used effectively with adolescent and adult learners as well (Ballard, 1992; Cooper & Brown, 1992; Elbow & Belanoff, 1986; Nolan, 1991; Rousculp & Maring, 1992; Valeri-Gold, Olson, & Deming, 1991; Werner, 1992).

If one were assessing learners' progress in an integrated program, portfolios would include samples of their writing. However, other types of information can be appropriate. Samples of creative activities, such as instructional activities in which learners outline passages or generate questions about materials that they have read, could become part of a reading assessment portfolio. Anecdotal records observing the responses of adult learners to instructional activities could also be included. And portfolios might contain data about the frequency with which learners attended instructional sessions or the length of time that they were occupied by different learning tasks.

Attitudinal information could be reported anecdotally or with a structured inventory such as that in Exhibit 3–6. Depending on the liter-

---

Exhibit 3–6
An Attitude Inventory That Can Be
Administered Orally or in Writing

Name_____

Date _____

1. When reading, I become nervous if_____

_____

(continued)

Exhibit 3–6 *(continued)*

2. Something I would like to change about these lessons is_____

_____

3. My favorite place for reading is_____

_____

4. A job that I would like to have and for which reading is important is_____

_____

5. If I could read any type of material, I would choose_____

_____

6. If someone cannot read, people might think_____

_____

7. It is difficult to read something if_____

_____

8. What I like best about these lessons is_____

_____

9. I become confused when reading if_____

_____

10. I cannot read when_____

_____

11. I would be less nervous about reading if_____

_____

12. When I have to do lessons on the computer, I feel_____

_____

13. The best thing I ever read was_____

_____

14. When I'm asked to read aloud, I feel_____

_____

acy skills of the learners, a decision would be made about whether an attitude inventory like that in Exhibit 3–6 should be administered orally or in writing.

Alternatively, an attitude inventory could be based on observations. An observational inventory does not require instructor and learner interaction. It could be completed by instructors at intervals and then incorporated into the learners' portfolios (Exhibit 3–7).

Exhibit 3–7
**An Attitude Inventory That Is Completed
as Learners Are Observed**

Name_____

Date _____

1. reads often   reads rarely

             1   2   3   4   5   6   7

2. reads for short periods   reads for long periods

             1   2   3   4   5   6   7

3. careless when reading   careful when reading

             1   2   3   4   5   6   7

4. anxious when reading   calm when reading

             1   2   3   4   5   6   7

5. frustrated by computer-reading activities   at ease with computer-reading activities

             1   2   3   4   5   6   7

6. sets low reading standards   sets high reading standards

             1   2   3   4   5   6   7

7. frustrated by group work   positive about group work

             1   2   3   4   5   6   7

(continued)

Exhibit 3-7 *(continued)*

8. does not read functionally   reads functionally

       1   2   3   4   5   6   7

9. not positive about workbook   positive about workbook
   activities   activities

       1   2   3   4   5   6   7

10. does not enjoy reading aloud   enjoys reading aloud

       1   2   3   4   5   6   7

Either interactive or observational attitude inventories could be devised to assess the attitudes of learners toward specific reading tasks or instructional activities. For example, a functional reading attitude inventory might ask persons to complete statements of the following sort:

- When I have to read a recipe, I feel . . .
- If I had to follow a bus schedule, I would . . .
- The hardest part of reading a map is . . .
- One of the most confusing things in the newspaper is . . .
- Telephone directories would be easier to use if . . .
- If I could change one thing about a bank statement . . .
- If I made a mistake when reading a menu, it probably would be . . .

Another type of item that could be part of a portfolio would be examples of spelling. Response to structured reading activities could also be appropriate, especially when these were annotated with supplementary information, such as observations about the attitude of the learner during the activities. Tape-recorded interviews and conversations can also be useful components of portfolios. Figure 3–12 illustrates several different types of information that could be part of an assessment portfolio.

Summary

Assessment of adult literacy is a complex process. Although useful in this process, formal tests contain biases that can invalidate the results of the tests. The validity of tests can be increased by complementing

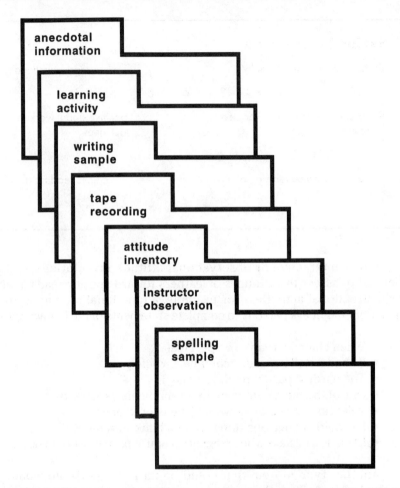

Figure 3-12. Types of materials that can be part of an assessment portfolio.

group-administered tests with individually administered achievement tests or individually administered reading tests.

The validity of formal tests can be confirmed if the results of the tests are coupled with supplementary data. Examples of useful and available supplementary data would be those resulting from the analysis of oral reading errors. A functional reading inventory, a cued reading inventory, a global knowledge of print inventory, or a portfolio could be other opportunities for gathering supplementary assessment data.

CHAPTER

4

Literacy Instruction for Adults With Developmental Disabilities

T hough developing the literacy of adults with disabilities is a complex problem, the diversity of viewpoints about how to define adult literacy may itself be a factor contributing to the complexity of this problem (Cervero, 1985). For example, illiteracy has been defined objectively as the inability to recognize common words (Bishop, 1988). However, illiteracy has been defined also as a wide range of subjective behaviors, including behaviors as sophisticated as the ability to solve complicated, printed problems (Guthrie & Kirsch, 1984; Harman, 1986).

According to subjective definitions, literacy begins at the point where individuals cannot achieve goals with print that they set for themselves. Consequently, some persons may be viewed as illiterate if they cannot read to solve day to day problems with print in the environment. Other adults may be viewed as illiterate if they cannot read well enough to pass a test for a high school equivalency diploma. And still other adults may be considered illiterate if they cannot complete college level assignments with print (Bender 1991; Hayes, 1993).

Chisman (1990b) defined literacy from a functional perspective. He included not only reading and writing but mathematics and problem solving as areas in which individuals could be illiterate. Additionally, he argued that functional communication in the standard language of a community could be a component of literacy.

In view of the subjectivity of many definitions of adult illiteracy, it is not surprising that there is uncertainty about the number of persons who are illiterate. Even less surprising, there is uncertainty about the optimal programs for teaching reading to adults who are illiterate. When one expands the consideration of adult learners to adult learners with disabilities, considerations about optimal literacy programs become even more complex.

Among adults who have not learned to read, some have disabilities that have been diagnosed, some have disabilities that have not been diagnosed, and some are illiterate solely as a result of factors unrelated to their disabilities. Because adults who have not learned to read may receive assistance through programs designed for persons with disabilities or through general adult education services, the professional literature from both special education and adult education is relevant to instructional practices for adults with disabilities.

Six Approaches To Instruction

There are many materials, organized programs, and services for adults who are illiterate. This aid may be available through the federal, state, or local government. Or it may be available through churches, service clubs, private organizations, or volunteers. Table 4–1 lists a group of prominent organizations that provide information about literacy programs for adults.

Despite the multiplicity of materials and organizations, there are only six popular approaches for organizing instruction. Most programs exemplify one of these approaches or are a variation of one of these six. These approaches have been used by adults with disabilities as well as by adults without disabilities. The six approaches, highlighted in Figure 4–1, include computer-assisted programs, skills-based programs, whole language programs, psychoeducational programs, programs that employ children's materials, and functional reading programs.

Table 4–1 Organizations That May Provide Information About Adult Literacy Programs

American Association for Adult and Continuing Education, 112 16th St., NW. Suite 420, Washington, DC 20036

American Library Association, Office of Literacy Outreach Services, 50 E. Huron St., Chicago, IL 60611

Association for Community-Based Education, 1805 Florida Ave., NW, Washington, DC 20009

Business Council for Effective Literacy, 1221 Avenue of the Americas, New York 10020

Clearinghouse on Adult Education and Literacy, U. S. Department of Education, 400 Maryland Ave., SW, Mail Stop 7240, Washington, DC 20202-5515

Division of Adult Education and Adult Literacy Initiative, U. S. Department of Education, 400 Maryland Ave., SW, Mail Stop 7240, Washington, DC 20202-5515

International Reading Association, 800 Barksdale Rd., P. O. Box 8139, Newark, DE 19714-8139

Laubach Literacy International, 1320 Jamesville Rd., Syracuse, NY 13210

Literacy Research Center, University of Pennsylvania, 3700 Walnut St., Philadelphia, PA 19104-6216

Literacy Volunteers of America, 5795 Widewaters Parkway, Syracuse, NY 13214

National Clearinghouse for Applied Linguistics, 1118 22nd St., NW, Washington, DC 20037

National Coalition for Literacy, Indiana University, School of Education, Bloomington, IN 47405

Skills-based programs emphasize the orderly acquisition of reading strategies. These programs postulate an organizational base that identifies the skills required for learning to read. In addition to being identified, critical reading skills are sequenced from less difficult to more difficult in order to facilitate the acquisition of those skills. Although the organizational base is varied among programs, phonetics is the most common base. Phonetic skills are popular because these can enable readers to decipher words that they do not recognize visually.

In contrast to skills-based programs, whole language programs build on the aptitude that learners exhibit in oral communication. The primary material used for instruction in whole language programs is material that the learners themselves have created. These materials are created from transcriptions of the learners' speech. Instruction is

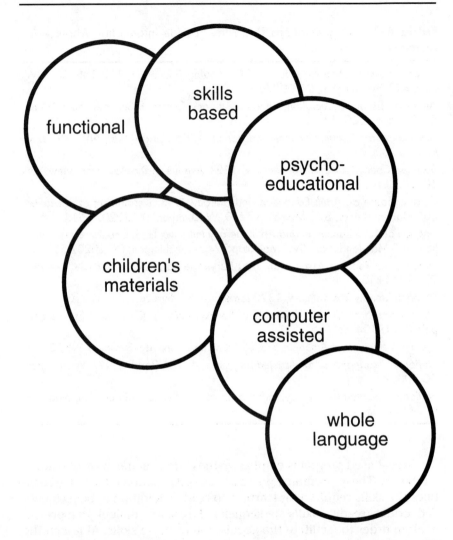

Figure 4–1.   Six popular programs of literacy instruction for adults with disabilities.

presented in a communicative context that enables learners to see the purposeful rationale for each activity. In skills-based programs, words, grammatical rules, and concepts are mastered in a predetermined order that is the same for all learners. In whole language programs, the order for acquiring skills is based on the patterns of vocabulary, grammar, and meaning that characterize the language of individual learners.

Computer-assisted instruction is not so much an independent approach to learning as it is a format for presenting instruction. Computer-formatted instruction can incorporate any of the other instructional approaches. Nonetheless, computer-assisted instruction is often discussed separately from the other programs because of its technical peculiarities and the practical implications of those technical features. Computer-assisted instruction has also been signaled out because of its widespread use and potential to eventually dominate the field of adult literacy education.

Psychoeducational instruction emphasizes the selection of reading materials that embody issues of genuine importance to adult learners. Although the optimal material for this type of instruction will vary among learners, there are predictable concerns that all adults are likely to confront at different times during their lives. These predictable concerns provide high interest topics about which instructors can assemble collections of materials for adult learners. As with computer-assisted instruction, psychoeducational instruction can overlap with one of the other programs. Because psychoeducational programs emphasize the content of the material that will be employed during instruction rather than the format of the instruction, psychoeducational programs can be complemented by skills-based instruction or whole language instruction.

Programs that employ children's materials do so because proponents are attempting to regulate the sophistication of the materials to which adults are exposed during instruction. However, there is a risk that learners may feel it is demeaning to read materials aimed at young learners. To prevent feelings of this sort from undermining a program, learning to read children's materials can be represented as a component of a program that trains adults to help young children. Adults may be motivated to read children's material if they view that learning as an instructional responsibility that will enable them subsequently to read to youngsters. The children to whom adults read may be enrolled in community programs. Or the children may even be persons in the families of the adult learners. In each case, adults and children, both of whom are learning to read, are matched as tutors and learners. And both the children and the adults have opportunities to benefit from the program.

Functional reading programs emphasize print in the environment. Unlike skills-based programs, in which the tasks can lack verisimilitude, functional programs present readers with problems like those that the readers confront in their daily lives. Approaches to reading that integrate literacy skills with job skills are popular examples of functional reading programs.

Although the preceding approaches are presented in separate chapters in this book, the different types of adult literacy programs can overlap when they are actually implemented. For example, whole language approaches emphasize writing, attempting to build reading instruction on the naturally developing communicative competencies that learners demonstrate as they attempt to understand the writing system. Because of the opportunities to facilitate letter formation, spelling, and grammar through computers, there are opportunities to combine computer-assisted literacy programs with whole language approaches (Wangberg, 1986). Journals, correspondence, guided writing, and multiple creative activities can be initiated, maintained, and generalized within the context of computerized instruction (Church & Bender, 1989; Kearsley, Hunter, & Furlong, 1992; McKenna & Robinson, 1993).

In addition to opportunities for combining computers with the writing portions of a whole language approach, there are opportunities to combine computerized instruction with all of the literacy approaches. Because of the structure, organization, and specification of precise objectives within skills-based learning approaches, computerized versions of skills-based programs can be devised with less difficulty than for other types of instructional programs. If skills-based materials rely heavily on drills, the materials that incorporate the drills could be computerized. Any of the other approaches that employed drills could be readily combined with computers as well.

In addition to drilling, popular formats for computerized instruction include tutorials and simulation. Tutorials provide direct instruction about new skills that learners are developing. Computerized direct instruction about vocabulary, grammar, concepts, comprehension skills, and study skills could be combined with programs that are skills-based, psychoeducational, functional, or focused on children's materials. Simulation software provides a real world representation of situations and encourages learners to become familiar with those events or to solve problems against the background of those events. Computerized simulations can complement whole language approaches as well as programs that are skills-based, psychoeducational, or functional. Simulations could also encourage learners to prepare for reading to children as part of an approach that employs children's materials. Within programs that employed children's materials, computers could also enable learners and their instructors to monitor simulated activities that the learners would later initiate with children.

Combining computerized instruction with other approaches to literacy instruction can preserve the advantages of the other approaches and actually enhance those approaches through the distinctive advantages of computerization. Examples of distinctive advantages could be opportunities for immediate feedback, maintenance of records, improved motivation, alternative formats for lessons, progressive sequencing of learning units, individualization of programs, acceleration of learning tasks, streamlining of administrative tasks, reduction in costs, and expansion of the number of learners with whom instructors can interact.

Any of the six approaches can be combined with each other in an eclectic program. For example, learners might be exposed to both whole language literacy strategies and skills-based strategies. However, because the approaches are based on different assumptions, instructors need to ensure that integrated programs do not cause confusion. Confusion might result if activities from distinct approaches influenced learners' expectations about the procedures, scope, and goals of their instructional programs.

Clear perceptions by learners about the purposes and foundations for reading strategies might be enhanced if strategies from one program are not merely appropriated but adapted to complement those in another program. For example, skills-based exercises can complement whole language approaches if the skills-based exercises rely on the vocabulary, grammar, and concepts that learners use in their writing. Adapted skills-based lessons of this sort can be less disruptive within a whole language program than a set of skills worksheets that could supplement whole language lessons but which were not synchronized to the language that learners used in their whole language activities nor to the content of the passages that the learners created in those lessons.

In a similar fashion, instructors could adapt whole language strategies so that these complemented skills-based programs. As an example, vocabulary recognition is taught in contrasting ways within skills-based programs and whole language approaches. Whereas skills-based programs postulate a precise scope and progressive sequence of vocabulary to which learners are exposed, whole language programs focus on the communicative language of learners when selecting vocabulary for instruction. If instructors in skills-based programs bridge these alternative procedures for selecting vocabulary, they can benefit from the distinct advantages of each approach. Instructors can bridge the two alternatives by continuing to use the sequencing of skills specified within skills-based programs as the basis for designating vocabulary that is instructionally appropriate. They can use the sequencing of skills to identify target words that are analogous to words from learners' personal lexicons. As a result of supplementing skills-based activities with the vocabulary that learners use regularly and that is meaningful to them in their everyday lives, learning can be more effective. As a consequence, learners' ability to generalize and their motivation to acquire and retain reading vocabulary can be improved within skills-based programs. These benefits can result without risking the confusion that would ensue if the format, expectations, and philosophy of instruction were changed dramatically during alternating instructional activities.

Within an eclectic program, techniques from the six programs might be kept intact without much adaptation if they were arranged in stages. These nonadapted strategies could then be arranged sequentially within a program. As an example, Jones (1981) recommended that whole language and skills-based activities be used with adult learners who are illiterate. However, because of the reading precision that can be gained through skills-based training, he recommended that this training follow the initial intuitive learning that can be developed through whole language instruction.

When designating instructional programs for specific learners, one must consider practical factors such as the availability of materials, the training of instructors, the goals of the program, the amount of time available by instructors, the amount of time available by learners, and cost effectiveness. Though the relative strengths and weaknesses of programs are linked to practical considerations, strengths and weaknesses are tied to instructional factors as well. An example of such a factor would be the transfer of learning to real world situations. Another example could be the adaptability of programs to the individual physical, psychological, and linguistic needs of persons with disabilities. Additional instructional factors for evaluating programs may include the opportunities for both immediate and sustained reinforcement, the continuity of the instruction, and motivation of adults to learn within the program (Figure 4–2).

Personality, Cognitive Traits, and Group Traits

Strengths and weaknesses of the instructional approaches, as well as multiple practical factors, can influence the specific literacy approach that instructors select. However, personality variables may influence the degree to which learners are successful with a specific program. As such, personality factors, as well as cognitive traits and group traits, should influence this selection of instructional programs.

There can be great variance in the personalities of adults with disabilities. Personality traits can be sufficiently influential to predetermine

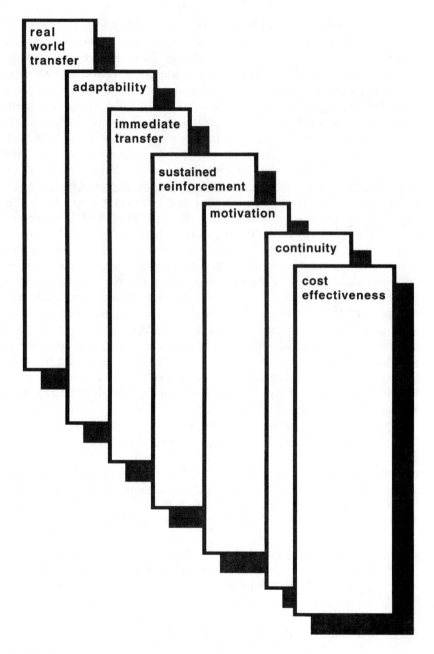

Figure 4–2. Instructional factors on the basis of which adult literacy programs are evaluated.

learners' attitudes toward specific instructional programs. For example, persons attracted to technology would respond to computer-assisted instruction differently from learners who are intimidated by technology. Persons who insisted on participating in the planning and the selection of materials for their instruction would not benefit to the same extent from a skills-based program as someone who followed structured plans more submissively. Figure 4–3 illustrates the relationship between personality factors and programs compatible with those personality factors.

As a corollary to this issue, one can question the degree to which the attitudes of instructors and administrators toward instructional changes influence the type of learning that transpires, the degree of learning that transpires, and even whether learning transpires. In a model for implementing computerized education, Hummel and Archer (1993) addressed attitudes of teachers and administrators as factors that could influence the success of computer innovations. Giordano (1993) reviewed research about attitudes of teachers toward mathematics as a factor contributing to successful learning by persons with disabilities who were being instructed by those teachers. Teacher attitudes are part of the context of reading instruction. The context for reading instruction, along with the learner and the text, is part of a tripartite approach to ensuring that reading assessment and instruction are developed on a comprehensive base. Several informal inventories have been designed to assist instructors in evaluating their own attitudes toward reading, reading assessment, and reading instruction (Kinney & Harry, 1991; Lipson & Wixson, 1991; McKenna & Robinson, 1993).

In addition to personalities, attitudes, and values of both instructors and learners, the cognitive styles of learners may be an additional factor that can predispose them positively or negatively toward specific instructional approaches (Jarvis, 1983). Learners might exhibit a variety of cognitive profiles, emphasizing or suppressing information that can be visual, auditory, or kinesthetic. The following examples highlight several potential cognitive processing differences:

- learners who are active versus learners who are passive
- learners who are impulsive versus learners who are reflective
- learners who prefer concrete data versus learners who prefer abstractions
- learners who focus on the overall organization of data versus learners who can dispense with this pattern

As an example of the impact that cognitive style can have on the development of literacy skills, learners with visually dominated cogni-

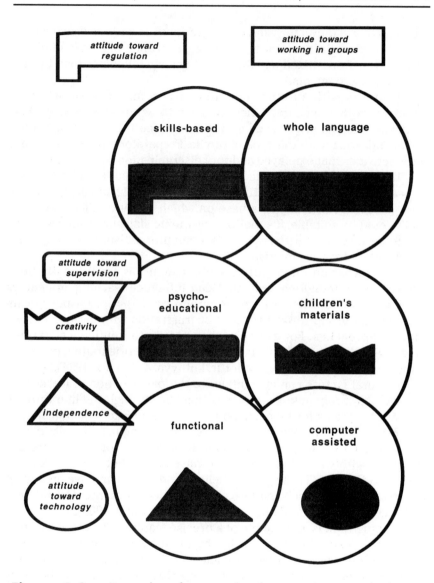

Figure 4–3.   Examples of personality features that can predispose learners toward literacy programs.

tive styles might learn to read best with instructional approaches that encourage them to see written passages. Most functional reading programs emphasize whole word recognition, which builds on learners' abilities to use the shapes and configurations of words as visual cues to identification. In functional reading programs, learners might be exposed to words fixed as labels on items surrounding them in their learning environments.

Learners with auditory cognitive styles might learn best with approaches that encourage them to listen to words or sentences. Phonetically oriented skills-based systems might be the optimal approach for an individual with this type of profile. Preparatory for reading, readiness activities that employed auditory discrimination could be effective.

Learners with kinesthetic cognitive styles might learn best in programs that encourage them to write words. A whole language program that encouraged writing as a base on which reading skills were to be built could be suitable. If superior kinesthetic skills predisposed learners to be successful with keyboards, computer-assisted learning might be an optimal avenue for instruction.

As a variation on cognitive style, which has traditionally been viewed as an individual trait that can influence learning, educators have questioned whether there are group traits that predispose members of that group toward success or frustration with certain instructional approaches. For example, group traits that influence learning might pertain to gender, social class, age, sexual orientation, or exceptionality (Banks, 1994; Traustadottir, Lutfiyya, & Shoultz, 1994).

Cultural factors can also influence the participation of learners in educational programs. Two themes that run through the literature on literacy programs for bilingual and nonnative speakers of English concern the need to incorporate learners' native language linguistic abilities and their distinctive background experiences, for the culture and language with which individuals are raised contribute to their values, beliefs, and goals. These values, beliefs, and goals can have an impact on cognitive style, social patterns, and reactions of learners to different models of instruction (Cloud & Medeiros-Landurand, 1989).

Competition is an example of a precise feature of instructional programs that can influence learning by persons from diverse cultures. Competition can be positive for some learners and negative for others. If adult learners respond suitably, competitive situations can be used. When competition has negative effects on learning, the instructional strategies that are competitive can be adapted or eliminated.

Similar to the different responses to competition, learners can respond differently to the ways that they are grouped during instruction. Whereas some persons learn best in isolation, others prefer group learning. In cultures where cooperative patterns of social interaction characterize the day to day routines, persons from those cultures may respond best to instructional grouping that reflects those patterns (Baca & Cervantes, 1989; Bloome, 1987; Castaneda, 1976; Chan & Rueda, 1979; Fillmore, 1981; Field & Aebersold, 1990).

Another factor that instructors need to consider is the reaction that adults who are not proficient in English may exhibit to instruction that may only be available in English. For example, individuals who are not literate and who are in the initial stages of acquiring English will wish understandably to rely on literacy instruction in their native languages. However, whether instruction is presented in persons' native languages or in English, that instruction will have the greatest impact if it is perceived by individuals as relevant to their personal experiences. Because these experiences may include employment, social interactions, societal issues, home tasks, or supervision of children, functional literacy programs or a psychoeducational program can be suitable. If bilingual instructors or linguistically sensitive instructors are available, whole language programs provide opportunities to incorporate the learners' language as well as their distinctive background experiences (Flores et al., 1985; Heald-Taylor, 1986; Perez & Torres-Guzman, 1992; Peyton & Reed, 1990; Riggs & Allen, 1989; Smallwood, 1991). The relevance of instructional programs can be further increased if the learners themselves participate in the selection of materials, instructional techniques, and scheduling (Riggs & Allen, 1989).

Figure 4–3 indicates the relationship between personality traits and instructional programs. Illustrations similar to Figure 4–3 could be adapted using other factors such as cognitive style, group traits, characteristics of instructional programs, or practical factors. All of these elements are potentially relevant to decisions about the best practice for adult literacy instruction.

Summary

Six approaches for developing the literacy of adults with disabilities were identified. The approaches included computer-assisted programs, skills-based programs, whole language programs, psychoeducational programs, children's materials programs, and functional literacy programs. The programs can be evaluated on the basis of whether the skills developed within those programs transfer to real world situations. Other areas in which the programs can be evaluated include opportunities for immediate and sustained reinforcement, long term continuity of instruction, motivation, cost effectiveness, and ability to meet the needs of individual adult learners with disabilities.

The many adult literacy programs that are available may strike some critics as a sign of disorganization. However, the diversity among adult learners comprises personality traits, individual cognitive traits, and group traits. In view of this great diversity, multiplicity of instructional approaches may be an asset rather than a weakness, for the opportunity to select and adapt programs from a varied instructional menu could be essential to locating the best solutions to literacy problems.

CHAPTER

5

Computer-Assisted Literacy Programs

with
Linda Leeper and Jana Siegel

S tudies have indicated that adults learning to read have benefited from computer-assisted instruction (Anderson, 1991; Askov & Turner, 1989; Wangberg, 1986). Finnegan and Sinatra (1991) reviewed formats for computer-based literacy instruction such as word processing, databases, spreadsheets, and graphics. The authors concluded that all of these types of programs could be effective. They listed specific examples of software from these categories that could be helpful to adult learners at different levels of reading achievement. Church and Bender (1989) identified instructional software in the following categories: drill and practice, tutorials, games, simulations, and problem solving. They cautioned that it was the responsibility of individuals who were instructing persons with disabilities to decide which categories of software, if any, were appropriate for the learners with whom they interacted.

Woodward and Gersten (1992) reviewed research studies indicating that students with disabilities in high school special education programs and their nondisabled peers spent comparable amounts of time on computer-assisted instruction. However, the learning of persons with disabilities was focused about drill and practice software while the learning of individuals without disabilities involved this type of software only occasionally.

Cochran and Bull (1993) identified three general areas in which computers could be used to help individuals with communication disorders: instruction, evaluation, and augmented or alternative communication. With reference to instruction, computers can function as teachers, providing information sequentially and reinforcing correct responses to lessons. Computers can be a context for instruction, comprising a source of printed and pictorial material that can stimulate interaction between the instructors and the learners. And computers are recording systems that can keep useful data to be consulted by both learners and instructors.

Raskind (1994) identified computer programs that could help adults with learning disabilities develop literacy skills. The programs included word processing, spell-checking, proofreading, outlining, abbreviation expanding, speech recognition, speech synthesis, optical character recognition, and personal data managers. Raskind emphasized that these programs could be used for computer-assisted instruction or as a component of adaptive processing. When used as part of instruction, the goal of the technology is to directly promote learning. However, when employed in an adaptive fashion, the goal of technology is not to instruct learners but rather to enable them to compensate for their disabilities (Raskind, 1994).

As an example of how computers can enable persons with disabilities to achieve goals that might otherwise be inaccessible, computers have been equipped with adaptive devices that convert printed materials into spoken words. This adaptation allows users to understand material that they cannot read independently (Kelly, 1993). In addition to education and communication, there are numerous opportunities for computers to help persons with disabilities in other areas of their lives, such as recreation, leisure, health maintenance, home management, mobility, and daily living (Chandler, Czerlinsky, & Wehman, 1993; Hannaford, 1993). Even when the goal of computerized learning programs is to help learners develop specific academic skills, the learners will inevitably develop computer skills that may transfer to computerized tasks in other academic or nonacademic areas (Anderson, 1991).

Sometimes, the indirect benefits of computerized technology are not adequately appreciated. Computerized technology can enable persons with disabilities to establish routines in their daily living schedules. Equally impressive, computers can enable persons with disabilities to experience the independence that results from the ability to vary these routines at will (Smull & Danehey, 1994). Because most computerized recreation is interactive, the stimulation that it may provide to persons with disabilities can be more beneficial than noninteractive types of recreation such as television viewing (Masters et al., 1993). Familiarization with the use of computers can be a bridge for individuals with physical and multiple disabilities to employment that involves computer related tasks (Sowers & Powers, 1991).

Table 5–1 lists the names and addresses of companies that develop or distribute computer software for literacy programs. By contacting these firms, instructors can receive information about programs that are available as well as the content and format of the programs.

Multiple factors should influence the selection of software. These factors could concern the physical facilities in which instruction would take place, the type of computers available, accessibility of facilities, accessibility of computers, accessibility of programs by persons with disabilities, attitudes of the instructional staff, attitudes of the learners, cost, curricular goals, training of instructors, and convenience. Table

Table 5–1 Companies That Publish or Distribute Computer-Based Literacy Materials

Academic Software, 1415 Queen Anne Rd., Teaneck, NJ 07666

American Education Computer, 2450 Embarcadero Way, Palo Alto, CA 94303

American Micro Media, 19 N. Broadway, Red Hook, NY 12571

Britannica Software, 345 Fourth St., San Francisco, CA 94107

Cambridge Development Laboratory, 42 4th Ave., Walthan, MA 02154

Design Ware, 185 Berry St., San Francisco, CA 94107

Developmental Learning Materials, 200 Bethany Dr., Allen, TX 75002

Follett, 4506 Northwest Hwy., Crystal Lake, IL 60014

Holt, Rinehart & Winston, 1627 Woodland Ave., Austin, TX 78741

Houghton Mifflin, Dept. 67, Mount Support Rd. CN9000, Lebanon, NH 03766-9000

Learning Company, 6493 Kaiser Dr., Fremont, CA 94555

Learning Lab Software, 8833 Reseda Blvd., Northridge, CA 91324

Mind Play, 82 Montvale Ave., Stoneham, MA 02180

National School Products, 101 E. Broadway, Maryville, TN 37801-2498

Random House Media, 400 Hahn Rd., Westminster, MD 21157

Scholastic, P. O. Box 7502, 2931 E. McCarty St., Jefferson City, MO 65102

Simon & Schuster, P. O. Box 2987, New York, NY 10185

Sunburst, 39 Washington Ave., Pleasantville, NY 10570

5–2 identifies sample questions one could ask when evaluating the suitability of computer literacy programs for adults with disabilities. Also contained within Table 5–2 are questions that could be helpful in the evaluation of software for computer literacy programs.

Anderson (1991) reviewed software compatible with adult literacy programs. Although he endorsed the use of this software, he admitted that there was a "strong case to be made for the development in all countries of indigenous software" (p. 208). Critics of the technology

Table 5–2 Sample Questions for Evaluating the Suitability of Computer Literacy Programs for Adults With Disabilities

1. Can the program be used with adaptive devices such as a touch screen or modified key board?
2. Will the program be viewed as one intended for children?
3. Can activities and drills be interrupted by learners if they become tired or frustrated?
4. Can learners get help at any time within the program if they are unclear about how to proceed?
5. Can the size of printed information and visual displays on screens be adjusted?
6. Can time limits for activities be expanded or eliminated?
7. Can activities be completed cooperatively?
8. Are records of successful learning preserved?
9. Are incorrect responses explained adequately to the learners?
10. Do the literacy skills that are targeted transfer to real world reading materials?
11. Does the program include activities that reinforce the learning on the computer but which do not require the computer?
12. Is the availability of computers to learners in proportion to the time required to learn the skills at the computer?
13. Does the operation of the program assume prerequisite computer literacy skills?
14. Does the program complement other available programs that can precede, supplement, or proceed this program?
15. Can the program be accessed by learners independently for self-study?
16. Are graphics appropriate and motivating for persons with disabilities?
17. Are graphics appropriate for males and females?
18. Are graphics appropriate and motivating for persons from a range of backgrounds and from diverse cultures?
19. Is there a clear relationship between the skills that are targeted and the learning activities?
20. Is there sufficient diversity with the activities to keep learners motivated?

and software that Anderson espoused would argue that personalized contexts are required at more refined levels than those set by national boundaries. This is especially true in a diverse society such as that within the United States where the factors that influence learning may originate in different ethnic groups, languages, geographical regions, religions, cultures, ages, and gender.

Fine (1991) reviewed testimonials in support of computer-assisted learning. She suggested that adults who use computers develop positive impressions of themselves because they can control the format, difficulty, and pace of instruction to a greater extent than persons in non-computerized programs. Additionally, computer-centered activities can reduce peer pressure and the embarrassment that adult students may feel if responses made in groups are corrected by instructors. And because computer-assisted instruction simultaneously teaches computer literacy as well as reading and writing skills, the approach may prepare learners to be successful with technological tasks in employment, leisure, and daily living (Anderson, 1991; Chandler et al., 1993; Hannaford, 1993). The tasks for which computers are preparatory might involve computers themselves or analogous equipment such as an automated teller machine, a VCR, or an automated appliance.

Criticism of Computer-Assisted Approaches

Cuban (1986) provided an historical review of technology in education since 1920. He pointed out that emerging technologies had failed to live up to the predictions made by enthusiastic advocates about the critical role of these innovations within instruction. High cost, lack of auxiliary personnel, and unreliable equipment have been pervasive factors limiting the influence of instructional technologies that relied on film, radio, television, and computers. Computer technology has frequently been imposed on instructional staff rather than selected in response to needs of learners that the staff has identified. When this circumstance is combined with the other factors, the failure of some instructors to be enthusiastic and confident about computers hardly seems surprising.

Although she did not offer data to dispute the claims about learning made by advocates of computer-assisted literacy instruction, Bishop (1988) dismissed computers as "expensive gadgets" that were not cost effective. For example, the number of learners who can benefit from computer-assisted instructional programs can be limited because of the relatively prohibitive price of computers compared to the price of printed instructional materials.

Computers are linked often to approaches in which learners master skills in a progressive, serial order. Because such approaches do not result in immediate achievement, the use of computers in programs where there are high rates of student turnover has been discouraged (Bishop, 1988). Despite these potential drawbacks, Bishop did admit that computer-assisted instruction could be alluring to adults who might not be motivated to perform comparable activities with a pad, pencil, and workbook.

Jacobson (1993) pointed out several weaknesses that could characterize computer-assisted approaches to adult literacy. Some of these weaknesses are intrinsic to the software itself and may be the result of limited financial incentives for computer software producers to develop adult literacy programs. Other limitations could be the result of an experientially and linguistically diverse population for which computer programs lack sufficient adaptability to be suitable, a scarcity of teachers who are well informed about computer technology, and a lack of research data demonstrating that learners have made meaningful gains after using computer-assisted literacy programs.

Rinsky (1993) highlighted a common vocabulary problem of computer literacy programs. For even when these programs are intended to present introductory vocabulary, the instructions for employing the programs may contain interactive vocabulary that falls outside the range of beginning readers. Examples of frequently occurring vocabulary with which readers are likely to be unfamiliar include *answer, catalog, command, continue, control, correct, cursor, escape, finish, incorrect, joystick, memory, paddle, password, practice,* or *repeat*.

Although acknowledging that computers have great potential benefits as instructional tools, Maddux (1993) noted predictable but inappropriate expectations about computers that should be considered before computerized instruction is adopted. For example, there is a tendency to believe that once computerized instruction has been initiated, superior learning will follow automatically. The corollary of this tendency is a belief that whenever learning has been linked to computers, the quantity and the quality of that learning has advanced. The computerization of learning activities can lead to a misplaced commitment to those activities. This commitment can be based not on the demonstrated value of the activities but on the money and time that was invested to computerize the instructional tasks. Finally, because persons expect too much from computers, they may misperceive the role of the computer as supplanting rather than supplementing human decision making.

Reviewing literature about the use of computers by adolescents with disabilities, Woodward and Gersten (1992) questioned whether computerized instruction had enabled learners to master curricular objectives. Among the factors they cited as limiting the effectiveness of computerized instruction were an overreliance on drill and practice software, limited access to computers, and a poor understanding by both instructors and learners about how computerized programs complement the goals of the traditional curriculum.

Response To Criticism

Church and Bender (1989) noted emotional factors that can predispose persons to resist computerized instruction. They wondered if computerized instruction didn't challenge some individuals because of the disruptive changes that it entailed in the established routines of instructors. Some instructors may view computerized changes as implicit, negative criticism of programs to which they have made contributions. And some persons may fear the imposition of a requirement that they develop the technical skills to manage computers. Such views can foster personal attitudes that reduce the effectiveness of computerized instruction.

Church and Bender (1989) suggested techniques for reducing the resistance to computers that might be displayed by instructional staff. A key recommendation was to initiate a planning and evaluation process in which all staff members affected by new technology were encouraged to participate. Other suggestions were to educate instructors about the advantages of technology and to form an advisory board of staff members to make decisions about introducing new technology.

Responding to criticism that computers are not cost effective, Packer and Campbell (1990) argued that the cost effectiveness of computers could not be assessed accurately because there are not adequate evaluative data about the learning potential of computers. Even when cost prohibits each learner from having unlimited access to a computer, there are instructional techniques for adapting to such a situation. For example, instructors can project the output from a single machine for the benefit of all of the members of a group, encourage team learning, and employ individualized sessions on computers to supplement non-computerized instruction (McKenna & Robinson, 1993).

Disagreeing with the argument that computer programs necessitate regimentation, Hayes (1993) highlighted adaptability as an advantage of computers when these are used to instruct persons with learning disabilities. For example, learners who have problems with handwriting can benefit from the printed output of computers. Learners who have problems with spelling, vocabulary, or grammar can be aided by computer programs that check spelling, suggest synonyms, or review grammar. Although the adaptability of computers is not comparable to that of instructors who modify lessons based on the responses of students, there are multiple examples of software with sufficient adaptability to be used effectively by persons with learning disabilities (Majsterek & Wilson, 1989).

Ylvisaker, Szekeres, Harwick, and Tworek (1994) noted that learning environments can be structured with computers in ways that cannot be controlled in other types of instruction. This is an advantage for persons who have disabilities that reduce their attentiveness, such as acquired brain injury. And when learners require extended drill and practice exercises, computers can be effective in situations where the patience of instructors would wear thin. For similar reasons, computerized instruction with controlled rates for the presentation of new information or the review of previously learned information can be especially useful as part of instructional programs for learners with severe disabilities (Thousand & Villa, 1993).

Because some computer programs present training that is divorced from real life situations, the skills that are developed with the programs may not transfer to functional contexts. By ensuring that computer training is linked to the social or academic objectives that have been set for learners in the noncomputerized portions of their instructional programs, the probability of functional learning is increased (Ylvisaker et al., 1994).

Adult literacy software may exhibit drawbacks in content, instructional design, record keeping, and the ease with which it can be used by learners (Reid, Allard, & Hofmeister, 1993). By critiquing programs, instructors can become aware of negative features and then adapt instruction to minimize the effects of these drawbacks. With regard to content, instructors can question whether content is presented logically, clearly, and in a manner that generalizes to other types of learning, and is responsive to objectives that have been defined for a precise audience (Reid, Allard, & Hofmeister, 1993). Questions about design could focus on whether the program contains adequate variety, differential response modes, adjustable rates of instruction and response, sensitivity to diverse responses from learners, and suitable types of feedback (Reid, Allard, & Hofmeister, 1993). After reviewing checklists, questionnaires, and forms developed to help instructors critique computer software, Church and Bender (1989) noted the following common categories among the questions on these items:

- instructional content
- use of graphics, color, text, and sound

- software objectives
- appropriateness of lesson pacing, ability levels, ease of use, and presentation of content
- software product information such as title, publisher, and computer format
- user manuals and documentation

The precise questions that instructors of persons with disabilities would pose would depend on the characteristics of the learners with whom they were interacting and the instructional expectations of the software that was being employed (Ylvisaker et al., 1994). Exhibit 5–1 is an example of a checklist that instructors could devise to evaluate software. As a result of a careful critique with such a checklist, instructors might make a decision about whether to employ a specific computer program. Alternatively, instructors could decide to use that program in an adapted fashion to compensate for potential weaknesses that the critique had revealed.

Exhibit 5–1
Computer Software Checklist

Software_____

1 ----- 2 ----- 3 ----- 4 ----- 5
inferior   average   superior

precise instructions	1 ----- 2 ----- 3 ----- 4 ----- 5
interesting content	1 ----- 2 ----- 3 ----- 4 ----- 5
adult orientation	1 ----- 2 ----- 3 ----- 4 ----- 5
compatible with adaptive devices	1 ----- 2 ----- 3 ----- 4 ----- 5
absence of gender bias	1 ----- 2 ----- 3 ----- 4 ----- 5
diverse activities	1 ----- 2 ----- 3 ----- 4 ----- 5
stimulating graphics	1 ----- 2 ----- 3 ----- 4 ----- 5

(continued)

Exhibit 5-1 *(continued)*

legible print on screen	1 ----- 2 ----- 3 ----- 4 ----- 5
on-screen help	1 ----- 2 ----- 3 ----- 4 ----- 5
accurate	1 ----- 2 ----- 3 ----- 4 ----- 5
suitable language	1 ----- 2 ----- 3 ----- 4 ----- 5
appropriate activities	1 ----- 2 ----- 3 ----- 4 ----- 5
user friendly	1 ----- 2 ----- 3 ----- 4 ----- 5
challenging	1 ----- 2 ----- 3 ----- 4 ----- 5
difficulty can be regulated	1 ----- 2 ----- 3 ----- 4 ----- 5
length of sessions can be regulated	1 ----- 2 ----- 3 ----- 4 ----- 5
can be interrupted	1 ----- 2 ----- 3 ----- 4 ----- 5
does not assume prerequisite computer skills	1 ----- 2 ----- 3 ----- 4 ----- 5
self-correcting	1 ----- 2 ----- 3 ----- 4 ----- 5
records performance	1 ----- 2 ----- 3 ----- 4 ----- 5
allows user cooperation	1 ----- 2 ----- 3 ----- 4 ----- 5
transfers to other computer programs	1 ----- 2 ----- 3 ----- 4 ----- 5
transfers to noncomputerized materials	1 ----- 2 ----- 3 ----- 4 ----- 5
generalizes	1 ----- 2 ----- 3 ----- 4 ----- 5

perfect score:	**115 pts**
above average score:	**>69 pts**
average score:	**69 pts**
below average score:	**<69 pts**

Church and Bender (1989) described computer programs that could be employed to teach reading and the skills related to reading that are found in kindergarten through high school curricula. The programs they identified emphasized skills in the following areas: recognizing letters of the alphabet, spelling, using phonetics, recognizing facts, recalling facts, organizing, sequencing, drawing inferences, identifying main ideas, predicting, generalizing, and forming judgments.

Software that was not designed to teach a precise reading skill could still be used as part of an instructional program that would develop that skill. For example, game software may not have been designed to teach specific literacy skills; nonetheless, games can help persons stay on task, work toward goals, learn how to interact with computers, and remain motivated. As such game software could develop skills and behaviors that might transfer to computerized lessons that do teach or reinforce specific reading skills (Church & Bender, 1989). In a similar fashion, simulation software, which encourages learners to model real life situations, or problem-solving software, which encourages learners to use discovery learning approaches, can develop global skills that transfer to instructional programs that highlight academic drilling, practice, and tutorials (Church & Bender, 1989).

Church and Bender (1989) also identified software intended to expand the productivity of instructors by managing the auxiliary instructional tasks and record keeping that can be associated with teaching reading. These tasks can include creating and grading tests, duplicating, responding to inquiries, distributing messages, computing statistics, keeping a log, devising worksheets, maintaining professional contacts with electronic mail, and accessing software through telecommunication networks (Kearsley et al., 1992).

In order to best meet the individual needs of learners with disabilities, some instructors may wonder whether they should design their own computerized learning programs. For teachers who do decide to create their own programs, the effort required to do so can be reduced if they employ authoring systems, which are programs that contain multiple cues to assist inexperienced users in developing instructional software. However, even these authoring systems can be cumbersome, complex, and frustrating. Church and Bender (1989) recommended that instructors ask the following types of questions before investing time and funds with authoring systems:

- Are traditional teaching approaches better suited to the learning objectives than computerized instruction?
- Are there available software packages that could adequately meet the needs of the learners?

- Do instructors have the motivation, time, and resources to learn and use the authoring system?

Increasing Accessibility To Computers

Before computers can be used by individuals with disabilities, computers must be physically accessible. For example, there are assistive devices to position computer key boards for increased accessibility. Chandler, Czerlinsky, and Wehman (1993) reviewed assistive technology devices that could increase the accessibility of computers for persons with physical handicaps. Among the devices they reviewed were headpointers for persons who cannot press keys with their fingers and expanded keyboards that require only a single light touch by users. Inge and Shepherd (1995) identified technology that could be employed as alternatives to keyboards for persons with disabilities when they entered data into computers. In addition to adapted keyboards with special formats and keys, their list included optical scanners, power pads, joysticks operated by the movement of the tongue against the roof of the mouth, and multiple alternatives to the typical mouse. In all, they listed 37 alternative input devices that could be paired with distinctive profiles of ability or weakness in areas such as gross motor movement, fine motor control, fine motor accuracy, control of facial muscles, vision, and auditory sensation. Additional adaptive devices for computers can include voice input, special switches, Morse code, light pens, touch screens, pressure plates, as well as voice and Braille output for information displayed typically on computer monitors (Alliance for Technology Access, 1994; Burkhead, 1992; Pesta, 1994).

Although computers are still not accessible to all individuals with disabilities, there have been remarkable advances in this area during the past decade. Table 5–3 lists some of the companies that have developed modified keyboards for use by persons with handicaps.

Internet Resources for Adult Literacy

The *internet* is a computer-accessed channel to information about numerous educational topics, including *adult literacy*. The advantages of this on-line type of communication is that current information is disseminated quickly, widely, and inexpensively. A disadvantage of on-line communication can be that the information, though more current than that disseminated through printed journals, can be poorly edited, inaccurate, and confusing.

Table 5-3   Companies That Provide Keyboards Adapted for Persons With Disabilities

Ability System Corp., 1422 Arnold Ave., Roslyn, PA 19001

William Bradford, Publ., 310 School St., Acton, MA 01720

Comput Ability Corp., 400000 Grand River, Suite 109, Novi, MI 48375

Hach Associates, P. O. Box 11754, Winston-Salem, NC 27116

Jordan & Associates, 1127 Oxford Ct., Neenah, WI 54956

Polytel Corp., 1287 Hammerwood Ave., Sunnyville, CA 94089

Psychological Corp., 555 Academic Ct., San Antonio, TX 87204

Unicorn Engineering, Inc., 5221 Central Ave., Suite 205, Richmond, CA 94704

Words +, Inc., 4421 10th St. W., Suite L. P. O. Box 1229, Lancaster, CA 93535

Zygo Industries, Inc., P.O. Box 1008, Portland, OR 97207-10008

Table 5–4 identifies information that can be accessed through the computerized internet. These resources are continuously being updated, revised, and expanded. The table lists available resources using the following categories: national nongovernmental programs, federal programs, state–local programs, university programs, search directories, lists, electronic journals, and usenet groups. All of these computerized sites contain potentially useful information about adult literacy. Some of the sites are more formal than others. Generally, the resources become less formal as one progresses through the categories in the table, from national nongovernmental programs to usenet groups. Actual exploration of information sites is the only route through which users can make realistic decisions about the usefulness of particular sites to them.

Adult Literacy and New Technologies is an internet information site that can be accessed through an electronic address (*e mail*). In this case the electronic address is: *http://litserver.literacy.upenn.edu/intro-ltl.html. Adult Literacy and New Technologies* is the information clearing house for the *Literacy Technology Laboratory* (LTL). This laboratory was established by the National Center on Adult Literacy (NCAL), a unit of the U.S. Department of Education to help adapt new technologies to adult literacy learning and instruction. The LTL promotes the use of effective instructional software, hardware, and networking solutions in adult literacy education, attempting to advance software development efforts by responding to information needs of both practitioners and developers. As with many of the listings in Table 5–4, *Adult Literacy and*

Table 5–4   Internet Resources for Adult Literacy

National Nongovernmental Programs

National Center on Adult Literacy (NCAL)
(*e mail:* http://litserver.literacy.upenn.edu/) Established in 1990 by the U.S. Department of Education, this center provides information such as newsletters, abstracts of research projects, listings of commercial adult literacy software, a list of free adult literacy software, technology information, and a list of literacy internet sites. *(Several of these sites are described in other citations within this table.)*

Current NCAL Research Projects
(*e mail:* http://litserver.literacy.upenn.edu/ncal-current-proj.html) This site includes descriptions of current NCAL research.

NCAL Adult Literacy Software Database
(*e mail:* http://litserver.literacy.upenn.edu/softdatabase.html) This database describes software available for demonstration and review in the Literacy Technology Laboratory (LTL) at NCAL. This extensive list has software titles, publishers, and brief descriptions. NCAL does not make recommendations about the usefulness of the software.

Adult Literacy and New Technologies (LTL)
(*e mail:* http://litserver.literacy.upenn.edu/intro-ltl.html) This site is an information clearing house for the LTL and was established to help adapt new technologies to adult literacy learning and instruction. The laboratory promotes the use of effective instructional software, hardware, and networking solutions for problems in adult literacy education. It attempts to advance software development by responding to the needs of both users and developers.

NCAL Publications
(*e mail:* http://litserver.literacy.upenn.edu/ncal-pubs-list.html) NCAL publishes technical reports, occasional papers, and policy briefs about adult literacy.

Federal Programs

National Adult Literacy and Learning Disabilities Center
(*e mail:* http://novel.nifl.gov/nalld/nalld_states.html) Established by the Academy of Educational Development, this center connects users to resources throughout the country. Among the resources listed are state departments of adult education, literacy resource centers, vocational rehabilitation agencies, and professional associations.

National Institute For Literacy (NIFL)
(*e-mail:* http://novel.nifl.gov/) This institute links users to current events, recent information, literacy forums, and other literacy resources. The available information has focused more on general literacy than adult literacy.

(continued)

Table 5–4 *(continued)*

State–Local Programs

Greater Pittsburgh Literacy Council (GPLC)
(*e mail:* http://letters.com/gplc/) Information is focused about literacy in the Pittsburgh area. Some articles on adult literacy are also available. GPLC connects to *Project Literacy,* which matches volunteer tutors to adults who need assistance learning to read and write.

Michigan Literacy Resource Council (MLRC)
(*e mail:* gopher://edcen.ehhs.cmich.edu:70/11/edcen.resource/rfrm/slrc) Located at Central Michigan University, MLRC provides information about programs in Michigan. It is linked to adult literacy publications, such as the State Literacy Resource Center Bibliography.

Minnesota/South Dakota Regional Adult Literacy Resource Center
(*e mail:* http://www.cybernetics.net/users/sagrelto/elands/home.sgm) Among the information in this center is the *Internet Directory of Literacy and Adult Education Resources* (*e mail:* http://www.cybernetics.net/users/sagrelto/elands/home.htm) and the *Ohio Literacy Resource Center* (*e mail:* http://archon.educ.kent.edu/contents.html) The center is linked to information about legislation, funding, state agencies, and projects promoting adult literacy and adult education.

University Programs

Drexel University Adult Literacy Home Page
(*e mail:* http://www.drexel.edu/outreach/home.html) This site contains information about governmental support for adult literacy programs and literacy in general. Information is available about legislation and funding in Philadelphia, Pennsylvania, and the country.

Search Directories

Education Resources
(*e mail:* http://archon.educ.kent.edu/edu.html) This site is linked to useful connections, such as state literacy resources, libraries, and internet directories. The state resources to which it is linked include the *Indiana Literacy and Technical Education Resource Center, the Virginia Adult Education and Literacy Network,* and the *Texas Literacy Resource Center.*

Yahoo-Educational Literacy
(*e mail:* http://www.yahoo.com/Educational Literacy/) This site connects to the *Greater Pittsburgh Literacy Council, Media Literacy On-Line Project, NCAL, NIFL, OLRC, Texas Literacy Resource Center,* and the *Urban Education Web.*

Media Literacy On-Line Project
(*e mail:* http://interact.uoregon.edu/MediaLit/HomePage) Originating at the University of Oregon, this site is connected to multiple media links. Although resources directly applicable to adult literacy are limited, there are numerous resources about general literacy.

(continued)

Table 5-4   *(continued)*

Other Resources

AEDNET archives
(*e mail:* http://alpha.acast.nova.edu/education/aednet.html) Operated by the *Adult Education Program* at Nova Southeastern University, AEDNET is a forum for current discussions about adult education and an archive for previous discussions.

National Resource Centre for Adult Education and Community Learning, New Zealand
(*e mail:* http://actrix.gen.nz/users/ncr/index.html) This center contains multiple links to information about adult education.

Dr. E's Eclectic Compendium of Electronic Resources for Adult/Distance Education
(*e mail:* http://www.oak-ridge.com/ierdrepl.html) This site lists electronic resources for adult education.

Internet Directory of Literacy and Adult Education Resources
(*e mail:* http://www.cybernetics.net/users/sagrelto/elands/home.htm) Sponsored by the Minnesota/South Dakota Regional Adult Literacy Resource Center, electronic resources such as journals and news groups are identified.

Lists

AEDNET: Adult Education Network
(*e mail:* listserv@alpha.acast.nova.edu.) Hundreds of individuals interested in adult education have participated in this international electronic network. Researchers, practitioners, and graduate students are among those who have discussed adult and continuing education. In addition to discussions, information about conferences and special events is featured. *New Horizons in Adult Education,* an electronic journal, is distributed through AEDNET.

DDFIND-L-
(*e mail:* listserv@gitvml.bitnet.) This general forum about disabilities includes adult education and literacy issues as well as links to other internet sites geared toward specific disabilities or medical concerns.

NLA: National Literacy Advocacy List
(*e mail:* majordomo@world.std.com) Sponsored by the National Literacy Advocacy Alliance, this list provides information and discussions about adult literacy education and adult learning in general.

Electronic Journals

CATALYST: Community Colleges
(*e mail:* listserv@vtvml.bitnet or listserv@vtml.cc.vt.edu) This is an electronic version of *CATALYST,* a journal for community college educators.

HORIZONS: New Horizons in Adult Education
(*e mail:* listserv@alpha.acast.nova.edu) Current as well as back issues of *New Horizons in Adult Education* can be accessed via AEDNET *(referenced elsewhere in this table).*

(continued)

Table 5–4   (continued)

Usenet Groups

Alternative Adult Literacy
(*e mail:* alt.adult.literacy) This source contains information about learners, tutors, and instructors involved in adult literacy programs.

Miscellaneous Education of Adults
(*e mail:* misc.education.adult) This source contains discussions about adult education.

Alternative Education of the Disabled
(*e mail:* alt.education.disabled) This source contains information about education of persons with physical and mental disabilities.

New Technologies contains connections that enable users to transfer to other sites on the internet containing related information.

As an example of how this laboratory has promoted the development of technology through information, the LTL has undertaken an extensive survey of computer use in adult literacy programs. The survey enabled researchers to inventory the technology holdings of literacy programs, explore practitioner attitudes toward computer-assisted instruction, and examine the barriers to the use of technology in adult learning programs. The report, entitled Tools for a Lifetime, is available at this internet site.

Although the amount of information on the internet can be daunting, the internet is an opportunity for persons to be members of the community of individuals who are working to improve adult education and literacy. It can be particularly rewarding when individuals have a forum for sharing insights, strategies, or useful solutions, thereby compounding the impact of their insights and instructional techniques. The information in Table 5–4 may help practitioners, researchers, and students make contacts with other individuals interested in adult literacy, participate in discussion groups, locate publications, gain access to computer software, discover critical reviews of materials, learn about alternative programs, designate suitable instructional strategies, and detect relevant research.

Assessment

Most computerized literacy programs are capable of maintaining records about the amount of time that learners have spent on specific activities. These records may also indicate how often learners were successful when responding to computerized questions, problems, or drills. As such, computer-based approaches to adult literacy simplify criterion-based testing, in which the progress of learners on tasks is referenced to their earlier performance on the same or comparable tasks.

In addition to tests that merely record data, there are programs that interpret the performance of the persons taking those tests. An advantage of computer-based test interpretation is that computers apply decision rules more consistently than do people (Witt, Elliott, Kramer, & Gresham, 1994). Additionally, computers do not exhibit the examiner biases that can characterize the scoring of individual instructors (Hasselbring & Moore, 1990).

An advantage of computer-administered tests is that instructors can develop banks of questions from which test items that are appropriate for individual learners can be drawn (Witt et al., 1994). Even if learners take the identical test repeatedly, the content can be rearranged easily each time the test is taken. As a result of opportunities available on the computer, learners can participate in drill and practice activities that are simultaneously practice tests (Retish, Hitchings, Horvath, & Schmalle, 1991). Such tests can reduce the aversion that some learners may exhibit to what they perceive as a forced interaction with computers (Witt, Elliott, Kramer, & Grisham, 1994).

Computer-adaptive testing represents another advantage of computer-administered tests (Mehrens & Lehmann, 1987). Computer-adapted tests can regulate factors such as amount of response time or level of difficulty for the persons taking the tests. For example, if persons are having difficulty responding to individual items on tests, less difficult items are presented. Conversely, if individuals are progressing through test items without making any errors, more difficult items are presented. In both cases, the total number of items in the test to which the examinee would be exposed would be reduced. As a result, the testing time would also be reduced. Learners would not be as bored or tired as they might be with nonadapted tests, and a positive self-image could be maintained by persons who otherwise would not respond repeatedly to items on tests.

If learners are using word processing to respond to items on tests, instructors can use the computer to provide responses to remarks made by learners (Bratcher, 1994). These remarks can be evaluative, informing the learners about their progress in a unit, or the remarks could be part of a dialogue in which instructors comment upon the content of the material about which the students are reading and writing.

Clear advantages of computer-based assessment are ease of administration and efficient, accurate, and rapid scoring. Computer-analyzed tests also enable instructors to search for patterns in the responses of individual learners on both standardized and informal tests (Wallace et al., 1992). These patterns could be used to diagnose individual learning patterns and to identify optimal types of instruction for those individuals (McCleod & Cropley, 1989). Although warning that the programs to aid in error analysis were limited, Hasselbring and Moore (1990) noted that programs were being developed that would provide additional opportunities for error analysis.

Johnson (1988) developed a list of questions to assist instructors when purchasing a computer-based assessment program. The following questions, many of which would also be appropriate to help make decisions about tests that instructors might devise themselves, are based on items in Johnson's list.

- Are required documents and instructions included?
- Are supplementary materials computerized?
- Can the program be adapted to complement a variety of curricula?
- Does the program generate logically and progressively sequenced objectives?
- Can scoring be adapted on the basis of both chronological and mental ages?
- Are the materials to which the test is synchronized current?
- How much time and effort will be saved by the program?
- Does the program generate printed reports that can be custom-tailored for individual programs, learners, and administrators?
- Has the program been piloted?
- Does accompanying data indicate that the program is valid and reliable?

Computer-based literacy programs are not distinct approaches to instruction, as are skills-based instruction or whole language literacy instruction. Instead, computers offer a distinct format for instructional programs that might be based on the skills approach, the whole language approach, or one of the other approaches. Consequently, computer-based programs complement other systems of instruction. Depending on the type of instruction with which a computer program were associated, the system of assessment suitable for that type of instruction would be equally appropriate for the complementary computer program.

Despite these similarities between approaches to computerized assessment and the systems of instruction that the systems complement, computers involve a format for providing information and responding that can restrict or amplify learners' performance. Restricted performance can result when computers are unfamiliar, intimidating, or inaccessible to users. But special opportunities for learners to excel during testing may be available during computerized testing. The following list identifies characteristics of computer interactions that may enhance learners' performance during practice sessions to prepare them for tests:

- opportunity to practice responding to questions in a highly structured situation
- ability to easily edit, revise, or reverse responses
- opportunity to develop or transfer self-management and decision-making skills
- opportunity to experiment with different test-taking strategies
- opportunity to practice responding to the same test items in different orders, for different lengths of time, and with different degrees of attentiveness
- opportunity to nurture motivation when testlike activities are presented in a format that learners perceive as novel

If learners were to respond positively to these computerized practice opportunities, their performance on computerized tests would be enhanced as well.

The assessment of individual learners may be tied to the assessment of computerized instruction. In this case, instructors may evaluate the program at the same time they are evaluating the progress of individual learners. The evaluation can be done formatively, as instructors develop the program, or summatively, after they achieve a major milestone in the development of a program (Kearsley et al., 1992). Although either type of evaluation can rely on quantitative measures, such as standardized tests, or qualitative measures, such as interviews with participants, qualitative data can be especially useful during the implementation stage of a program (Kearsley et al., 1992).

Summary

Computers can function as teachers, as a context for instruction, and as recording systems that can keep useful data to be consulted by both learners and instructors. Although there can be problems with computer-assisted instruction, such as cost, physical accessibility, and inappropriately sophisticated technology, there are clear advantages as well. Several of these advantages are opportunities for increased independence during learning, higher motivation for adult learners, and the development of technological skills that can transfer to other areas of learning and to functional living.

Although the cost can restrict the availability of computers to learners, there are instructional techniques for adapting to this situation, such as the use of a projector to display the output from a single machine for the benefit of several learners. Although the adaptability of computers is not comparable to that of instructors, computer programs do not necessitate regimentation. For example, learners with specific problems can be aided by computer programs that check spelling, suggest synonyms, or review grammar. Computerized instruction with controlled rates at which new information is presented or at which previously learned information is reviewed can be especially useful as part of instructional programs for learners with severe disabilities.

Instructional software includes programs that can be categorized as drill and practice, tutorials, games, simulations, and problem solving. Because the content, design, and practicality of specific software can limit the benefits of that software for individual learners, instructors can critique software, questioning whether content is presented logically, clearly, in a manner that generalizes to other types of learning, and responds to defined learning objectives. Several approaches to critiquing programs were reviewed.

CHAPTER
6

Skills-Based Programs

Programs that employ skills-based instruction are extremely popular. Skills-based programs incorporate structure and organization that reduce the minimum level of training required for instructors. Because of this structure, there is an increased probability that learners can maintain continuity in their learning should they transfer from one skills-based program to another or from one instructor to a different instructor.

Proponents of skills-based programs sometimes refer to these approaches as ones involving direct reading instruction (Carnine, Silbert, & Kameenui, 1990). The term *direct reading instruction* is well grounded in the tradition of skills-based learning. As an example, Betts (1946) referred to directed reading activities in the textbook that he wrote in the forties. However, the recent popularization of this term may result more from the virulent debates between advocates of holistic approaches and skills-based approaches than it does from attention to tradition. Because their academic adversaries have described themselves as attentive to the *whole learner*, some promoters of skills-based programs may have felt that they were being depicted as advocates of a fragmented and artificial approach to education. By referring to their approach as *direct instruction* rather than skills-based, they placed the rhetorical burden upon their opponents, who could now be depicted as supporters of nondirect instruction.

If learners are being successful in a set of sequenced, skills-based materials, it is easy to recommend subsequent learning activities that build on this successful learning. Similarly, if learners are not progressing adequately, one can ratchet down the instruction to a lower level within these structured programs.

Searfoss and Readence (1994) noted that, though learning procedures varied among the different skills-based programs, three stages typically characterized the materials: preparation for reading, guided reading, and postreading activities. The initial stage, preparation, might include building of background information, introduction of new vocabulary, motivation, and setting a goal for reading. The second stage might include oral reading, silent reading, and response to comprehension questions. Postreading activities might include activities such as the development of skills in comprehension, decoding vocabulary, critical reading, studying, writing, listening, and oral language.

Carnine, Silbert, and Kameenui (1990) noted that skills-based materials should reflect six characteristics of direct reading instruction. These characteristics were the specification of objectives, designation of reading strategies, development of teaching procedures, selection of examples to illustrate the reading strategies, sequencing of skills, and provision for practice and review. These criteria could be the basis for selecting instructional materials, adapting instructional materials, or incorporating general reading materials into instructional programs. Betts himself (1946) had recommended a five-step approach to direct reading instruction: preparation, guided silent reading, development of comprehension, development of skills, and generalization. These five steps are still the prototype for the majority of learning programs intended for adolescents and young adults (Orlich, Harder, Callahan, Kravas, Kauchak, Pendergrass, & Keogh, 1985) as well as the majority of high school reading programs intended for this group (Richardson & Morgan, 1994).

Multistep procedures of the type used in direct reading activities could be a basis with which to develop instructional materials that had the characteristics of skills-based materials. Such instructor-developed materials would be in formats that would complement the packaged materials in skills-based programs. Instructor-developed materials would be appropriate when incorporating texts that were not designed to be part of a structured program into a structured program. McKenna and Robinson (1993) proposed a three-stage approach to help learners comprehend content area texts not designed specifically for reading instruction. They recommended prereading strategies such as building prior knowledge and introducing learners to technical vocabulary. To supplement actual reading, they recommended setting well-focused goals and employing written guides to help students focus on key materials. Examples of postreading strategies included questioning and direct instruction.

Questions, which could be oral or in writing, could be devised by instructors spontaneously, as part of dialogues with students, or prior to the instructional activities in which learners would respond to questions. Questioning could be directed from instructors to learners, from learners to instructors, from students to each other, or to persons outside the learning environment. Learners could also monitor their own comprehension by generating questions for themselves and attempting to answer these questions.

Rather than classifying this entire three-stage approach to teaching as direct instruction, McKenna and Robinson labeled it the *explicit teaching model* and designated direct instruction as an element within the postreading phase that followed guided reading. They perceived direct instruction as an opportunity for instructors to model strategies that they wished learners to adopt, to assess learners' progress in achieving instructional objectives, and to encourage transfer of learning between the diverse strands of the curriculum. McKenna and Robinson cautioned that the development of direct instruction lessons and materials is a teacher-organized technique that is successful only when instructors develop precise learning objectives. However, they supported the technique because it is buttressed by a broad base of research and is conductive to clearly defined, sequential planning.

Because of the structure, organization, and specification of precise objectives within skills-based learning materials, computerized versions of skills-based programs can be devised with less difficulty than for other instructional programs. For the same reason, it is relatively simple to develop and coordinate supplementary instructional activities for skills-based programs.

When one uses computerized materials, those materials represent a series of decisions that would typically be made by the teachers employing instructional programs. For example, in computerized instruction, specific concepts, features of text, types of information, or vocabulary are emphasized, de-emphasized, or suppressed (Readence, Bean, & Baldwin, 1992). Although teachers can select materials in which these types of decisions have been made already by the authors, the designation of materials constitutes a decision for which instructors must still be responsible.

For example, teaching vocabulary to learners by means of computers illustrates the decisions for which instructors are responsible. Individual instructors who help learners comprehend passages about specific topics are the persons best qualified to make decisions about which words are critical and which are expendable in those passages (Moore, Moore, Cunningham, & Cunningham, 1994). Although a panel of expert educators can develop vocabulary software that reflects key concepts within passages, instructors are better able to identify vocabulary that is relevant to a passage and that also complements the abilities, backgrounds, and learning patterns of individuals (Alvermann & Phelps, 1994). Only instructors can ensure that learners are internalizing vocabulary in a way that promotes their ability to read independently (Herber & Herber, 1993). When instructors participate in the development or adaptation of computerized vocabulary lessons, they are empowered to make the decisions they should be making about the content and format of those lessons.

Although computerized drills are especially popular, they may not be substantively distinct from the drills with paper and pencil that these supplement or replace. For this reason, computerized drills have been referred to derogatorily as electronic workbooks. However, genuine advantages result from computerizing skills-based drills. Some of these advantages include opportunities for immediate feedback, individualized assessment, custom-tailored drills, and a motivating format (McKenna & Robinson, 1993). As a result of these opportunities, instructors may be able to assemble a complete package of supplementary and remedial instructional materials to complement skills-based programs (Carnine et al., 1990).

Neither the designation of skills-based programs by administrators nor the use of skills-based materials by instructors indicates a lack of sophistication by those persons. To the contrary, adaptive implementation of skills-based approaches requires sensitivity and professional expertise. One can extend a remark about the guitar to skills-based approaches. A master of the guitar was questioned about why the guitar was such a popular instrument. She answered that it was the easiest instrument to teach oneself to play. Attempting to embarrass the accomplished musician, the interviewer than asked why she had devoted her life to such a simple instrument. She responded confidently that, though it was the easiest to learn, it was the most difficult to master.

In a comparable way, skills-based programs do not assume a high degree of sophistication among instructors as a condition for initially being implemented. Inadequate preparation of both instructors and administrators in adult literacy programs is a problem of sufficient magnitude that it can restrict the effectiveness of any instructional program (Foster, 1990; Jacobson, 1993). The instructors in these programs are often volunteers with limited training. Nonetheless, when instructors use organized packages of skills-based instructional materials, they can become somewhat autonomous facilitators who can interact with a relatively large number of learners (Crowley-Weibel, 1992).

When skills-based programs are presented by means of computers, the reliance on instructors with extensive knowledge about literacy instruction may be reduced even further (Anderson, 1991). However, because computer-assisted literacy approaches can make distinct demands for technologically sophisticated instructors, there still may not be a net gain in the overall effectiveness of such programs (Jacobson, 1993).

Criticism of Skills-Based Programs

Despite the popularity of skills-based adult literacy programs, the use of such programs with adults who do not speak English is controversial. Green (1989) discouraged the use of these programs because vocabulary and grammar can be isolated in an artificial fashion that restricts the communicative skills of persons learning to speak and read in English. The perception that one can transfer communicative skills from one's native language to the reading of English is critical to the successful literacy learning of non-English speakers.

Montero-Sieburth (1990) reviewed educational programs in which Hispanics had participated and concluded that education for adult Hispanics "needs to be organized around their issues, rather than on set objectives that have little to do with their lives" (p. 110). Because vocabulary and grammar are academically restricted in skills-based programs, it can be difficult to locate or create passages with topics corresponding to issues that learners view as meaningful.

The need that literacy instruction be viewed as meaningful is not limited to adults who are not proficient speakers of English. This is also a characteristic of effective instruction for elderly adults. For example, DeSanti (1979) conducted a study indicating that the comprehension of elderly readers decreased when they perceived that their instructional programs were emphasizing basic skills rather than personally relevant issues.

The structured organization of skills-based programs allows vocabulary and grammar to be isolated. One can then manipulate vocabulary and grammar to create a hierarchy of skills. These skills can progress logically from simple to more elaborate tasks in a fashion that is somewhat unnatural but which nonetheless can simplify learning. For example, if adults have learned a generalization about the short sound of the letter *a* when it occurs between two consonants, one could construct a passage in which words that conformed to this rule were presented frequently in grammatically noncomplex sentences. The following passage might be used:

The fat rat sat on a hat.

The cat spoke to the fat rat.

"Sit on a mat and not on a hat," said the cat.

"I'll sit on a hat," said the fat rat.

"Then, I will give you a pat," said the cat.

As is the case in the preceding illustration, the hierarchy of skills used in skills-based instructional programs is geared usually to phonetic principles. Phonetics are intended to help readers pronounce words that they would recognize in oral discourse but which they don't yet recognize visually. Reliance on restricted phonetic patterns can limit the creativity of the authors of skills-based materials. As a consequence, the resulting materials, though instructionally elegant, can lack verisimilitude. Certainly, the preceding passage about the fat cat does not resemble the materials that adult learners would confront on a daily basis and which they would be motivated to read.

Even if instructors had the time and ingenuity to devise realistic, phonetically constrained passages about family matters, current events, or workplace issues, there is a pervasive criticism that challenges all artificial learning materials. The use of learning materials that have been edited to eliminate the phonetic irregularities that occur typically in English writing may cause learners to rely excessively on phonetics as a reading strategy. The learners may be confused and disheartened when they subsequently discover that reliance on phonetics is less productive with everyday reading materials than it was with the structured materials that they encountered in their literacy programs.

Response to Criticism

Despite these problems, there are ample testimonials in support of phonetically based skills programs. Chall (1984) argued that adult learners should master phonetic principles because these skills constitute a stage through which all developing readers, including adult learners, must pass. Bishop (1988) described the benefits of the Nellie Thomas approach to adult literacy instruction, a predominantly skills-based program that contained a robust portion of phonetic learning. Crowley Weibel (1992) and Jones (1981) described phonetic approaches associated with the Laubach literacy programs that have been used for over 60 years in adult education programs. The extensive use of skills-based adult literacy programs by a wide range of professionals and volunteers during an extended period may be the most convincing evidence validating any of the approaches to adult literacy instruction.

Skills-based instructional materials are organized with sequenced skills that are limited by stages through which learners progress. This structure can be an obvious advantage for some learners and instructors. However, if it becomes disadvantageous, instructors can employ adaptations (Searfoss & Readence, 1994). The following examples illustrate adaptations to skills-based materials:

- adjust the lengths of the sessions allowed for timed activities
- allow different learners to progress through skills-based materials at variable rates
- allow learners to select passages or activities
- ask learners to identify the techniques they are employing to read passages or answer questions
- assess learners' progress often
- encourage learners to paraphrase passages that they have read
- encourage persons to identify the learning goals for skills-based activities
- ensure that activities are presented in a format that the learners find motivating
- interview learners about the suitability of the pacing and content of skills-based activities
- link reading to functional writing
- link reading to other academic activities
- modify passages or comprehension questions so that they are best suited for learners
- promote cooperative problem solving by learners
- supplement reading with oral discussion
- supplement skill-centered exercises with meaning centered activities

- supplement skills-based activities with demonstrations, simulations, games, role playing, or independent research that encourages learners to generalize the skills they have developed in structured activities
- supplement skills-based materials with literature and functional reading materials

Sample Activities

Instructors wishing to use a skills-based approach often purchase materials that contain passages to be employed during reading instruction. Decisions about the words in these passages and the order in which the words are to be learned have already been made by the persons who have developed those instructional materials. Activities synchronized to these passages may have been selected and arranged in workbooks. Computer software, tape-recorded activities, special magazines, and simplified newspapers are examples of other resources that may be available to support skills-based programs.

Although many persons have learned to read effectively as a result of being matched with a comprehensive program of materials and activities, skills-based instruction can be implemented in an alternative, adaptive fashion. Using the principles that support skills-based programs, instructors can assemble custom-designed materials that respond to the unique backgrounds and interests of adult learners.

For example, as part of a phonetic approach to literacy instruction, instructors could organize words into clusters. Groups of words that begin with the same consonant, blend, or digraph might be a basis for these clusters. Using this technique, learners could associate words with which they were not familiar with those words that they could recognize already.

Exhibit 6–1 is an example of a worksheet with which instructors could identify a group of words containing common consonants. The target words indicated on this worksheet normally would be words that the learners had already mastered. Alternatively, target words could be the initial words to be learned among a cluster of words.

Exhibit 6–2 contains the same worksheet illustrated in Exhibit 6–1, but completed for a specific adult learner. This learner was already able to recognize the three target words *hat, cat,* and *dog.* Because the adult learner for whom this worksheet was designed was employed in a construction job, the words selected for association with the target words were terms relevant to his occupation. The purpose of this

Exhibit 6–1
Consonant Worksheet for Use in Skills-Based Instruction

B b (bat)   target word: _____

_____

_____

_____

_____

_____

C c (car)   target word: _____

_____

_____

_____

_____

_____

D d (dog)   target word: _____

_____

_____

_____

_____

_____

Exhibit 6–2
Completed Consonant Worksheet for Use
in Skills-Based Instruction

B b (bat)   <u>target word</u>: _hat_ _____

                  hand _____

                  hit _____

                  hoe _____

                  hard hat _____

                  _____

C c (car)   <u>target word</u>: _cat_ _____

                  coveralls _____

                  _____

                  _____

                  _____

                  _____

D d (dog)   <u>target word</u>: _dog_ _____

                  dig _____

                  dirt _____

                  _____

                  _____

                  _____

worksheet is to identify new words that begin with the same consonants as the target words. These complementary words, which form the clusters, have been identified by the instructor in Exhibit 6–2.

The words that are linked to the target words could be reviewed in drills or reinforced in passages that instructors created. Or the new words could be used in instructor assisted writing activities. These writing activities would result eventually in the creation of materials that could be used as part of reading instruction.

Exhibits 6–3 through 6–11 contain examples of other worksheets that can be employed in skills-based literacy programs. The worksheets illustrate how blends of consonants (such as *bl, cl,* or *fl*) can be the basis for organizing words for instruction. Other samples of planning worksheets for skills-based lessons that are illustrated in this chapter are listed below:

- Worksheet Using Digraphs
- Worksheet Using Word Stems
- Worksheet Using Compound Words
- Worksheet Using Phonics Generalizations about Vowels
- Worksheet Using Phonics Generalizations about Consonants
- Worksheet Using Phonics Generalizations about Accenting
- Worksheet Using Generalizations about Pluralization
- Worksheet Using Common Prefixes

The worksheets included in this section, as well as many of the materials incorporated within skills-based programs, employ terms such as *blend, compound word,* and *digraph.* These terms, as well as other terms used frequently in skills-based programs, are listed and defined in Table 6–1.

Critiquing Skills-Based Programs

As with all approaches to literacy, skills-based literacy programs can be swords with two edges. A program that can be beneficial to some learners can be harmful to others. The compatibility of skills-based literacy materials with other materials that learners have already used successfully is a critical factor influencing whether skills-based programs will be beneficial.

Table 6–2 contains sample questions that could help instructors evaluate the suitability of skills-based materials for adult learners with

Exhibit 6–3
Worksheet Using Blends to Organize Words for Instruction in Skills-Based Programs

bl (blue)   target word: _____

_____

_____

_____

_____

cl (clean)   target word: _____

_____

_____

_____

_____

fl (fly)   target word: _____

_____

_____

_____

_____

(continued)

Exhibit 6-3 *(continued)*

Other blends that can be the basis for grouping words:

- br
- cr
- dr
- fr
- gl
- gr
- pl
- pr
- sc
- scr
- shr
- sk
- sl
- sm
- sn
- sp
- spl
- spr
- st
- str
- sw
- thr
- tr
- tw

Exhibit 6–4
Worksheet Using Digraphs *(i.e., consonants which, when combined, produce a sound that is distinct from that they would otherwise produce)* to Organize Words for Instruction in Skills-Based Programs

ch (child)   target word: _____

_____

_____

_____

_____

_____

sh (ship)   target word: _____

_____

_____

_____

_____

_____

th (the)   target word: _____

_____

_____

_____

_____

_____

(continued)

Exhibit 6–4 *(continued)*

th (thick) target word: _____

_____

_____

_____

_____

_____

ph (phone) target word: _____

_____

_____

_____

_____

_____

wh (where) target word: _____

_____

_____

_____

_____

_____

Exhibit 6–5
Worksheet Using Word Stems to Organize Words for Instruction in Skills-Based Programs

_ ab (cab)   target word: _____

_____

_____

_____

_____

_____

_ am (ham)   target word: _____

_____

_____

_____

_____

_____

_ad (bad)   target word: _____

_____

_____

_____

_____

_____

(continued)

Exhibit 6–5 *(continued)*

Other word stems that can be the basis for grouping words:

_a	_eak	_ife
_ace	_eal	_ig
_ack	_eam	_ight
_ade	_ear	_ike
_ag	_eat	_ile
_ain	_ed	_ill
_ake	_ee	_im
_all	_eed	_in
_ame	_eek	_ine
_amp	_eem	_ing
_ance	_een	_ink
_and	_eep	_int
_ane	_eer	_ip
_ang	_eet	_ire
_ank	_eight	_irt
_ap	_ell	_ish
_ar	_en	_iss
_ark	_end	_it
_arm	_ent	_itch

(continued)

Exhibit 6-5 *(continued)*

_art	_est	_ite
_ash	_et	_ive
_ass	_ew	_ix
_at	_ib	_o
_atch	_ick	_oach
_aught	_id	_oak
_ay	_ide	_oal
_ead	_ief	_oam
_oam	_ote	
_oan	_ough	
_oast	_ought	
_ob	_ould	
_obe	_ounce	
_ock	_ound	
_od	_ouse	
_ode	_ove	
_og	_ow	
_oil	_owl	
_oin	_ub	
_oke	_uck	
_old	_ude	

(continued)

Exhibit 6–5 *(continued)*

_ole	_ue
_oll	_uff
_ome	_ug
_ood	_ull
_ook	_um
_ool	_umb
_oon	_ump
_oop	_un
_op	_unch
_orn	_unk
_ort	_unk
_ose	_unt
_oss	_ush
_ost	_ust
_ot	_ut
	_y

Exhibit 6–6
Worksheet Using Compound Words to Organize Words
for Instruction in Skills-Based Programs

air_____   target word: _____

_____

_____

_____

_____

_____

back_____   target word: _____

_____

_____

_____

_____

fire_____   target word: _____

_____

_____

_____

_____

_____

Exhibit 6–6 *(continued)*

Other word parts that can be the basis for grouping compound words:

any_	hand_	ring_
base_	horse_	rip_
basket_	house_	run_
bath_	herd_	shoe_
bed_	ice_	short_
black_	in_	side_
blue_	lady_	sun_
bull_	line_	sweet_
candle_	look_	thunder_
car_	lunch_	turn_
cat_	mad_	under_
check_	man_	up_
cow_	night_	wind_
dog_	note_	wood_
down_	no_	work_
ear_	off_	yard_
eye_	out_	year_
farm_	over_	
finger_	pan_	
flash_	pay_	

(continued)

Exhibit 6–6 *(continued)*

foot_	pick_
fruit_	pig_
god_	pin_
grand_	pine_
green_	play_
gun_	police_
half_	race_

Exhibit 6–7
Worksheet Using Phonics Generalizations About Vowels to Organize Words for Instruction in Skills-Based Programs

If a word contains only one vowel, that vowel is usually short (*it*)

target word: _____

_____

_____

_____

_____

_____

(continued)

Exhibit 6–7 *(continued)*

If a one-syllable word ends in *e*, the *e* is usually silent and the other vowel is long (*hate*)

target word: _____

_____

_____

_____

_____

_____

If *i* is followed by *gh* or *ld*, the *i* is usually long (*high, mild*)

target word: _____

_____

_____

_____

_____

If *o* is followed by *ld*, it is usually long (*hold*)

target word: _____

_____

_____

_____

_____

_____

(continued)

Exhibit 6–7 *(continued)*

If two vowels occur together in a one-syllable word, the first vowel is often long and the second vowel is silent (*goat*)

<u>target word</u>: _____

_____

_____

_____

_____

_____

Exhibit 6–8
Worksheet Using Phonics Generalizations About Consonants to Organize Words for Instruction in Skills-Based Programs

If *c* is followed by *e*, *i*, or *y*, it is usually soft (*center, city, cycle*); otherwise, it is usually hard (*cup*)

<u>target word</u>: _____

_____

_____

_____

_____

(continued)

Exhibit 6–8 *(continued)*

If *g* is followed by *e, i,* or *y,* it is usually soft (*gem, giant, gymnasium*); otherwise, it is usually hard (*gun*)

<u>target word</u>: _____

_____

_____

_____

_____

_____

If the suffix *ed* is preceded by *t* or *d,* it is usually pronounced as a separate syllable (*patted, padded*); otherwise, the *ed* usually is not pronounced separately (*piled*)

<u>target word</u>: _____

_____

_____

_____

_____

_____

Exhibit 6–9
**Worksheet Using Phonics Generalizations About Accenting
to Organize Words for Instruction in Skills-Based Programs**

**The first syllable of a two-syllable word is usually accented
(*pony*)**

target word: _____

_____

_____

_____

_____

**The root of a word with a prefix or a suffix is usually accented
(*descended*)**

target word: _____

_____

_____

_____

_____

_____

(continued)

Exhibit 6–9 *(continued)*

The first part of a compound word is usually accented (*baseball*)

target word: _____

_____

_____

_____

_____

_____

If a word ends with the suffix *tion*, the syllable before it is usually accented (*demonstration*)

target word: _____

_____

_____

_____

_____

_____

_____

Exhibit 6–10
Worksheet Using Generalizations About Pluralization to
Organize Words for Instruction in
Skills-Based Programs

**Most words are made plural by adding *s* to the singular form
(*dog–dogs*)**

target word: _____

_____

_____

_____

_____

**Most words ending in *ch, s, sh, x,* and *z* are made plural by
adding *es* to the singular form (*catch–catches; pass–passes;
dish–dishes; box–boxes; fizz–fizzes*)**

target word: _____

_____

_____

_____

_____

(continued)

Exhibit 6–10 *(continued)*

Most words ending in *y* preceded by a vowel are made plural by adding an *s* (*monkey–monkeys*)

target word: _____

_____

_____

_____

_____

_____

Most words ending in *y* preceded by a consonant are made plural by changing the *y* to *i* and adding *es* (*penny–pennies*)

target word: _____

_____

_____

_____

_____

_____

(continued)

Exhibit 6–10 *(continued)*

Most words ending in *f* or *fe* are made plural by changing the *f* or *fe* to *v* and adding *es* (*calf–calves; wife–wives*)

target word: _____

_____

_____

_____

_____

_____

Many words are made plural irregularly (*foot–feet*)

target word: _____

_____

_____

_____

_____

_____

Exhibit 6–11
Worksheet Using Common Prefixes to Organize Words
for Instruction in Skills-Based Programs

ap   *to or toward (approach)*

target word: _____

_____

_____

_____

_____

_____

co   *together or with (cooperate)*

target word: _____

_____

_____

_____

_____

_____

de   *down, from, or away (decline)*

target word: _____

_____

_____

_____

_____

_____

(continued)

Exhibit 6–11 *(continued)*

Other common prefixes that can be the basis for grouping words:

a	(from)	equi	(equal)	neo	(new)
ab	(from)	ex	(from)	non	(not)
ac	(to)	extra	(outside)	ob	(against)
acro	(top)	fore	(before)	omni	(all)
ad	(toward)	hemi	(half)	op	(against)
alt	(high)	holo	(whole)	pan	(all)
ante	(before)	homo	(same)	poly	(many)
anti	(against)	hyper	(excessive)	post	(after)
auto	(self)	hypo	(less)	pre	(before)
bi	(two)	ideo	(idea)	pro	(for)
bio	(life)	il	(not)	pseudo	(false)
cent	(hundred)	im	(not)	quad	(four)
co	(together)	in	(within)	quasi	(seemingly)
com	(together)	inter	(between)	quint	(five)
con	(together)	intra	(among)	re	(again)
contra	(against)	ir	(not)	retro	(backwards)
counter	(against)	kilo	(thousand)	semi	(half)
dec	(ten)	macro	(large)	soli	(alone)
deci	(ten)	magn	(large)	sub	(under)
di	(apart)	mal	(bad)	super	(above)

(continued)

Table 6–1   Vocabulary and Terms Used Frequently in Skills-Based Programs

affix: same as *prefix*

analytical phonics: approaches to instruction in which learners infer phonics generalizations about groups of words exhibiting those generalizations

blend: several consonant letters that occur together so that the sounds that they produce in isolation are preserved (*examples—bride, cry, drive*)

compound words: words formed from other words (*examples—spaceship, baseball, backfire*)

context: information from a source other than an unfamiliar word that indicates the meaning of that unfamiliar word (context can be *syntactic* or *semantic*)

decode: decipher unfamiliar words by applying phonics generalizations

digraph: two consonants that occur together and which produce a sound different than that which they would produce in isolation (*examples—phone, thick, where*) (a diphthong may be referred to as a *vowel digraph*)

diphthong: two vowels that occur together and which produce a distinct sound (*examples—oil, boy, auto*)

encode: learners apply phonics generalizations to written words that they do not know how to spell

grammar: the rules that govern the assembling of well-formed sentences

(continued)

137

Table 6–1 *(continued)*

linguistic phonics: approaches to instruction in which learners associate groups of words that exhibit common phonics generalizations

morpheme: subcomponents of words that indicate meaning

orthography: the system by which words are spelled

phoneme: the smallest units of spoken words

phonics: approaches to reading instruction that encourage learners to verbalize the sounds of letters in words with which they are unfamiliar (see *analytical phonics, linguistic phonics,* and *synthetic phonics*)

phonology: the academic study of the sounds used in speech

prefix: a syllable that occurs at the beginning of a word or word part and that emphasizes or changes meaning (*examples–income, convert, review*)

r-controlled vowels: vowels which, when followed by the letter *r,* produce a distinct sound (*examples—her, bird, burn*)

root: the portion of a word that remains after prefixes or suffixes are removed (*examples—invert, inspire, replay*)

schwa: an amorphous vowel, resembling somewhat the sound of short *u,* and written phonetically as an upside down e̲ (*examples–the final vowel sound in letter, vision, lesion*)

scope and sequence of skills: see *scope of skills* and *sequence of skills*

scope of skills: a list of the precise skills that are emphasized in instructional materials

semantic context: use of meaningful cues surrounding unfamiliar words to guess the meaning of those unfamiliar words (example—She prefers to drink her coffee with both cream and _____.)

semantics: the rules that govern the assignment of meaning to groups of words

sequence of skills: a list of the order in which instructional materials introduce precise skills

sight words: words that occur frequently and that readers should be able to understand without decoding *(examples—the, in, to)*

stem: a base for forming families of words (*examples—cab, ham, bad*)

structural analysis: deciphering the meaning of words by attention to prefixes, suffixes, and roots

syntactic context: use of grammatical cues to guess the meaning of unfamiliar words (example—The coat was a rich shade of _____.)

syntax: same as *grammar.*

synthetic phonics: approaches to instruction in which learners are presented with phonics generalizations that they apply to novel words

Table 6–2 Sample Questions for Evaluating the Suitability of Skills Based Materials for Adults with Disabilities

1. Are there reading aids to help the learners be as independent as possible when using the materials?
2. Are the learning exercises linked in a logical fashion?
3. Are instructions for learners expressed in a clear and concise manner?
4. Are there supplementary pictorial cues to assist readers?
5. Are the formats of the exercises suitable for adults?
6. Is the content of passages interesting to adults?
7. Are spaces for writing answers to questions adjacent to the problems?
8. Is the amount of space for writing answers adequate?
9. If learners must purchase the materials, is the cost affordable and reasonable?
10. Is the type legible and appropriate?
11. Is the size of the margins adequate?
12. Are headings, subheadings, italicized print, and bold print present and adequate?
13. Are answers to exercises contained in the learners' books or available to learners?
14. Are there other complementary materials to which learners can refer or to which they can progress?
15. Is successful completion of drills and activities designed to reinforce adult learning?
16. Can the materials be adapted to compensate for the effects of cognitive disabilities on learning?
17. Are the materials relevant to learners from diverse cultures?
18. Are the materials motivating to males and females?
19. Do the materials have a scholastic or real world orientation?
20. Can the activities be completed by learners working in groups?

disabilities. This table could also prepare instructors for adapting skills-based materials to increase the effectiveness of those materials. Exhibit 6–12 contains a checklist that could be helpful when performing such critiques.

Assessment

Assessment may be more straightforward in skills-based programs than in other instructional approaches. When skills are isolated and sequenced, tests can measure the competencies for which learners are accountable at different stages in the instructional program. The majority of reading tests that are on the market complement skills-based instructional programs. The popularity of tests that complement

Exhibit 6–12
Skills-Based Materials Checklist

Material_____

1 ----- 2 ----- 3 ----- 4 ----- 5
inferior   **average**   **superior**

precise instructions	1 ----- 2 ----- 3 ----- 4 ----- 5
interesting content	1 ----- 2 ----- 3 ----- 4 ----- 5
adult orientation	1 ----- 2 ----- 3 ----- 4 ----- 5
reading aids	1 ----- 2 ----- 3 ----- 4 ----- 5
absence of gender bias	1 ----- 2 ----- 3 ----- 4 ----- 5
diverse activities	1 ----- 2 ----- 3 ----- 4 ----- 5
pictorial cues	1 ----- 2 ----- 3 ----- 4 ----- 5
legible print	1 ----- 2 ----- 3 ----- 4 ----- 5
suitable format	1 ----- 2 ----- 3 ----- 4 ----- 5
adequate margins	1 ----- 2 ----- 3 ----- 4 ----- 5
adequate headings	1 ----- 2 ----- 3 ----- 4 ----- 5
appropriate activities	1 ----- 2 ----- 3 ----- 4 ----- 5
adequate space for writing answers	1 ----- 2 ----- 3 ----- 4 ----- 5
challenging	1 ----- 2 ----- 3 ----- 4 ----- 5
supplemented with complementary materials	1 ----- 2 ----- 3 ----- 4 ----- 5
answers to activities available to learners	1 ----- 2 ----- 3 ----- 4 ----- 5
reasonable cost	1 ----- 2 ----- 3 ----- 4 ----- 5
adaptable on the basis of disabilities	1 ----- 2 ----- 3 ----- 4 ----- 5

(continued)

Exhibit 6–12 (continued)

sensitive to diverse cultures	1 ----- 2 ----- 3 ----- 4 ----- 5
allows learner cooperation	1 ----- 2 ----- 3 ----- 4 ----- 5
transfers to real world	1 ----- 2 ----- 3 ----- 4 ----- 5

perfect score:	**100 pts**
above average score:	**>60 pts**
average score:	**60 pts**
below average score:	**<60 pts**

skills-based instructional programs is an indication of the popularity of the programs themselves. The popularity may also indicate the relative ease with which skills-based tests can be devised. And the popularity of skills-based tests indicates the difficulty of devising tests to assess instructional programs that are not skills-based.

Because skills-based instruction is competency based, most instructional programs include assessment instruments as part of a complete package of materials. As such, tests that are linked to the precise competencies being emphasized within instructional programs can be included with those programs. The synchrony between assessment materials and instructional materials is an attractive feature of skills-based programs. This advantage of skills-based programs may be especially attractive when adults are preparing to pass specific tests, such as those associated with earning a high school equivalency diploma, entry into the armed services, admission to a labor organization, or job advancement.

Summary

Skills-based programs represent the most popular approach for developing adult literacy. Because of the structured organization within these programs, learners can maintain continuity in their learning should they transfer between programs. This structure facilitates the development of a complete package of instructional materials that can supplement the primary instructional program.

Skills-based programs can be packages of learning materials and activities. The elements of these packages, already developed, are designed to be implemented in a sequential fashion. However, skills-based generalizations can be used in an adaptive fashion, by helping adults learn clusters of novel words. This adaptive approach makes greater demands on instructors, but it allows instructors to reinforce the interests of learners through the personalized selection of vocabulary. The adaptive approach to skills-based instruction also raises the likelihood that learners will retain and transfer skills.

Because the majority of reading tests attempt to measure precise skills, there are many commercially distributed instruments to complement skills-based instructional programs. Additionally, assessment instruments that are custom-tailored to individual skills-based programs are usually included as components of those programs. The availability of carefully developed, standardized tests that are precisely synchronized to skills-based programs is a factor contributing to the popularity of these programs.

Instructors can critique the content and format of materials to help them evaluate the suitability of skills-based materials for individual learners. This type of critique can also assist instructors when they are adapting skills-based materials for individual learners. Additional aspects of skills-based programs that could be focused upon in a critique would be supplementary materials, reinforcement of adult learning, or the correspondence of learning materials to the interests of the learners.

CHAPTER
7
Whole Language Programs

Whole language programs were originally devised to teach young learners to read by encouraging them to rely on their oral language competencies. Unlike the predetermined routes along which learners progress in skills-based programs, whole language programs allow participants to pursue personalized learning paths.

A fundamental assumption of whole language programs is that learners who are placed in literacy-rich environments will naturally channel the communicative aptitude evident in their oral language toward problems of reading and writing (Goodman et al., 1988). This assumption about the natural acquisition of literacy skills is similar to that which some researchers believe is the explanation for the development of oral language skills in the first place. For though regimented speech and language exercises may be appropriate as clinical intervention for persons with communication disorders, such activities are unnecessary for persons with normally developing communication. Proponents of whole language approaches believe that learning to read and write can follow a natural path of development that is comparable to that of oral communication.

Criticism of Whole Language Approaches

Although few persons would argue with the potential benefits of whole language approaches to literacy, these benefits are not assured for all participants in the programs. Whole language programs can be effective when two conditions are met. One of these conditions is that the instructors must have a reasonable degree of sophistication about teaching, managing an instructional program, customizing learning materials, and about the acquisition of reading. Additionally, effective programs assume that both teachers and learners will devote a sustained amount of time to the tasks in the programs.

Because of the structure and regimentation that characterizes skills-based programs, learners can transfer easily between programs or from one teacher to another. In contrast, whole language programs can be extremely personalized. Consequently, eccentric features within these personalized programs may restrict learners from transferring the skills developed in one setting to different instructional settings.

Response to Criticism

The practical demands of whole language instruction may dissuade some persons from employing programs based on it. Nonetheless, the advantages of whole language instruction can be sufficiently impressive to outweigh these practical difficulties. A major difficulty is the management of the program. As an example of a solution to this problem, there are instructional models that illustrate how instructors can develop libraries of customized reading materials through writing samples that are shared among the members of a group or even written collaboratively by group members.

For example, Stasz, Schwartz, and Weeden (1991) described a whole language program in which the primary materials for instruction were chronicles written by adults about their lives. Opportunities for instruction emerge at three stages of such group activities: during the assisted creation of the chronicles, while persons are learning to read the chronicles to others, and at the times when learners are reading chronicles from other group members. Wangberg (1986) described a similar program where the work associated with transcribing, revising, and copying chronicles for other group members was minimized through the use of computers. Kazemac (1988), reviewing research on both reading and women's issues, argued that whole language programs involving collaboration and group interaction not only minimized practical problems of implementation but were well suited to the collaborative learning styles that can characterize females. Furthermore, both the content and the format of education should be sensitive to adult females with disabilities who may have special needs that result from their dual identities as females as well as persons with disabilities (Deegan & Brooks, 1985).

Other reports (Barasovska, 1988; Crowley-Weibel, 1992; Keefe & Meyer, 1991; Ross, 1989; Soifer, Irwin, Crumrine, Honzaki, Simmons, & Young, 1990; Wangberg, 1986) have underscored the value of instructional programs in which adults incorporated reading, writing, and oral communication as they shared or collaborated on the creation of communicative materials. Both the creation and sharing of these materials provided opportunities for adult learners to develop and retain literacy skills.

Eliciting Oral Language

Eliciting speech samples that have sufficient length, novel vocabulary, grammatical diversity, and conceptual richness can be challenging when working with adults who are not literate. Kennedy and Roeder (1975) provided step by step examples of how to elicit writing samples from adults and then later use these samples for reading instruction. But the challenge of eliciting instructional materials can be compounded when a whole language program is designed for adults with disabilities.

When one is having difficulty obtaining suitable speech samples from adults with disabilities, instructors may use partially complete sentences to elicit speech. For example, adult learners might be cued with the phrase, "*I wish that.*" After the adult responds, the instructor can follow up with appropriate questions about the basis for that wish. Other partially complete sentences reflecting the *wish* motif can be devised.

- I wish I could be
- I wish my spouse would
- I wish my children would
- A job I wish I could have is
- I wish I didn't ever have to
- More than anything in the world, the thing I wish I could have is
- If I were able to live anywhere, I would wish to live
- If I could have any power, I would wish that I could
- Something I would never wish for is
- The person I wish I could be is
- If I could travel anyplace, I would wish to visit
- If I were to be an animal, I would wish to be
- If I could eliminate one thing from the world, I would wish to eliminate
- If I could change one thing about myself, I would wish

Figure 7–1 is an illustrated worksheet containing a set of partially complete sentences. The partially complete sentences are intended to elicit a response about fear, a topic that likely will be viewed as meaningful. The resulting sentences could be the basis for whole language reading activities. Figures 7–2 through 7–7 are similar illustrated worksheets designed to develop language samples on the following topics:

Something that frightened me was...

This was so frightening that...

If this ever happened again, I would wish that...

The reason I feel this way is....

Figure 7–1.   Fear worksheet.

The worst injury would be one where...

If I were injured in this way, people might treat me as if...

If I had this type of injury, I would...

The reason I feel this way is....

Figure 7-2. Injury worksheet.

An animal that is dangerous would be...

Some reasons why this animal is so dangerous are that...

If I ever were face to face with this type of animal, I would...

The reason I feel this way is...

Figure 7–3. Animal worksheet.

The worst type of illness is one in which...

If I had to be around people with this illness, I would...

If I developed this illness myself, I would want to...

The reason I feel this way is...

Figure 7–4. Illness worksheet.

The best friends are ones who...

If I had no friends, I would...

The reasons that some persons do not have friends are...

The reason I feel this way is...

Figure 7–5. Friendship worksheet.

When one dies, what happens is...

What may happen after my own death is that...

When I am dead, the persons who knew me may...

The reason that I feel this way is...

Figure 7–6. Death worksheet.

Persons that you don't know could...

One of the reasons that strangers might speak to you is that...

When you meet a stranger, it is best to...

The reason I feel this way is...

Figure 7-7. Stranger worksheet.

- injury
- animals
- illness
- friendship
- death
- strangers

Additional worksheets could be developed that are better suited to the precise backgrounds, attitudes, values, and goals of the specific adult learners with whom instructors would be working.

Combining Whole Language With Skills Activities

Some proponents of whole language literacy instruction may view skills-based programs as philosophically incompatible with their programs. A chasm of hostility often separates advocates of the two approaches when the context is elementary reading instruction. However, when the focal group shifts to adults or persons with disabilities, instructors tend to exhibit less ideological loyalty and more pragmatism. Within special, remedial, and adult education, whole language instruction is potentially relevant to all programs because it is an additional instructional option for learners who have not learned to read in other programs. However, whole language instruction may require scaffolding from skills-based instruction in order to assure that adults with disabilities achieve their highest potential as learners.

Several skills-based activities can be combined readily with whole language instruction. Three formats for skills-based programs that complement whole language instruction especially well are closure activities, question sets, and sorting activities.

Closure Activities

Closure activities, often referred to as *cloze* activities by teachers, consist of passages that have been spoken by learners and then transcribed. The transcription may have been performed by the instructor, an instructional assistant, or another adult. These transcribed passages are then altered by the deletion of words, phrases, or sentences.

For example, if persons used several words that rhymed (*bat, flat, that*), these words would form a cluster. The learners would be presented with a transcription of the passage in which those words had originally occurred. However, the clustered words would have been deleted from the passage. As the learners attempted to fill in the missing items, they could be cued by the content of the passage, which would be a transcription of a meaningful event that they had recounted in their own language. After the missing words were recognized successfully, that cluster of words would in turn become a set of target words with which new words that followed the same pattern could be associated.

Exhibit 7–1 is a worksheet indicating how a closure activity could be designed. Adult learners can be permitted to examine the original transcription while attempting to decipher the missing words from the altered passage, as they are encouraged to do in Exhibit 7–1. Alternatively, learners could be encouraged to first examine the original transcription, which could then be removed from view. After the original passage had been removed, learners could attempt to fill in the missing items on the closure worksheet. The decision about whether learners would have access to the original transcription while completing the

---

Exhibit 7–1
Closure Worksheet Based on a
Transcription of Adult Speech

So when it was my turn to bat, I got the heavy metal bat. On the second pitch, I hit the ball where their manager was sitting. He was so fat. But he ducked out of the way when the ball came. He was so mad. And everybody laughed.

So when it was my turn to ___, I got the heavy metal bat. On the second pitch, I hit the ball where their manager was sitting. He was so ___. But he ducked out of the way when the ball came. He was so mad. And everybody laughed.

target word: _____

_____

_____

_____

_____

exercise would depend on the judgment of the instructor about which format would best benefit an individual learner.

Exhibit 7–1 is a sample of a closure worksheet from which words that rhyme have been deleted. However, there are multiple opportunities for designating clusters of target words that would be deleted and then become the basis for instructional exercises. For example, one could delete all of the proper nouns in a passage. One might delete proper nouns wherever these occurred, or one might delete items on their second or third occurrence. The decision about the optimal pattern of deletion would depend on the instructor's judgment about which pattern was in the learner's best interest.

Parts of speech, such as prepositions, verbs, or articles, could be other possibilities for clusters of words that would be deleted. One could delete numerical information, names of places, dates, or any grouping of terms that occurred in a passage elicited from the learners. The only limitation on the designation of clusters for specific adults would be that the category of items in the clusters must be reflected in the transcribed speech of those adults.

Question Sets

Question sets are an opportunity to elicit samples of speech that can be incorporated into whole language instruction for adults with disabilities. Question sets comprise common questions that generalize to all narrative passages. For example, adult learners may have spoken at some length about their diverse experiences as part of a cooperative learning activity. If they are beginning readers, they would be frustrated if they tried to read samples of sentences that had been selected from all of the sentences that they might have spoken.

Instead, the content of their conversation can be reorganized and abbreviated with question sets. A simple question set might consist of the following five questions:

- Who was involved?
- Where did it take place?
- When did it take place?
- What happened?
- Why is this important?

Question sets can be used to reduce complex conversations for incorporation into instructional activities. However, question sets can also be used to help persons with limited speech focus on key elements in episodes that they are attempting to recount. If persons are capable of recounting only several observations about their experiences, question sets can direct them to critical dimensions of those episodes. Once an experience is described in terms of the dimensions that are evident in question sets, those responses become more like a passage that has been written by someone other than the learner. As such, question sets can encourage the development of skills that may transfer to other materials. Additionally, responses to question sets have the prerequisite information that will enable adult readers other than the author to share and understand those passages.

Once readers understand the five questions within a question set, the first three questions can be reduced to *who, where,* and *when.* If one were using a question set to reduce a complex conversation to a manageable form, the instructor and the adult learners might refer to a transcription of the original conversation in order to complete their responses. However, because learners' responses to question sets provide an orderly and predictable basis for instruction, responses to question sets rather than transcriptions of original conversations would be used for learning activities.

An advantage of question sets is that the completion of the question set would, by itself, instruct learners about fundamental reading comprehension skills. As the skills of the readers developed, they could use the identically structured question set that they had used to help them comprehend their personal narratives to understand passages that had been written by others. These passages written by others might include narrative passages from magazines or books.

Exhibit 7–2 is an example of an instructional worksheet based on a question set. This worksheet uses a question set as the basis for isolating a target word. This target word can be linked with a cluster of synonyms. The synonyms in the cluster could include words that were outside the oral vocabulary of the adult learner for whom the lesson was being developed. The learner would thus have an opportunity to learn new vocabulary by associating it with vocabulary terms that he or she had used already to describe a familiar incident.

Sorting

Once an oral language sample has been elicited, instructors have opportunities to employ sorting activities. Sorting activities encourage learners to manipulate cards on which are written words, phrases, or sentences that they have used in their oral conversation.

The words from an oral language transcription might be recorded individually on cards. For example, the words from the passage tran-

---

Exhibit 7–2
Example of an Instructional
Activity Worksheet Using a Question Set

Who?

When?

Where?

What happened?

Why is this important?

Target word: _____
                    _____
                    _____
                    _____
                    _____

---

scribed in Exhibit 7–1 are recorded in Exhibit 7–3. If each of these words were placed on a card, learners could sort through the deck, arranging the words in different ways. If the word cards had been shuffled randomly, learners might try to sort out the words that began with a specified consonant, such as the letter *m*. Or they might be given a target word with a short *a*, such as *bat*, and asked to sort out the other words with short *a*. They might sort out single syllable words, two syllable words, or words with more than two syllables. Learners could use several cards or they might employ a larger set. The cards employed in a sorting activity could all be drawn from a transcription or from several transcriptions reflecting different topics.

Exhibit 7–3
The List of Words from the Speech Transcription in
Exhibit 7–1 as the Basis for Multiple Sorting Activities

and	metal
ball	my
bat	of
but	on
came	out
ducked	pitch
everybody	second
fat	sitting
got	so
he	the
heavy	their
hit	to
I	turn
it	was
laughed	way
mad	when
manager	where

Even learners who are unable to recognize the printed words from their own speech can still be successful with simple sorting activities. For example, if learners were asked to solve tasks with cards that had words they had spoken printed on them, they might be successful by using a select feature. Referring back to Exhibit 7–3, the initial consonants with which words began might be sufficient to sort out those words that were similar to *bat* or *mad*. If an instructor pronounced the words as the learner examined each card, this might enable the learner to use phonetic cues to differentiate words.

Sorting activities can be combined with closure exercise. A learner could be asked to sort words into the sequence in which those words had been deleted from a transcribed passage. Alternatively, a learner might be asked to pick out those words from a deck of word cards that could complete sentences devised by the instructor. For example, a learner might be asked to pick out those words from Exhibit 7–3 that could complete sentences of the following types:

I am _____.

John is _____ .

It is _____ *ball.*

She could _____.

Types of Learners for Whom Whole Language Instruction Can Be Appropriate

Jones (1981) reviewed research on the psychology of adult learning and concluded that both skills-based instruction and whole language instruction complemented essential stages in the acquisition of literacy by adults. However, he discouraged exclusive exposure to skills-based programs, because, "this instruction is maximally effective only after the learner has acquired insight into the reading process . . . pertaining to content with which he is interested and familiar" (p. 81). As such, Jones supported the use of whole language programs during the initial phases of reading instruction, to be followed by skills-based instruction.

Whole language approaches have been used extensively and successfully with adult learners who speak languages other than English. Studies have confirmed that whole language approaches are effective with linguistically diverse learners because the programs build on the learners' background experiences, cultural values, and linguistic patterns (Anderson & Barnitz, 1984; Green, 1989; Montero-Sieburth, 1990; Paul, 1986).

Because whole language programs facilitate social interaction, older persons are another group for whom these programs can be suitable. Opportunities for social interaction and input about the schedule, format, and content of reading instruction can be essential to positive literacy programs for the elderly (Bernazza-Haase, Robinson, & Beach, 1979; Heilsel & Gordon, 1984; Kingston, 1979; Rigg & Kazemek, 1983; Robinson & Bernazza-Haase, 1979). Because psychoeducational approaches have many of these same advantages, these are also popular as literacy programs for the elderly (Bernazza-Haase et al., 1979; Rigg & Kazemek, 1983).

Assessment

Because both the content of instruction and the schedule for acquiring specific reading skills are variable among learners in whole language programs, assessment in whole language programs is complex. This complexity represents a major obstacle that might dissuade some instructors from using whole language programs. The issue of assessment would be especially relevant for instructors preparing learners for skills-based tests to enter into a profession, graduate from a program, or participate in any event for which passing a test was conditional.

The long-range effectiveness of whole language programs has in many cases been based on testimonials from the instructors and participants in these programs. Such testimonials are a type of evidence about the learning that has transpired. However, the objectivity of testimonials can be questioned. If one supplements whole language instruction with skills-based drills of the type that have been described in this chapter, these activities will increase the likelihood that persons who have learned to read with whole language programs will demonstrate those skills on skills-based tests.

Nonetheless, whole language instruction is not taught in a format that prepares persons as effectively for performance on standardized tests as does skills-based instruction. Additionally, proponents of whole language instruction have expressed reservations about the use of skills-based tests to measure progress in whole language programs that proceed from a distinct philosophy about the nature and goals of reading (Goodman et al., 1988).

The most common approach for assessing progress of learners in whole language programs is through portfolios that indicate the learning that has transpired. The portfolio can contain evidence of responses to activities by learners. These learning samples could be completed pages from workbooks, printouts of computer drills, writing samples, diaries, and artistic works. This evidence may be supplemented with annotated observations in which instructors indicate the affect exhibited by learners during the exercises.

Samples of reading by learners can also be included in portfolios. The samples may consist of tape recordings or transcriptions of reading that have been diagnostically annotated with one of the techniques explained in Chapter 3. These samples of reading, as well as the responses to learning activities, would be dated so that a person examining the portfolio could form an impression of how the learner had progressed during the course of instruction (Froese, 1991).

A third category of item that would be present almost certainly in a portfolio would be information about the attitudes of learners. This information could include observations about the responses of learners to structured inventories, such as those included in Chapter 3. Or the information could be gathered informally as instructors made notes about conversations, interviews, and personal interactions with learners.

The portfolio might contain information about punctuality, participation in group activities, time on task, and comments made by peers. Although such information would be circumstantial, it could be useful when attempting to form a comprehensive perspective about learners' progress.

Another type of information that could be included in a portfolio would be responses by learners to standardized tests. Though the validity of these tests could be questioned when applied to adult learners in whole language programs, the probability of an incorrect evaluation would be reduced if the test results were viewed in the context of a cumulative file that exhibited the strengths and weaknesses of learners in response to a wide range of literacy learning tasks.

Summary

Whole language programs develop literacy skills with activities that integrate speech, writing, listening, and reading. The primary material used for instruction is based on narratives created by the learners themselves. Once these narratives have been created, instructors have opportunities to reinforce basic skills using those materials. If adults with disabilities are having difficulty providing speech samples that are a suitable basis for instruction, techniques such as closure, question sets, and sorting can help to elicit those speech samples.

Whole language approaches to literacy instruction have been criticized because of the difficulty of managing the programs, the requirement that instructors be somewhat skilled, and the complexity of the assessment associated with the programs. Techniques that employ group and cooperative learning were reviewed as solutions to problems of managing whole language programs. And portfolio assessment has been proposed as a means of organizing assessment within these programs. Examples of lessons were illustrated to assist inexperienced instructors while they experiment with whole language instruction.

Whole language instruction is useful because it represents an instructional alternative for individuals with disabilities who have not responded to the other literacy programs available. Whole language instruction can incorporate learners' language, values, attitudes, goals, and patterns of social interaction. As such, it may be especially suited as a literacy program for individuals from special groups, such as older persons, females, and members of ethnic and cultural minorities.

CHAPTER

8

Psychoeducational Programs

L iteracy programs can be thought of as equations. The equations contain variables with different weightings assigned to them. The weightings assigned to all of the variables within a program are likely to be different from each other. From program to program, the weights assigned to the identical variables would certainly be different. For example, every literacy program attends to variables such as backgrounds of the learners, primary language of the learners, sequencing of skills to be mastered by learners, availability of printed materials, access to computers, relevance of learning materials to the personal concerns of learners, and qualifications of the instructors. However, not all programs allocate a comparable amount of attention to each of these variables. The backgrounds of learners, the language of learners, and the qualifications of instructors are examples of factors that would be weighted more heavily in whole language programs than in skills-based programs; a greater proportion of the total energy in whole language programs is consumed by these three factors. Conversely, the sequencing of skills is an example of a factor that would be weighted more heavily in skills-based programs than in whole language programs.

In psychoeducational programs, the most heavily weighted factor would be the materials used for learning; for these materials should be perceived by learners as personally relevant. The insistence that reading materials exhibit personal relevance is derived from strategies used by therapists in psychology, which explains the origin of the term *psychoeducational*. Scully and Johnston (1991) discussed the similarities between psychoeducational instruction and psychotherapeutic techniques. They concluded that psychoeducational instruction could lead to the development of insights by adults that were comparable to those gained during psychological therapy.

Criticism of Psychoeducational Programs

Psychoeducational programs combine the advantages of literacy instruction and psychological therapy. One might anticipate that the time spent considering meaningful issues would detract from the literacy progress that learners could be experiencing. However, when persons are learning to read with materials that they perceive as potential solutions to their personal problems, the intensity of their learning may be increased qualitatively even if it is diminished quantitatively.

Nonetheless, one must question whether instructors will be prepared to address issues that will be raised inevitably by learners when they are learning to read materials that have been selected because they are controversial, provoking, and challenging. Additionally, what is the likelihood that instructors in adult literacy programs will have the knowledge, sophistication, or background to recognize the problems that persons are experiencing, let alone recommend materials for instruction that complement those problems?

Assuming that instructors can designate materials that correspond to the meaningful issues that adults encounter, how are literacy skills to be taught in the context of these materials? In skills-based programs and computerized literacy programs, skills to be mastered are isolated and arranged in an orderly progression. In whole language instruction, the learning of skills is always at the appropriate level for learners since the learning is synchronized to transcribed passages of the learners' own language. However, in psychoeducational programs, the materials that will meet the personal, psychological needs of learners are likely to exceed their emerging skills as readers. How does one prevent learners from becoming frustrated by materials which they may be motivated to read but which exceed their competence?

Response to Criticism

Although psychoeducational programs, which are sometimes referred to as bibliotherapeutic programs, can be employed by trained therapists (Lombana, 1992), the programs do not necessarily assume that instructors will be experienced counselors and psychologists. Instructors in adult literacy programs can devise psychoeducational programs by surrounding learners with materials that deal with the predictable problems, crises, and concerns likely to be encountered by adults.

It is a maxim of adult learning that learners respond to materials that emphasize topics of interest to them. As such, instructors can attempt to surround learners with predictably high-interest materials. These materials can be popular books and periodicals or materials that have been designed for adult learning. Collins (1990) compiled a bibliography of adult education materials for use in adult literacy programs. This bibliography had been restricted to materials that had been edited to simplify their use with learners with limited skills. The materials in the bibliography were arranged according to topics, which would simplify the identification and selection of resources suited for specific learners.

Instructors could easily compile a customized bibliography that best reflects the interests of learners with whom they are interacting. Sources of materials for such a bibliography could be publishers of adult literacy materials. Table 8–1 contains a list of such publishers.

As adults with disabilities are likely to respond to fiction or nonfiction books that focus on their own disabilities, instructors of adults with disabilities may wish to consult topical bibliographies highlighting such issues (Azarnoff, 1983; Baskin & Harris, 1984; Baston & Bergman, 1985; Friedberg, Mullins, & Weir-Sudiennik, 1992; LiBretto, 1990; McKee, 1987; Quicke, 1985; Ziegler, 1980). Although many of the books discussing issues about disabilities are aimed at an adolescent audience, these materials can still be appropriate for adults who are learning to read. Even books targeted for preadolescents might be appropriate if these are incorporated into literacy programs employing children's materials (see Chapter 9). Turock (1982) reviewed printed resources that could be especially appropriate for mature and older adults involved in psychoeducational programs.

As adult learners encounter materials that interest them, instructors can explore issues provoked by those materials and teach reading skills simultaneously. Table 8–2 contains sample questions that can help instructors estimate the suitability of general books and periodicals for incorporation into instruction. Exhibit 8–1 contains a checklist

Table 8-1   Examples of Companies and Organizations That Publish Reading Materials Aimed at Adult Education

Addison-Wesley—World Language Division, Jacob Way, Reading, MA 01867

Amsco School Productions, 315 Hudson St., New York, NY 10013

Center for Literacy, 3723 Chestnut St., Philadelphia, PA 19104

Contemporary Books, Dept. S90, 180 N. Michigan Ave., Chicago, IL 60601

Dynamic Programs, P. O. Box 5466, Trenton, NJ 10011

Fearon, 500 Harbor Blvd., Belmont, CA 94002

Free Library of Philadelphia (Reader Development Program), Logan Sq., Philadelphia, PA 19103

Globe, 200 Old Tappan Rd., Old Tappan, NJ 07675

Harcourt Brace, 6277 Sea Harbor Drive, Orlando, FL 32887

Houghton Mifflin, 101 Campus Dr., Princeton, NJ 08504

Jamestown, P.O. Box 9168, Providence, RI 02940

Janus, 2501 Industrial Pkwy. W., Haywood, CA 94545

Lifelong Learning Books—Scott Foresman, 1900 E. Lake Ave., Glenview, IL 60025

Literacy Volunteers of America, 5795 Widewaters Pkwy., Syracuse, NY 13214

Longman, 95 Church St., White Plains, NY 10601

New Readers Press, Dept. 78, Box 131, Syracuse, NY 13210

Prentice-Hall, 200 Old Tappan Road, Old Tappan, NJ 07675

Scholastic, P. O. Box 7501, 2931 E. McCarty St., Jefferson City, MO 65102

Steck-Vaughn, P. O. Box 26015, Austin, TX 78755

that could also be helpful when evaluating books or periodicals for use in psychoeducational programs for adults with disabilities.

The reading skills that learners develop in psychoeducational programs can be identical to the skills that they would have acquired with other literacy approaches. However, proponents of psychoeducational programs have argued that the impact of instruction about those skills is enhanced by virtue of the learners' motivation (Scully & Johnston, 1991). This motivation is linked to the personal relevance of the instructional materials as well as to the bonding that may form between instructors and learners who interact with high-relevance materials. By directing readers to materials that are instructionally suitable and that correspond to topics that the learners themselves have selected, the instructors may develop both literacy skills and a rapport with learners. These opportunities might not be available in another type of literacy program.

Table 8-2 Sample Questions for Measuring the Suitability of Books or Periodicals for Instruction to Adults With Disabilities

1. Does the book or periodical appear to be intended for adults?
2. Is the content of the book or periodical motivating?
3. Are features such as titles, headings, table of contents, or an index present and appropriate?
4. Are illustrations available and useful?
5. Is the length of sections, chapters, or articles suitable?
6. Is the material to be read independently; is the size and format portable and convenient?
7. Is there adequate room in the margins for taking notes or for writing questions?
8. Is the content of the materials relevant to males and females as well as persons from a range of backgrounds?
9. Does the content of the material relate to issues of concern to persons with disabilities?
10. Will the vocabulary, grammar, or concepts in the book or periodical frustrate developing adult readers?

After reviewing nearly six hundred articles, reports, and books about adult literacy, French (1987) concluded that the most effective programs are adult-oriented, involve the learners in decision making, and emphasize reading as comprehension. The initial two characteristics are more or less compatible with all of the approaches to adult literacy. However, not all literacy programs highlight comprehension with equal effectiveness.

Psychoeducational programs, like whole language programs, emphasize comprehension rather than the mastery of skills that may be viewed by learners as isolated, disjointed, and abstract. Consequently, psychoeducational programs have been used successfully for instruction with adults from linguistically and culturally diverse backgrounds, for the selection of socially and personally relevant reading materials can be critical when attracting, retaining, and motivating diverse learners to adult instruction (Diaz-Lefebvre, 1990; Montero-Sieburth, 1990).

Integrating Skills Instruction into Psychoeducational Programs

For psychoeducational programs to be employed successfully with learners with disabilities, reading skills may have to be taught and rein-

Exhibit 8-1
Books or Periodicals Checklist

Material_____

1 ----- 2 ----- 3 ----- 4 ----- 5
inferior   average   superior

interesting content	1 ----- 2 ----- 3 ----- 4 ----- 5
adult orientation	1 ----- 2 ----- 3 ----- 4 ----- 5
absence of gender bias	1 ----- 2 ----- 3 ----- 4 ----- 5
legible print	1 ----- 2 ----- 3 ----- 4 ----- 5
suitable format	1 ----- 2 ----- 3 ----- 4 ----- 5
adequate margins	1 ----- 2 ----- 3 ----- 4 ----- 5
challenging	1 ----- 2 ----- 3 ----- 4 ----- 5
reasonable cost	1 ----- 2 ----- 3 ----- 4 ----- 5
sensitive to diverse cultures	1 ----- 2 ----- 3 ----- 4 ----- 5
useful illustrations	1 ----- 2 ----- 3 ----- 4 ----- 5
suitable length	1 ----- 2 ----- 3 ----- 4 ----- 5
appropriate size	1 ----- 2 ----- 3 ----- 4 ----- 5
content relevant to persons with disabilities	1 ----- 2 ----- 3 ----- 4 ----- 5
suitable vocabulary	1 ----- 2 ----- 3 ----- 4 ----- 5
suitable grammar	1 ----- 2 ----- 3 ----- 4 ----- 5
suitable concepts	1 ----- 2 ----- 3 ----- 4 ----- 5

perfect score: ....80 pts
above average score: ....>48 pts
average score: ....48 pts
below average score: ....<48 pts

forced through structured activities. The clustering techniques that were recommended to integrate skills instruction into whole language programs can be equally appropriate for developing skills in psychoeducational programs. For example, instructors can identify target words that occur in materials in which adult learners are interested. These target words can then be used to form clusters of new words that adults will learn.

Clustering activities, as well as closure and sorting activities, can be effective for developing word identification skills in psychoeducational programs. However, since the focus of psychoeducational programs is the development of comprehension skills, what would be activities for developing rudimentary comprehension skills in these programs?

Question set activities, reviewed in Chapter 7, could be applied effectively to psychoeducational programs. However, outlining activities would be appropriate as well. Because outlining strategies generalize to all types of materials, these strategies can be particularly suited to the diverse materials that instructors are likely to encounter in psychoeducational programs.

Chronological Outlines

The simplest type of outline is a time line, or chronological outline. As adult learners read a passage, or listen to a passage being read, they make notes along a line. The span of the line on which they are progressively taking notes represents the span of a passage that they are reading or to which they are listening. The passage might be a portion of a paragraph, a paragraph, an article, or a book.

Figure 8–1 illustrates a chronological outline developed in response to a narrative passage. Some outlining strategies require that readers comprehend, recall, and then reconfigure the content of a passage after they have completely read that passage. Because the events listed on a chronological outline can be assembled in the same order that they are listed in the original passage, a chronological outline can be created even while learners are reading or listening to a passage.

Webbing

When learners create a web, they identify key concepts, events, or details. The details may be from a passage, chapter, article, or book that they are reading or to which they are listening. Unlike a chronological outline, a web does not require that events be recorded in temporal order. The learners can place the recorded information in balloons.

Mack finds the bottle

He calls Louise

**He tell Louise he knows
about her drinking**

She gets help

Louise tries to stop drinking

And Mack gets help for drugs

Figure 8–1.   Chronological outline.

If desirable, the size of the balloons can indicate the importance of the information recorded within them. The appropriate arrangement for the balloons is a decision made by individual learners.

The balloons within a web can be connected with lines. The lines connecting two balloons show that the content in those balloons is connected. The lines also indicate the relationship between the balloons. The specific relationship symbolized by each connecting line is indicated through a word or phrase that has been written on each line. Figure 8–2 illustrates the use of a web for a narrative passage.

Summary Forms for Outline Activities

The information upon which learners are concentrating when they read or listen to passages may be in narrative or nonnarrative formats. Chronological outlines are appropriate for narrative materials. Webs are appropriate for narrative or nonnarrative materials. However, readers are likely to find that nonnarrative materials are more difficult to outline with these techniques. For readers who are frustrated, instructors can use summary outline forms that they devise.

Exhibit 8–2 is an example of a form with which learners could outline nonnarrative materials. This form could be expanded or reduced based on the skills of the learners, the scope of the assignment, and the nature of the material being read.

Outline forms can also be devised for narrative materials. Outline forms for narrative materials might be effective learning instruments for persons who have progressed well with outline forms that have been applied to nonnarrative materials. Additionally, outline forms for narrative materials can be useful as instructional materials that can simply alter the pace or format of routine activities. Exhibit 8–3 is an example of a form for organizing narrative materials.

Critical Reading Activities

Critical reading is sometimes associated with the final stage of literacy development. For instructors who do assume this perspective, critical reading may seem inaccessible to beginning adult readers with disabilities. However, because psychoeducational programs employ materials that are intended to stimulate, confront, and challenge the participants, critical responses to materials by learners is to be expected. As such, critical reading can be not only appropriate but even necessary for beginning adult readers in psychoeducational programs. Additionally, because adults tend to view themselves as independent, responsible, motivated, and empowered, they may insist that they have the opportunity to learn critical reading.

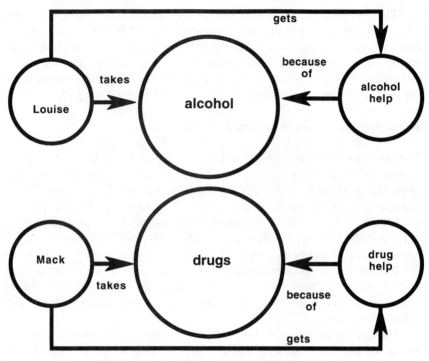

Figure 8–2. Web outline.

The critical reading tasks that are set for college students in their humanities and science classes would be inappropriate for adults with disabilities who are developing initial reading skills. Nonetheless, there are critical reading activities that can be appropriate for persons with very limited literacy skills. As an example, an instructor could read an argumentative, persuasive, or controversial passage with an adult learner. If the learner were unable to participate in the reading of the passage, the instructor could read the passage aloud, pointing to the words as they were spoken. The instructor might draw a circle and label that circle with the major premise of the passage that had been read. Within the circle, any material from the argument that was relevant to the premise would be outlined. The reader would compare and contrast the material arranged within the circle with that on the outside of the circle. The reader would question whether the substantiating information in the circle was adequate and persuasive. He or she could then decide whether the goal of the author who wrote that passage had been substantiated effectively.

Exhibit 8–2
Outline Form for Nonnarrative Materials

Title _____

Author(s) _____ When Printed _____

Questions asked:

Answers to the questions:

Why I agree with the answers to the questions:

Why I disagree with the answers to the questions:

In addition to the critical reading activity that was just described, the following 10 activities can be appropriate for developing critical reading skills in psychoeducational programs. All of these critical reading activities might be appropriate for beginning adult learners with disabilities.

Exhibit 8–3
Outline Form for Narrative Materials

Title _____

Author(s) _____ Year Printed _____

Time _____

Location _____

Characters: Descriptions:

Key Events:

What I liked best:

What I liked least:

Bias Estimation

In this instructional exercise, the learners read a passage about a controversial topic. If the learners cannot read the passage independently, the instructors may read the passage orally, pointing to the words as they are said. Learners are asked to place a "+" symbol next to words with a positive connotation and to place a "−" symbol next to words with a negative connotation. After summarizing the number of positive and negative terms on a worksheet (Exhibit 8–4), the learners attempt to assess whether the authors of the passage they have analyzed were supportive, negative, or neutral about the topic of that passage.

Exhibit 8–4
Critical Reading Worksheet—Bias Estimation

Name _____

Date _____

Title of Material _____

Positive Terms   _____

Negative Terms   _____

Conclusion _____

_____

*[**Directions to the Instructor:** The learner reads a paragraph about a controversial topic. If the learner cannot read the passage independently, you may read the passage orally, pointing to the words as you say them. Ask the learner to place a "+" symbol next to words with a positive connotation and to place a "−" symbol next to words with a negative connotation. After summarizing the number of positive and negative terms on the worksheet, the learner should assess whether the author was supportive, negative, or neutral about the controversial topic.]*

Argument Analysis

Adult learners are given a passage about a controversial topic. The readers are encouraged to read that passage. If the learners cannot read the passage independently, the instructors may read the passage orally, pointing to the words as they say them. Using a worksheet (Exhibit 8–5), the readers then attempt to identify the goal of the author's argument. On that same worksheet, they list facts in the passage that they feel might persuade readers to accept the author's goal for their argument.

Exhibit 8–5
Critical Reading Worksheet—Argument Analysis

Name _____

Date _____

Title of Material _____

Purpose of the Argument _____

Persuasive Facts _____

_____

_____

_____

_____

[Directions to the Instructor: *The learner reads a paragraph about a controversial topic. If the learner cannot read the passage independently, you may read the passage orally, pointing to the words as you say them. The readers identifies the goal of the author's argument and then lists facts in the passage that the author has included to persuade readers. The goal of the argument and the supporting details are written on the worksheet.]*

Question Generation

Learners are asked to read a passage about a controversial topic. The passage must contain several paragraphs. If the learners cannot read the passage independently, the instructors may read the passage orally, pointing to the words as they say them. The readers attempt to identify an implicit question that the authors are addressing as they present the information in each paragraph. A number is placed next to each paragraph that is analyzed. The implicit question for the content of each numbered paragraph is written next to the corresponding number on a worksheet (Exhibit 8–6).

Exhibit 8–6
Critical Reading Worksheet—Question Generation

Name _____

Date _____

Title of Material _____

Paragraph #   Question

_____   _____

_____   _____

_____   _____

_____   _____

_____   _____

*[**Directions to the Instructor:** The learner reads a set of paragraphs about a controversial topic. If the learner cannot read the passage independently, you may read the passage orally, pointing to the words as you say them. The reader identifies an implicit question that the author is addressing through the information that is presented in each paragraph. A number is placed next to each paragraph that is analyzed. The question corresponding to each numbered paragraph is written on the worksheet.]*

Identifying Persuasive Strategies

Adult learners read a passage about a controversial topic. The passage must contain several paragraphs. If the learners cannot read the passage independently, the instructors may read the passage orally, pointing to the words as they say them. Each paragraph in the passage is numbered. The readers then attempt to identify the persuasive strategies that the authors have employed in the numbered paragraphs. To indicate that a designated strategy was employed in a specific paragraph, the learners place the number of that paragraph next to the appropriate strategy on a worksheet (Exhibit 8–7).

Exhibit 8–7
Critical Reading Worksheet—Identifying Persuasive Strategies

Name _____

Date _____

Title of Material _____

Paragraph #   Strategy

_____   Statement That Makes One Feel Good

_____   Statement That Makes One Feel Bad

_____   Testimonial by a Famous Person

_____   Testimonial by an Ordinary Person

_____   Statement That "Everyone Is Doing This"

*[**Directions to the Instructor:** The learner reads a set of paragraphs about a controversial topic. If the learner cannot read the passage independently, you may read the passage orally, pointing to the words as you say them. After each paragraph is numbered, the reader identifies persuasive strategies that the author is employing in those paragraphs. The number that has been placed next to a paragraph is then written next to the appropriate strategy on the worksheet.]*

Color Coding Persuasive Strategies

The learners read a passage about a controversial topic. The passage must contain several paragraphs. If the learners cannot read the passage independently, the instructors may read the passage orally, pointing to the words as they say them. Each paragraph is numbered. Within the numbered passage, those paragraphs that are especially persuasive are colored by the learners using red markers. Paragraphs that are somewhat persuasive are colored with orange markers. Paragraphs that are significantly less persuasive or not persuasive are colored with green markers. The numbers that have been placed by the paragraphs are then written next to the appropriate colors and categories on a worksheet (Exhibit 8–8).

Exhibit 8–8
Critical Reading Worksheet—Color Coding Persuasive Strategies

Name _____

Date _____

Title of Material _____

Paragraph #   Strategy

_____   Red: .   Very Persuasive

_____   Orange: Somewhat Persuasive

_____   Green: Not Persuasive

*[**Directions to the Instructor:** The learner reads a set of paragraphs about a controversial topic. If the learner cannot read the passage independently, you may read the passage orally, pointing to the words as you say them. After the paragraphs have been numbered, the paragraphs that are especially persuasive are colored with a red marker. Paragraphs that are somewhat persuasive are colored with an orange marker. Paragraphs that are significantly less persuasive or not persuasive are colored with a green marker. The colored numbers that have been placed next to the paragraphs are then written next to the appropriate categories on the worksheet.]*

Summarizing Persuasive Phrases

The learners read a passage about a controversial topic. The passage must contain several paragraphs. If the learners cannot read the passage independently, the instructors may read the passage orally, pointing to the words as they say them. After the paragraphs are numbered, a persuasive phrase is identified in each paragraph. These key phrases are underlined by the learners. The number that has been placed by each paragraph is then written next to the key phrase from that paragraph on a worksheet (Exhibit 8–9).

Exhibit 8–9
Critical Reading Worksheet—Summarizing
Persuasive Phrases

Name _____

Date _____

Title of Material _____

Paragraph #   Key Phrase

_____   _____

_____   _____

_____   _____

_____   _____

_____   _____

[Directions to the Instructor: The learner reads a set of paragraphs about a controversial topic. If the learner cannot read the passage independently, you may read the passage orally, pointing to the words as you say them. After paragraphs are numbered, a key persuasive phrase is underlined in each paragraph. Using the worksheet, the learners place the number next to each paragraph next to the key phrase from that paragraph.]

Differentiating Relevant from Nonrelevant Details

The adult learners read a passage about a controversial topic. The passage should contain several paragraphs. If the learners cannot read the passage independently, the instructors may read the passage orally, pointing to the words as they say them. After the readers have numbered the paragraphs, they can examine the details that have been provided in each paragraph. They then attempt to identify a key question that is being implicitly answered through the details in each paragraph. Information that is relevant to that question is underlined and information that is not relevant to that question is circled. The number that has been placed next to each paragraph, the key question corresponding to each paragraph, and the results of the analysis of relevant and nonrelevant details are then written on a worksheet (Exhibit 8–10).

Overviewing

The learners are given a passage about a controversial topic. The passage must contain several paragraphs. The adult learners are instructed to read only the first and last paragraphs of the passage. If the learners cannot read these paragraphs independently, the instructors may read the two paragraphs orally, pointing to the words as they say them. The readers select several phrases from the introductory paragraph and several phrases from the concluding paragraph. The phrases are written in the appropriate sections on a worksheet (Exhibit 8–11). On the basis of the selected phrases that they have extracted from the passage, the readers attempt to infer the topic of the entire passage. They also attempt to infer the attitudes of the authors toward that topic.

Illustration Guide

The learners read a passage about a controversial topic. The passage must contain several paragraphs and it must include illustrations. If the learners cannot read the passage independently, the instructors may read the passage orally, pointing to the words as they say them. The illustrations in the passage are numbered. Next to each numbered illustration, a phrase is written by the learners about that illustration. The phrase as well as the number that has been placed next to each illustration is then written on a worksheet (Exhibit 8–12).

Exhibit 8–10
Critical Reading Worksheet—Differentiating Relevant from Nonrelevant Details

Name _____

Date _____

Title of Material _____

Paragraph #	Question	Relevant Sentences	Nonrelevant Sentences
_____	_____	_____	_____
_____	_____	_____	_____
_____	_____	_____	_____
_____	_____	_____	_____

*[**Directions to the Instructor:** The learner reads a set of paragraphs about a controversial topic. If the learner cannot read the passage independently, you may read the passage orally, pointing to the words as you say them. After the paragraphs have been numbered, the reader uses the details in each paragraph to identify a question that is being implicitly answered. Information that is relevant to that question is underlined and information that is not relevant to that question is circled. The number that has been placed next to each paragraph, the key question corresponding to each paragraph, and the results of the analysis of relevant and nonrelevant details are then written on the worksheet.]*

Summarizing with Topic Sentences

The learners read a passage about a controversial topic. The passage must contain several paragraphs. The passage should contain clear topic sentences that occur predictably at the beginning of each paragraph. The adult learners are directed to read only the topic sentence in

Exhibit 8–11
Critical Reading Worksheet—Overviewing

Name _____

Date _____

Title of Material _____

First Paragraph

_____

_____

Last Paragraph

_____

_____

Topic _____

Attitude _____

*[**Directions to the Instructor:** The learner reads only the first and last paragraphs of a passage about a controversial topic. If the learner cannot read the passage independently, you may read these two paragraphs orally, pointing to the words as you say them. The reader selects several phrases from the initial paragraph and several phrases from the concluding paragraph. The phrases are written in the appropriate sections on the worksheet. On the basis of this sampling of information, the reader attempts to guess the topic of the entire passage as well as the attitude of the author toward that topic.]*

each paragraph. If the learners cannot read these sentences independently, the instructors may read them orally, pointing to the words as they say them. After the paragraphs are numbered by the learners, the topic sentence in each paragraph is underlined. The number that has

Exhibit 8–12
Critical Reading Worksheet—Illustration Guide

Name _____

Date _____

Title of Material _____

Illustration #   Significance

_____   _____

              _____

_____   _____

              _____

_____   _____

              _____

_____   _____

              _____

[Directions to the Instructor: The learner reads an illustrated set of paragraphs about a controversial topic. If the learner cannot read the passage independently, you may read the passage orally, pointing to the words as you say them. The illustrations are numbered and a phrase is written about each illustration. The number that has been placed next to each illustration is then written next to the summary phrase on the worksheet.]

been placed next to each paragraph is then written on a worksheet next to a phrase that summarizes each topic sentence (Exhibit 8–13).

Exhibit 8-13
Critical Reading Worksheet—Summarizing
With Topic Sentences

Name _____

Date _____

Title of Material _____

Paragraph #   Topic Sentence

_____   _____

_____   _____

_____   _____

_____   _____

_____   _____

_____   _____

[Directions to the Instructor: The learner reads only the topic sentences in a set of paragraphs about a controversial topic. If the learner cannot read the sentences independently, you may read them orally, pointing to the words as you say them. Paragraphs are numbered and the topic sentence in each paragraph is underlined. The number that has been placed next to each paragraph is then written on the worksheet next to a phrase that summarizes each topic sentence. For this activity, reading materials should have clear topic sentences that occur predictably at the beginning of paragraphs.]

Assessment

Since the materials, the reading goals, the format of lessons, and the sequencing of skills in psychoeducational programs are individualized, assessing the progress of learners is complex. For this reason, a portfolio approach is likely to be employed.

Because psychoeducational programs can emphasize basic reading skills, a standardized, skills-based test could be a component of the portfolio. However, skills-based tests present assessment tasks in an isolated fashion that is distinct from the context in which those skills would have been presented in psychoeducational programs. Consequently, other types of information should be included in the learners' portfolios.

Curriculum-based assessment is a distinct type of testing that can supplement skills-based tests. Curriculum-based assessment enables instructors to define precise instructional goals and then monitor systematically if those objectives are achieved. Although curriculum-based assessment has been used extensively to measure whether learners are mastering word identification skills, the technique can be adapted to assess the comprehension skills that characterize psychoeducational programs (Howell, Fox, & Morehead, 1993).

In portfolios designed for learners who are in programs other than psychoeducational programs, information about the attitudes of learners would be useful but optional. In psychoeducational programs, information about attitudes would be critical. Information about attitudes would be needed at the beginning of an individualized instructional program in order to identify issues that were viewed as meaningful by learners. As learners developed literacy skills in the program, changes in attitudes would be monitored to observe whether the learners were making corollary changes in emotional, social, and psychological areas.

Information about learners' attitudes, biases, opinions, and values might be gathered by instructors through their interactions with learners. Recorded observations by instructors could be placed in learners' portfolios. Diaries, reports, collaborative projects, artistic creations, samples of lessons, and observations about learners by members of interdisciplinary teams could be additional opportunities to gather information for inclusion within portfolios. Psychologists and counselors could assist instructors as members of interdisciplinary teams within psychoeducational programs. Depending on the disabilities of the adult learners in the program, vocational rehabilitation counselors, speech–language pathologists, physical therapists, occupational therapists, and transition specialists could all contribute potentially to these teams.

Summary

Psychoeducational programs can reflect many of the priorities that adults identify for themselves in their own lives. As such, these programs motivate learners by reassuring them that the instruction is relevant to the issues and problems that they are confronting. Predictably, such programs are difficult to manage and instruct. Some of this difficulty can be reduced by the use of bibliographies that identify reading materials with topics that conform to those that the learners view as important. Additionally, one can complement psychoeducational programs with activities that reinforce essential comprehension skills and enable readers to use materials that would otherwise be frustrating to them. Chronological outlines, webbing, and summary forms are examples of complementary learning activities.

Because psychoeducational programs emphasize comprehension, these programs can be especially suited to critical reading instruction. Although viewed by some as the final step in the development of literacy, critical reading can be taught effectively to beginning learners with psychoeducational activities. These activities can enable learners to transfer to reading the critical thinking skills that they exhibit on an informal basis in their day to day oral transactions. Sample, introductory critical reading activities were reviewed.

CHAPTER

9

Programs That Employ Children's Materials

Because adult learners can exhibit the level of reading that would be appropriate for children, some instructors may be inclined to use instructional materials that have been designed for young readers. Though the content of materials intended for children would not be matched to the interest of adult learners, the controlled vocabulary, restrictions on complex grammar, simplicity of concepts, uniformity of format, and the sequencing of skills could be viewed as benefits that would outweigh this disadvantage.

Because of these benefits, even children's materials that are not part of structured programs, such as pieces of children's literature, can be useful for instruction. Samples of children's literature could be picture books, folk tales, fairy tales, fantasies, poems, realistic fiction, and historical fiction. Children's materials could even include picture books without any text; in these books, instructors and learners would generate suitable dialogue. And children's materials could be nonnarrative, such as expository books, textbooks, and reference books.

Children's materials can be made more attractive to adult learners if the adults perceive themselves as tutors for young children who are themselves learning to read. By assuming an instructional role, adults, who may be grandparents or parents, can become caregivers responding to basic needs that all children exhibit. Examples of universal, basic needs would be to accept, give love, belong, achieve, feel self-esteem, experience beauty, and participate in order (Burke, 1986). Adults as well as children can benefit from the symbiotic relationship that may develop during reading sessions (Glazer & Burke, 1994).

When adult learners read to children, there are opportunities to model behaviors that can impress the audience and the adults who are reading with values appropriate for all learners. Examples of these values are that reading is enjoyable, emotionally stimulating, social, and informative. The development of these values is a path to independent reading that will be personal and that may persist throughout individuals' lives (Collins & Cheek, 1993).

Alexis-Ford (1995) reviewed examples of educational programs to help African American learners with disabilities. There are distinctive family centered patterns of interaction between adults and children among many African Americans. Based on this interaction, programs that have included assistance from adults have been effective with learners from elementary school through early adulthood. In addition to parents, the instructors who have helped in these programs have included a broad range of volunteers. The potential benefits of community-based, family-centered programs such as those described by Alexis-Ford could extend to minority groups other than African Americans as well as to nonminority learners.

Dagostino and Carifio (1994) acknowledged that functional literacy was appropriate as a goal for all persons. However, they identified a higher order literacy that enables persons to read in an evaluative manner. They argued that basic literacy programs, while emphasizing functional literacy, should not exclude instruction about higher order literacy. Because of the complex social and psychological factors that can be present in children's literature, programs that employ children's materials may be able to inculcate evaluative reading skills effectively. Examples of evaluative reading skills might be using assumptions, intentions, attitudes, and biases to differentiate fact from opinion, reality from fantasy, or objective information from propaganda.

When preparing to share materials with children, adults master literacy objectives that will enable them to be successful. Children's literature can be especially suitable for helping adult learners as well as children master literacy objectives. Glazer (1986) illustrated a three-stage procedure for preparing to read books to children: preview the materials, make arrangements for the setting in which the book will be read, and practice the presentation. This type of careful, progressive preparation can provide the ideal opportunity for developing the skills of adult learners.

Glazer (1986) listed instructional goals to be set for children when adults read to them. The same goals could be suitable for the adult learners preparing themselves to read materials to children. Examples of goals could be the ability to weigh evidence, make appropriate choices, establish objectives, complete tasks, develop positive self-concepts, form values, understand emotions, and appropriately express feelings.

Glazer and Burke (1994) identified specific learning objectives that can benefit children to whom adults read. The same benefits can accrue to the adult learners who are preparing to read to the children. As an example, the following list identifies topics about which both children who are an audience for reading and adults who are learning to read to those children can acquire understanding.

- functions of print
- link between recall and printed text
- link between sounds and letters
- link between spoken language and written language
- nature of reading
- structures of stories
- types of books

The following list contains pretexts for actual lessons that could be implemented with most children's books.

- book care
- characters
- copyright
- dialogue
- facts and opinions
- fiction and nonfiction
- figures of speech
- graphic illustrations and photos
- indirect quotes and direct quotes
- inferences
- information about authors
- literary genres
- making predictions
- maps
- moods
- passages written in the first person and the third person
- plots

- points of view
- reading aids such as a table of contents, index, or glossary
- settings
- summary passages
- symbols
- tables and charts
- themes and morals
- titles and subtitles

The narratives in many children's books have predictable patterns of organization. These organizational patterns can be helpful to adult learners, for once a pattern is recognized, learners can use this information to infer a sequence of events while they are reading. As a result, word recognition, awareness of grammatical patterns, and comprehension can be facilitated. Predictable organizational patterns can also be used after the reading of a book to aid in the recall of events from that book. For example, readers of *The Gingerbread Man* will have repeated opportunities to grasp and generalize a pattern that characterizes all but the last of the gingerbread man's encounters with other characters in the story. As readers gain experience with books that have predictable patterns, they may recognize the pattern in a new book as a variation on one they have already discovered in a different context. Lynch (1986) identified predictable organizational patterns that included cause–effect, problem–solution, lists, and sequences.

If children are involved with instructional activities, adult learners assisting those children can develop insights about reading as they prepare to help with instruction. For example, Hagerty (1992) suggested several formats for instructional activities geared to children's books.

- Learners can complete sentences that prod reactions to specified features of books.
- Learners can write about a word, sentence, passage, or illustration from a book.
- Learners can complete forms that cue them about features such as characters, setting, time, plot, and theme.
- Learners can write short reports in which they evaluate the personality traits of characters.
- Learners can maintain journals in which an instructor responds to their comments about books.

Adult learners could act as facilitators for activities of this type. Additionally, adult learners could practice these activities with their own instructors in order to develop their confidence for modeling the activities to children.

Sometimes programs employing children's materials are managed in a fashion that can make them appear to be the antithesis of psychoeducational programs. After all, psychoeducational programs emphasize the personal relevance of the topics of instructional materials. In contrast, programs that employ children's materials may ignore personal relevance. However, the chasm separating programs that employ children's materials and psychoeducational programs may be bridged if adults are functionally motivated to read children's materials as a consequence of their roles as tutors to young learners.

Criticism of Programs That Employ Children's Materials

Newton (1980) expressed what came to be a prevailing opinion in the field of adult learning when she argued that adult learning should be oriented in the present. Present-oriented learning should emphasize learners' current status. For example, current status could be highlighted through the learners' social roles as parents, spouses, or workers. Additionally, present-oriented learning can highlight learners' membership in cultural, ethnic, and religious groups.

Jones (1981) identified practical factors that distinguished effective literacy instruction for adults from that which is effective for children. For example, the format of instruction could be influenced by the physiological and cognitive differences between adults and children. Other factors that could distinguish adult and child instruction could be the manner in which time was managed, the attentiveness of instructors to the previous experiences of learners, and recognition of the degree of learners' language development. Motivation, personal expectations, and the self-concepts of learners could also be the basis for differentiating programs that were respectively suited for children or adults. If one were to formulate an equation to calculate the benefits of approaches to instruct adults with children's material, any of the factors that have just been listed could influence that equation.

As many illiterate adults are poor, there can be factors associated with poverty that constitute an additional influence on the attitudes of poor adults toward literacy and literacy programs (Jones, 1981). These poverty-linked factors could include concerns about disapproval by illiterate peers, skepticism about a bond between literacy and employment, and questions about the assumption that literacy is an essential and prestigious personal achievement. When one adds to this equation the complications of physical, cognitive, and attitudinal problems that can be associated with developmental disabilities, the rationale for designing adult literacy programs distinct from those intended for children may seem striking.

Collins and Cheek (1993) noted advantages of using children's literature for instruction to children. The advantages included flexibility in grouping learners and in adapting instruction for their individual needs. However, they noted several practical restrictions on these programs. These restrictions would extend to adult literacy programs involving children's literature as well. Planning and record keeping could be more time consuming than in other literacy programs. Adult readers may have to judge whether books are appropriate for an audience of children. Books that are suitable or instructors with the skills needed to implement this type of program might be unavailable.

Response to Criticism

Sharp (1991) identified a predictable dilemma in adult literacy—the books that are psychologically, socially, and emotionally relevant to illiterate adult learners can contain such complex vocabulary, grammar, and concepts that the books are instructionally frustrating to novice readers. And though there are books that are instructionally suitable for adults, many of these materials are intended for young readers. There could be a resolution for this dilemma if learning to read children's books could be represented to adults as a functional type of learning.

Sharp (1991) suggested that the relevance of children's books for adults could be increased if the children's materials were depicted to adults as resources that the adults could use to help young children learn to read. For example, adult learners interacting with their own children might come to view children's books as important to them because of the impact that those books could in turn have on their children. But illiterate adults who had developed this perception would still require assistance meeting their own literacy needs before they could help their children. What would be the source of this support?

This assistance can be provided though community-based programs that develop the literacy skills of adults and children simultaneously. Several models for community-based, family-linked literacy programs have been developed in which adults and children interact during reading instruction (Laminack, 1989; McIvor, 1990; Nickse, 1990). Several of these models employed public libraries as the focal points for family-based literacy projects (American Library Association, 1990;

Monsour & Talan, 1993). Although children are often identified as the primary beneficiaries in the reports published about community-based programs, there are opportunities for adults to learn within these programs. The opportunities for adults can be as worthwhile as the opportunities for learning by children (Literacy Volunteers of America, 1991).

Because participants are providing useful services in community-based programs, there can be a reduction in the embarrassment that would otherwise be associated with preparation by adults to read children's books. The adult learners can receive assistance reading children's materials from instructors or from other adult learners who have successfully learned to read specific books. An audience of young persons may be drawn from the children in adult readers' own families. Children to whom adults can read may be identified also by the staff at day care centers or libraries.

In Chapter 4, Table 4–1 identified organizations that have provided resources and support for adult literacy programs. Although these organizations can be of assistance to all types of programs, this support can be critical to family-centered literacy programs that employ children's materials. This support can be especially important because of the informal organization and administration that often characterize family-centered programs.

The interest stimulated within children as they listen to or learn to read books may be increased if the children are allowed to earn inexpensive prizes and rewards. Examples of rewards could include pencils, stickers, books, magazines, field trips, coupons for restaurants, cinema passes, access to video games, or audiotapes. Exhibit 9–1 is an example of a form that can enable instructors to monitor adult learners' participation in this type of program. At the same time that records are being maintained about adult learners, the form allows instructors to record and tabulate the points toward prizes that are being earned by the children in the program.

A set of guidelines for promoting the employment of older adults in child care (Newman, Vander Ver, & Ward, 1991) recommends that older adults with disabilities be extended opportunities to work with young children in preschool settings. Such employment could provide effective settings for literacy programs in which adults as well as children benefit from reading children's materials.

Assessment

Assessing the progress of learners can be a troublesome feature of adult literacy programs that employ children's materials. Since these pro-

Exhibit 9-1
Example of a Form for Recording Books Read in a Children's Materials Program

Reading Record

Reader _____

Listener(s) _____

Book	Date	Time started	Time finished

1. _____

2. _____

3. _____

4. _____

5. _____

6. _____

7. _____

8. _____

9. _____

10. _____

Award toward which listeners are earning credits:

_____

grams are not intended to prepare adult learners to pass achievement tests, achievement tests could be inappropriate to assess the learning of participants in the programs. If one were considering a standardized test, questions of the following type could help with a decision about the effectiveness of a specific test (Searfoss & Readence, 1994):

- Would the standardized test or an informal test be appropriate?
- Does the test sufficiently reflect the learning one wishes to measure?
- If the test has a general scope, should it be replaced or supplemented with a more specialized test?
- Is the test better suited for initial screening rather than measuring achievement after instruction?
- Would an oral or a silent test be appropriate?
- Would a timed or an untimed test be appropriate?
- Will the results of the test have an impact on instruction?

Even after a decision is made to use a standardized test, instructors may modify the testing procedures. The following modifications, which were suggested by Collins and Cheek (1993) for increasing the validity of informal testing, can be equally appropriate for standardized tests: limit testing times according to students' abilities, employ various testing measures, reduce the formality of the testing situation, check the readability levels of all materials, ask for assistance from more experienced instructors, and verify test results against one's own opinions.

Peterson and Eeds (1990) suggested that the evaluation of young readers in literature-centered programs focus on data in each of the following categories: enjoyment, personal involvement, interpretation, making meaning, and insights into the structural elements of stories. A checklist of behaviors linked to these categories could be devised easily for adults learning to read children's materials.

Irwin (1991) recommended that instructors attend to situation- and text-related factors as well as reader-related factors when informally assessing comprehension. Situation-related factors are:

- physical environment
- student–teacher relationships
- students' perceptions of the purpose of reading
- teacher expectations
- suitability of format for assessing comprehension
- suitability of assessment questions

Text-related factors could focus on:

- readability level
- vocabulary
- sentence length
- organization

- number of concepts
- abstraction of concepts
- length of passage

Although quantitative measures are employed often as an indication of the effectiveness of family-centered and community-based literacy programs, these measures also could be used to assess the progress made by learners in those programs. The following list contains examples of quantitative measures that could be appropriate.

- a record of the number of times an adult learner participated in the program
- a record of the number of children with whom an adult learner interacted
- a record of the amount of time an adult learner spent interacting with children
- a record of the number of books an adult read to children
- a record of the number of other adult instructors an adult learner had assisted
- a record of the amount of time an adult learner spent assisting other adult instructors

In addition to quantitative information, the following types of supplementary, qualitative data can become part of assessment portfolios:

- recorded testimonials from an adult learner about the effectiveness of the program
- recorded testimonials from children about the books read to them by an adult learner
- recorded samples of an adult learner interacting with children
- recorded samples of an adult learner interacting with other adult learners
- observations by instructors about an adult interacting with children
- observations by instructors about the general literacy development of an adult learner
- anecdotal information from family members about behaviors of adult readers participating in the program
- attitudinal information about a learner

When involved in programs where they learn to read children's materials to an audience, adult learners may be motivated to self-monitor their reading. Program participants may be motivated to adopt self-monitoring strategies because of their joint identities as aides to young children and adult learners. Examples of self-monitoring activities would be *metacognitive strategies*, which are instructional exercises that improve learning by promoting awareness of learning (Baumann, 1988; Marzano, Hargerty, Valencia, & DiStefano, 1987). Three types of metacognitive processes are involved in reading: self-knowledge (recognizing one's strengths and weaknesses), task knowledge (understanding how different types of materials and tasks require distinct approaches to information processing), and strategy knowledge (awareness of functional strategies that enable one to achieve goals and then monitoring whether those goals are achieved) (Flavell, 1987; McNeil, 1984).

The application of metacognitive strategies to reading has been referred to as *metacomprehension* (Robeck & Wallace, 1990). Examples of metacomprehension by learners could be self-monitoring of their reading fluency and the degree to which they were understanding the intent of authors (Wong, 1991). Other indications of metacomprehension could be correcting errors, self-questioning, rereading of passages, and the use of contextual clues (Slavin, Madden, Karweit, Dolan, & Wasik, 1994).

Glazer (1992) identified prereading and postreading activities that could be opportunities for self-assessment. An example of a prereading activity would be making and confirming predictions about a book on the basis of a cursory examination of the cover, table of contents, or several passages. An example of a postreading activity would be recollecting key elements using organizational headings such as the book's introduction, setting, theme, plot, key episodes, and resolutions to problems.

Fitzgerald (1983) recommended that learners answer questions about passages, supplementing their responses with numerical codes that ranged from 1 (*not sure*) through 5 (*very sure*) as an indication of their degree of confidence in those responses. Describing a similar strategy, Smith and Dauer (1984) recommended that learners record and monitor their reactions to passages by annotating texts. For example, persons could make annotations with abbreviations of terms such as *agree, disagree, difficult, easy, confused*, and *clear*. Strategies of this sort require readers to evaluate whether goals that they have set while reading are being achieved.

Marzano, Hargerty, Valencia, and DiStefano (1987) recommended a general metacognitive strategy that could be applied to most materials. The strategy had six stages: relaxation, setting a goal, reading to accomplish that goal, monitoring what one is thinking, evaluating progress, and then evaluating whether one had been successful in achieving the goal that had been set. Davey (1983) suggested a five-step metacognitive activity that also could be applied to virtually any type of material. The five steps were: guessing the meaning of passages prior to reading, forming mental images while reading, combining information from passages with prior knowledge, monitoring comprehension, and correcting problems in the reading of passages as these are detected. Perhaps the most straightforward of the multistep metacomprehension processes was suggested by Brown (1980): reading, monitoring comprehension during reading, detecting problems in comprehension, and applying remedial strategies.

Garner, Alexander, and Hare (1991) recommended that instructors develop self-questioning strategies that were custom-designed to the needs of learners and the demands of specific materials. Custom-designed strategies could be effective when modeled by instructors or peer learners. To ensure that custom-designed strategies are comprehensive and can be modeled, instructors can task-analyze the steps and substeps in the strategies.

The results of self-assessment activities can be shared between adult learners and their instructors orally or through entries in response journals (Wollman-Bonilla, 1991). In response journals, learners record their reactions to materials that they have read. Instructors provide a written dialogue based on the journal entries. Opportunities for dialogue in response journals might be emotions elicited by passages, comparisons between the events in passages and the events in readers' lives, questions about passages, and questions about the process of reading. Journal entries by learners could be suggested by metacognitive activities. Careful analyses of the journal entries of learners can be occasions for instructors to assess the learners' reading processes, knowledge of the materials being read, and degree of engagement in the reading of those passages (Wollman-Bonilla, 1991).

Summary

Programs that employ children's materials may alienate adult learners who do not view these programs as responsive to adult issues and needs. Nonetheless, the programs can be managed in ways that eliminate this negative perception by adults. For example, adult learners can learn to read children's materials because they in turn will read those materials to young children. Under these circumstances, adults can be motivated to read children's materials because of their commitment to helping children. Additionally, if the materials adults are preparing to read are developmentally suited to their own level of reading, the adult learners can benefit as much as the children with whom they are interacting.

Another advantage of this type of program is that it can be organized informally in community settings. Adult learners often help other adult learners who are preparing to work with children, and this peer tutoring can be as productive as the interaction with children or with instructors in the adult literacy program.

One of the major drawbacks to this type of program is the difficulty of assessing the degree to which adult participants are benefiting from the program. Instructors can gather quantitative data, qualitative data, and the results of self monitoring activities into a distinctive type of portfolio. The data in such portfolios can be useful for evaluating individual learners as well as the effectiveness of the overall literacy program.

CHAPTER

10

Functional Reading Programs

Most literacy programs are delivered through free standing centers. These centers may be independent or they may be affiliated with community organizations such as libraries, schools, colleges, welfare agencies, churches, or service clubs. This model for organizing literacy programs has been employed to support instruction that has changed the lives of many persons who were illiterate. Nonetheless, this model has been criticized for having an insufficient impact on the literacy problems of adults.

Jacobson (1993) estimated that only 5% of the persons requiring assistance for illiteracy actually enrolled in programs, and that fewer than 20% of those enrolling showed progress equivalent to a gain of one grade level in their reading skills. Chisman (1990a) made similarly critical observations:

> It is inconceivable that we will be able to meet the needs of 20 to 30 million adults with limited basic skills, many of whom have pressing obligations at home and at work, by vastly increasing the number of free standing literacy centers. The only conceivable way to meet the demand is to place more emphasis on bringing literacy instruction to the people, rather than asking them to seek out a specialized location where they can find help. (p. 259)

Functional approaches to literacy are alternative programs that may not have the negative characteristics that Chisman and Jacobson were criticizing. Functional approaches are implemented within communities at the sites where specific literacy skills are actually employed. Functional approaches emphasize reading skills that involve learners' careers, home lives, personal relationships, and leisure activities.

Criticism of Functional Literacy Approaches

Functional literacy programs are attractive to instructors and learners because these programs can develop skills that adults can use immediately to solve literacy problems in their lives. Functional reading programs can have this immediate impact by encouraging learners to rely on whole word recognition strategies. Though functional literacy programs can be indispensable for learners who are incapable of mastering decoding skills, instructors need to be cautious that they do not stereotype all learners with disabilities as incapable of learning to use decoding strategies. An inappropriate stereotype of this type may persuade some instructors to believe that functional reading strategies are inherently better suited to the abilities of all learners with disabilities. Such an inappropriate bias can limit the literacy development of learners with disabilities (Buckley, 1995; Fowler, Doherty, & Boynton, 1995).

Functional reading programs are highly individualized. This high degree of individualization can create a difficulty in locating instructors who are competent to manage the program. Even after instructors are located, highly individualized functional reading programs can be difficult to implement because the programs require greater instructional preparation than alternative adult literacy programs. The increased demands on preparation by instructors can in turn restrict the number of learners with whom they can interact. This liability may seem especially disconcerting when one considers that the concern about limited impact on learners has been one of the chief incentives leading to the development of functional literacy programs.

Functional literacy programs are built on the backgrounds, values, and goals of the learners who participate. But there is predictable diversity among learners as a result of variable factors such as gender, culture, disability, community, career, and interest. How can instructors select materials and prepare instructional activities for learners with such predictable diversity?

Response to Criticism

There have been documented cases of successful functional literacy programs. Greenfield and Noguiera (1980) reported about instruction of adult learners in areas such as occupation, finance, health, and community issues. Biniakunu (1991) gave a detailed example of an episode in which adults from an African village were intrigued about learning to read when printed materials were linked to an environmental crisis in their community. And Rosow (1990) provided examples of how personally relevant consumer issues could be a pretext for literacy instruction with adults.

Alexis-Ford (1995) reviewed effective approaches to education that had been built on partnerships between African American youth and members of their communities. She identified the following topics that were addressed frequently in community-based instructional programs: motivation, advancement, cultural identity, decision making, goal setting, employment, self-advocacy, life skills, accessing information, community responsibilities, and mentor relationships. The format of these community-based programs included sessions that were conducted in schools, after school, on weekends, or as part of field trips, work shops, retreats, and special projects.

Such reports illustrate that adult reading programs can complement functional aspects of persons' lives. The programs that are reviewed in these reports exemplify the instructional philosophy of functional reading programs. This is an instructional philosophy in which "materials used to teach literacy skills . . . reflect the contexts within which those skills will be used, whether an adult's personal life, work life, or community involvement" (Fingeret, 1990, p. 27).

Community-based functional education programs are intended for groups of learners who exhibit predictable diversity. The professionals associated with some remedial educational approaches have maintained a bias about the cultural and linguistic differences exhibited by participants in the programs, viewing these differences as deficits that need to be eliminated before effective education can transpire (Alexis-Ford, 1995; Byrd, 1995; Harry, 1995). Because representatives of the community can be involved as instructors, peer tutors, mentors, and models, community-based, functional instruction has the potential to reduce bias while meeting the educational needs of multicultural learners.

The workplace may be the primary opportunity for developing functional reading programs. Given the staggering demographic data about adult illiteracy in the workplace (Skagen, 1986; Mikulicky, 1990), the usefulness of literacy programs that complement worksite skills is evident to employers. Harman (1986) pointed out that even persons who have learned to read are functionally illiterate if they cannot transfer those skills to the workplace.

One way to integrate literacy instruction into the workplace is through programs that help adults learn reading skills that are relevant to career performance (Chisman & Campbell, 1990; Mikulicky, 1990). To strengthen the perception of relevance, some employers have made instructional programs an accountable aspect of job responsibility (Rothwell & Brandenburg, 1990; Skagen, 1986; Workplace illiteracy, 1989).

Workplace literacy programs can have a synergistic impact on both employers and workers. The employers can benefit through the opportunity to employ workers with disabilities, through improved worker efficiency, and by having an organizational culture that acknowledges the appropriateness of including persons who exhibit a wide range of achievement within the workforce (Fabian, Luecking, & Tilson, 1994). And the workers can benefit through enhanced self-esteem and opportunities for career advancement (Newman & Beverstock, 1990).

Functional Reading Activities

Several popular curricula have highlighted opportunities for teaching functional literacy skills to adolescents and adults with disabilities. These curricula, referred to as *functional skills curricula*, are viewed by some as nonacademic approaches to instruction (Shapiro, Loed, Bouermaster, Wright, Headden, & Toch, 1993). However functional skills merely prepare individuals to be successful as adults in their communities. As such, the skills can be academic or nonacademic. The skills help individuals make adjustments with their daily living, occupations, or with personal and social issues (Brolin, 1995). Cronin and Patton (1993) identified major domains for functional curricula that included employment, education, home life, family, leisure, community, physical health, emotional health, personal relationship, and personal responsibility. Dever (1989) developed a functional curriculum for individuals who are mentally retarded. The curriculum was divided into categories that included vocation, leisure, travel, home, community, and personal skills. Functional reading, writing, and mathematics are clearly relevant to curricula that are organized in these fashions.

Employment has been identified consistently as a critically important domain within functional curricula. As such, career education can be viewed as the logical complement to functional curricula. Predictably, models of career education have been organized into strands that reflect major competencies within functional curricula. As an example, Clark and Kolstoe's model of career education (1995) included domains that included personal relationships, daily living skills, acquisition of occupational information, and development of appropriate values, attitudes, and habits.

Brolin's *Life-Centered Career Education* curriculum (1992) may be the most well known of the functional curricula. Brolin's curriculum was divided into three major sections: daily living, personal issues, and occupation. All three of these sections contained explicit lessons that relied on functional contexts to develop literacy skills. As an example, Brolin (1995) identified multiple instructional and supplementary materials to assist learners who were using his curriculum. Recommended printed materials were in areas such as citizenship, grooming, community, communication, applying for jobs, and maintaining a job.

Cronin and Patton (1993) illustrated opportunities for relating reading and writing to functional aspects of adults' lives such as employment, home, leisure, community, health, and personal relationships. They provided the following examples of functional reading activities:

- reading classified employment ads
- interpreting bills
- locating information about entertainment in a newspaper
- completing tax forms
- understanding directions for medicine
- understanding letters written by friends

Table 10–1 contains words and phrases that occur with high-frequency in the environment. The optimal list of functional words or phrases with which to begin or supplement a functional reading program would be devised individually on the basis of the personalities, surroundings, goals, and interests of specific adult learners. For persons with extremely limited reading skills, such personalized lists of functional words may constitute focal points for their literacy programs.

If learners responded positively to functional reading activities focusing on words that occurred frequently in their environments, instructors could supplement the list of words from the environment with words that occur frequently in functional printed materials. Table 10–2 contains high frequency words that occur in text. Recognition of these words could provide adult learners with the scaffolding to extract information from functional materials such as magazines, schedules, manuals, greeting cards, or the printed directions accompanying products.

Table 10–1   High-Frequency Words and Phrases in the Environment

BEWARE OF DOG	NO ADMITTANCE
BOYS	NO ENTRY
CAUTION	NO PARKING
CLOSE	NO SMOKING
CLOSED	NO SMOKING AREA
DANGER	NO TRESPASSING
DON'T RUN	OPEN
DON'T WALK	OUT
DOWN	POISON
EMERGENCY EXIT	PRIVATE
EMPLOYEES ONLY	PULL
EXIT	PUSH
FIRE ESCAPE	REST ROOMS
FOR RENT	RIGHT
FOR SALE	SLIPPERY WHEN
GENTLEMEN	WET
GIRLS	SMOKING
GO	SMOKING AREA
IN	STOOP
KEEP OUT	UP
LADIES	WET PAINT
LEFT	WOMEN
MEN	

Activities With Newspapers

The inexpensive and ubiquitous newspaper may be the functional reading material that is most popular among adults. Newspapers contain material on varied subjects and at different levels of difficulty. Because the information in newspapers is current and community-based, that information is likely to intrigue most adult learners. The following list highlights predictable types of information available in most newspapers:

- arts calendars
- charts
- classified ads
- comic strips
- directories of community services

Table 10–2   High-Frequency Words That
Occur in Text

a	I	then
all	if	there
an	in	these
and	into	they
are	is	this
as	it	to
at	like	up
be	may	was
been	more	we
but	my	were
by	no	what
can	not	when
could	now	which
did	of	who
do	on	will
each	one	with
for	or	would
from	out	you
go	see	your
had	she	
has	so	
have	some	
he	than	
her	that	
him	the	
his	their	
how	them	

- editorials
- employment information
- engagement and wedding information
- entertainment news
- feature stories
- financial information
- gardening news
- home maintenance information
- horoscopes
- hunting and fishing news
- letters to the editor

- movie schedules
- musical events
- news summaries
- obituaries
- photos
- police reports
- schedules of community events
- school news
- shopping information
- special topical reports
- sports information
- transportation information

Table 10–3 contains opportunities for teaching specific literacy skills with the newspaper. Skills that are illustrated in the context of the newspaper include vocabulary development, word attack, establishing personal references between readers and text, designation of analogous information, use of key words, critical reading, role playing, application of textual material to practical situations, and summarizing. These skills are explained and illustrated in the following sections.

Vocabulary Development

Learners can learn to read words that they encounter in newspapers. Some of these words will be ones with which they are already familiar and others will be new words. As part of vocabulary development, they can learn to recognize words with which they are orally familiar but which they cannot recognize in print. When they encounter words with which they are unfamiliar, they can initially learn the meanings of these words.

When they have developed the skills to recognize printed words with which they are already familiar orally, the learners can employ these words as target words in word clusters. The clusters enable the learners to use the pattern that is common to the words in the cluster as a mnemonic thread for associating those new words with the words they have already learned.

In newspapers, meaningful terms can be an effective pattern for forming clusters. For example, clusters might be created from words concerning civic events, weather, gardening, or sports. Interrelated words to be placed in meaningful clusters can be found in predictable sections of the newspaper. This predictability may help to eventually develop the learners' independence as readers when they consult newspapers.

Table 10-3 Literacy Lessons That Employ Sections of the Newspaper

Sections	Activities									
	Vocabulary	Word Attack	Personal Reference	Analogy	Key Words	Outline	Critical Read	Role Play	Application	Summarize
arts section	×	×	×	×	×	×	×			×
charts	×	×	×	×	×	×				×
classified ads	×	×	×	×	×	×			×	×
comic strips	×	×	×	×	×			×		×
community events	×	×	×	×	×	×				×
community services	×	×	×	×	×	×				×
editorials	×	×	×	×	×	×	×	×		×
employment information	×	×	×	×	×	×		×	×	×
feature stories	×	×	×	×	×	×	×	×		×
financial information	×	×	×	×	×	×	×	×	×	×

(continued)

Table 10-3 *(continued)*

Sections	Activities									
	Vocabulary	Word Attack	Personal Reference	Analogy	Key Words	Outline	Critical Read	Role Play	Appli-cation	Sum-marize
front page	×	×	×	×	×	×	×	×		×
gardening news	×	×	×	×	×	×	×	×	×	×
horoscopes	×	×	×	×	×	×		×	×	×
hunting and fishing news	×	×	×	×	×	×		×	×	×
letters to the editor	×	×	×	×	×	×	×	×		×
movie schedules	×	×	×	×	×				×	×
music calendars	×	×	×	×	×				×	×
news summaries	×	×	×	×	×	×	×	×		×
obituaries	×	×	×	×	×	×			×	×
photos			×	×				×		×
police reports	×	×	×	×	×	×		×		×

Word Attack

Word attack skills can enable learners to recognize the novel words that they encounter in print. Using the clustering technique, they can associate the novel words with "target words." The words grouped with the target words should exhibit a generalized regularity. Chapter 5 contains lessons and worksheets based on phonic regularities that could be employed to develop learners' word attack skills. Such worksheets could be used with newspapers or with any functional reading materials.

Personal Reference

Learners can be encouraged to see the personal relevance of the information in the newspaper. Perception of relevance can result from dialogue between the instructor and individual learners about material in the newspaper. The perception that materials in the newspaper are relevant to them may result also from the discussions among adult learners working in groups.

As the literacy skills of adult learners emerge, the personal impact of certain types of information will become greater. For example, those sections of the newspaper that recount local events should be of interest to most readers. If learners develop perceptions about the personal relevance of state, regional, national, and international events, information from newspapers that corresponds to these issues will become progressively interesting to them. To form these views, learners may require assistance from their instructors as well as their peer learners.

Analogy

Learners can become sensitive to the predicable types of information in newspapers if they designate analogous portions of the newspaper. For example, after a photograph, table, map, or retail advertisement had been highlighted, the learners could be encouraged to designate an item with a comparable format.

An analogy activity could be made more challenging if the learners were asked to focus on the content of material in the newspaper. For example, they might be requested to locate a letter to the editor that was sympathetic to one highlighted by the instructor. Or an editorial might be read which the readers were asked to contrast with other editorials, identifying the one with premises that were most like the original editorial.

Key Words

Within a passage, some words are more important than others. To help readers form this insight, instructors can use a highlighter to designate words that are essential for comprehension. When these key words are read, the passage is transformed into telegram like prose. These transformed passages can then be the basis for instruction.

As a result of this activity, passages that would overwhelm learners with limited literacy skills can be altered so that they are accessible to readers. Even passages with only several highlighted terms can be read when instructors and learners cooperate, with the instructors assisting the learners by verbalizing the unhighlighted words.

Critical Reading

Learners can apply critical reading strategies to passages in newspapers. If learners cannot read the passages, the instructor can read them to the learners, pointing to the words as the instructor says them. The passage can be analyzed subsequently.

Critical reading strategies can be extremely simple. For example, adult learners can be encouraged to determine the goal of a persuasively written passage and then to investigate whether there are details that would persuade readers to accept that goal. Chapter 8 contains illustrations of critical reading activities intended for psychoeducational materials. But these same activities could be employed effectively in a functional reading program with newspapers.

Role Playing

Using material from the newspaper, learners can interact with their instructors as well as with each other. For example, learners might adopt the attitudes of an author who had written a letter to the editor about a controversial topic. They would attempt to maintain those attitudes during a discussion. Editorials, feature stories, sports columns, or political cartoons could provide the same opportunity for role playing. If learners cannot read passages independently, the instructor can assist them. Role playing can be an aspect of a comprehensive instructional unit that had several literacy goals. For example, role playing could precede or follow instruction and activities about vocabulary or word attack skills.

Application

The relevance of many portions of the newspaper can be underscored if learners are challenged to apply the content of the passages that they have read. Many portions of the newspaper will contain information that may lend itself to application by learners. Sections on the weather, gardening, home management, careers, civic events, schedules, job opportunities, entertainment, and shopping contain recurring topics. These sections can provide opportunities for learners to comprehend passages by applying their content.

Summarizing Information

Summarizing is a technique that encourages persons to see what they have read as a whole rather than as a conglomeration of letters, words, and sentences. Learners can be instructed about summarized information with newspapers. As examples of predictable sources of summary information in newspapers, the front page, or the beginning of each major section, may contain encapsulated statements about major events. Headlines and subtitles are summaries of the passages to which they are connected. Tables, charts, and illustrations, as well as the captions for photographs, are additional examples of summaries on which learners can be encouraged to rely.

Assessment

Although precise skills are learned in functional reading programs, those skills are learned with materials that are in a distinct format from that in skills-based reading tests. Because skills-based tests have an academic orientation, this type of test, used alone, would not be the best measure of performance for learning in functional reading programs.

Curriculum-based assessment can be especially appropriate for functional reading programs. As with other types of assessment, curriculum-based assessment focuses on the instructional needs of learners. However, curriculum-based assessment assesses instructional needs by examining learners' continuing performance in response to actual instructional activities.

Algozzine (1991) identified four categories of information that can be subsumed under curriculum-based assessment. In addition to evaluations of learning environments, instructors can evaluate teaching strategies and samples of learners' responses to those strategies. The evaluations of learners' responses could be based on straightforward measures such as the number of items that were completed on worksheets or lengths of time required to complete assignments. The evaluations could be supplemented with more complex measures, such as analyses of patterns of errors made by learners on instructional assignments. Based on information from the previous three categories of evaluation, instructors could adapt instructional strategies and then observe the responses of learners to the adaptations. Variations of curriculum-based assessment can be extended to home, community, or workplace environments. This extension seems logical if one recognizes that curriculum, in addition to its academic identity, can be divided into four other domains: home, community, recreation, and vocation (Artensani, Itkonen, Fryxell, & Woolcock, 1995).

For example, functional reading skills can be developed as part of a workplace literacy program. The relationship between functional assessment and employment is well documented in the professional literature about functional curricula. Definitions from the early 1980s equated functional assessment with the measurement of those characteristics that facilitated or restricted individuals' employment (Brolin, 1995). Though more recent definitions have expanded functional assessment to include a range of environmental factors, employment has remained as a pivotal element among these factors. This link is well underscored in those sections of the Americans with Disabilities Act concerned with assessment (Feldblum, 1991; Parry, 1993; Wehman, 1993).

As part of a workplace literacy program, the employment environment can be evaluated to determine if it is suitable for developing literacy skills. This evaluation can be part of a general workplace assessment, such as that outlined by Everson, Burwell, and Killam (1995) for individuals who are deaf-blind. The workplace categories that they identified included:

- flexibility of scheduling
- availability and location of transportation
- mobility assumptions
- orientation assumptions
- requirement to cross streets
- requirement for independence
- requirement for self-initiating work
- strength and endurance requirements
- importance of appearance
- communication requirements
- required degree of attention to time
- required degree of attention to tasks

- social constraints
- need to adapt to changing routines
- attitudes of employers
- availability of reinforcements
- need for functional reading skills
- need for functional math skills
- vision prerequisites
- hearing prerequisites
- tolerance of employer to unusual behaviors related to disabilities

These categories are similar to those developed for persons with disabilities by Parent, Sherron, and Groah (1992). One distinctive category that was included in the checklist of Parent and her colleagues was *financial concerns*. Although Riches (1993) outlined a less comprehensive list of factors to be incorporated into a worksite evaluation, she included the important category of *job safety*, evaluating whether there were safety concerns and safety rules that could determine the suitability of specific job locations.

Within specific jobs, there will likely be job-related tasks that involve literacy. Evaluating the strategies that are designed to enable learners to complete job-related tasks, as well as evaluating the successful discharge of those tasks, can be critical measures for a modified curriculum-based assessment of the learning that takes place in work site functional reading programs. These records can be maintained by job supervisors or reading instructors.

Job responsibilities can be task-analyzed into major components and subcomponents so that instructors can identify, monitor, and develop the literacy competencies that are part of those tasks. Because these task analyses also enable learners to receive feedback about the source of any difficulties they are experiencing, the analyses provide the basis for the fourth component of a modified approach to curriculum-based assessment, the use of learners' responses to designate and adapt instructional strategies.

In many occupations, there are tests associated with job performance. The format of these tests may be written, requiring participants to read and respond to printed materials. This type of test measures literacy skills and employment skills simultaneously. When supplemented by performance checklists that have been completed by supervisors, written employment tests can comprise the core of an assessment portfolio that contains information about both literacy skills and employment skills.

Sometimes employment skills tests are linked to salary increases and promotion. Under these circumstances, workers may be motivated to develop the literacy skills required to improve their performance on the tests. Learners may even demand that the skills prerequisite to raising their scores on such tests become the instructional focus in functional reading programs.

If a portfolio to assess both literacy and employment skills were being assembled, specific categories of information should be part of the employment assessment. The following categories of information, based on recommendations from the National Association of Rehabilitation Facilities, are examples (Wehman et al., 1992):

- family and friends
- vocational skills
- learning characteristics
- employment history
- ecological information (e.g., community, residence, or transportation)
- individual preferences
- career planning

When one develops a portfolio that includes information about employment and functional literacy, quality of life can be included as a measure with which to assess the effectiveness of learning (Kiernan, 1995). Using this qualitative perspective, learning can be assessed on the basis of an individual's physical security, ability to achieve adult goals, and sense of personal satisfaction (Halpern, 1993).

General categories of observations that would be appropriate for a portfolio would be records of the number of tasks that had been completed successfully by learners, frequency with which tasks had been attended to by learners, duration of times spent at tasks, lengths of intervals between tasks, and performances on task-analyzed learning experiences (Lengyel & Evans, 1995). Other types of information that would be appropriate for a functional reading assessment portfolio would be data about attitudes of the learners while they were participating in functional reading programs, samples of learners' responses to instructional activities, and cumulative responses that indicate the development of literacy skills during specified periods.

Summary

Functional reading programs are employed often with adults with moderate or severe disabilities. The rationale is straightforward — if learners can master only a limited range of reading skills, they should focus on skills that will have an impact on their daily lives. Although functional reading programs are suitable for persons with limited aptitude in reading, these programs also can be suitable for adults with mild disabilities or adults without disabilities. As such, functional reading programs can be an optional type of instruction even for adults who would learn successfully in other literacy programs.

Functional reading programs are attractive because the programs can motivate learners though the acquisition of literacy skills that have an immediate effect on the problems they confront in their daily living, careers, and leisure. Functional reading programs also represent a potential solution to problems of workplace illiteracy, enabling workers to learn skills that are required to discharge their responsibilities and to advance to other types of employment.

CHAPTER
11

Multicultural Issues

with
Jozi DeLeon and Robert Ortiz

As multiculturalism has emerged as a primary characteristic of our society, multicultural learning goals have been emphasized within instructional programs. An example of a critical multicultural learning goal is the adaptation of instruction and materials so that persons from minority groups can achieve their full potential as learners. An additional goal is that learners develop insights into the abilities, needs, viewpoints, values, and goals of persons from other groups (Anderson, 1988; Banks, 1994; Gollnick & Chinn, 1990; Pai, 1990; Tesconi, 1990).

Sleeter and Grant (1987) reviewed definitions of multicultural learning and noted that race was the only element common to all of the definitions. Although multiculturalism is linked inextricably to race, other characteristics of learners, such as gender, social class, age, sexual orientation, and exceptionality may be appropriate elements of multicultural learning programs (Banks, 1994; Traustadottir et al., 1994). And because of pervasive poverty among ethnic minority groups, poverty itself can be a plausible characteristic of multiculturalism (Davidson & Koppenhaver, 1993; Hughes, 1989; Porter, 1989; Traustadottir et al., 1994; Wilson, 1989).

No matter what definition one adopts, culture and language emerge repeatedly as predictable obstacles encountered by learners in multi-cultural societies (Graham & Cookson, 1990). As evidence of the prevalence of this view, a substantial literature has developed about the impact of culture and language on services and education for persons with disabilities.

Cultural Diversity

Reports about persons with disabilities within culturally and linguistically diverse segments of the population indicate that the rates of incidence for disabilities within these groups are inordinately high (Dutton, 1985; Guendelman, 1985; Hispanic Americans Council on Scientific Affairs, 1991; Logue, 1990). For example, an analysis of data about the placement of minority learners in special education programs (Harry, 1994) has revealed overrepresentation by some minority groups. Afro-American and Hispanic students both were overrepresented in the category of learners who were *trainable mentally retarded*. Hispanics were overrepresented as *learning disabled* and blacks were disproportionately represented in the category of *severely emotionally disturbed*. Asian and white learners were disproportionately identified as *gifted and talented* while all other groups appeared underrepresented in this category.

Multiple and diverse factors can indirectly influence the disproportionate placements of persons from ethnic minorities in special education programs. An example would be the inability of individuals making the referrals and performing the assessment to distinguish individual and cultural differences from learning deficits. Additionally, the socioeconomic conditions found among certain culturally and linguistically diverse groups can affect development because of the impact that these conditions have on nutrition, prenatal care, and medical attention. As a consequence, socioeconomic conditions can contribute to the higher number of individuals with disabilities in certain groups.

Native Americans appear to be especially vulnerable to exhibiting disabilities as a result of distressing socioeconomic conditions. O'Connell (1987) reported that the rates of certain disabilities among adult American Indians was unusually high. These disabilities have included alcoholism (Kivlahan, Walker, Donnovan, & Mischke, 1985; May, 1986, 1988), mental health problems (May, 1987, 1988), communication disorders (Thielke & Shriberg, 1990), drug abuse (May, 1986), depression (May, 1987), and fetal alcohol syndrome (McShane, 1988).

In a 1987 survey, 33% of Afro-Americans and 27% of Hispanics were living in conditions below the poverty level. In contrast, the poverty levels among Asian Americans have been reported at approximately 10%, mirroring those of white Americans (Harry, 1992). These statistics about poverty among ethnic minorities are correlated with the data about their overrepresentation in special education. For as the percentage of individuals living in poverty increases, the percentage of individuals from those groups assigned to special education programs increases proportionately.

Cultural factors can also influence the participation of learners in educational programs. The cultural milieu in which individuals are raised contributes to their values, beliefs, and many components of their general life-style patterns. These values, beliefs, and general life-style patterns can have an impact on cognitive style, interaction styles with teachers and peers, and reaction to different types of reinforcement (Cloud & Medeiros-Landurand, 1989). Adults may have shed explicit aspects of cultures that could influence their dress, customs, selections of foods, and preferred pasttime activities. Although such individuals may appear to be fully acclimated to a distinct culture, implicit aspects of their previous culture can remain through adulthood, affecting their values and beliefs. If instructors working with diverse groups do not understand the influence of culture and language, they may assume that learners are unmotivated, uninterested, or unable to make progress.

The delivery of services to culturally and linguistically diverse groups is complex. The distinctive views and values of persons from ethnic minority groups can restrict the impact of service and educational models that were developed with nonminority populations (Christensen, 1989; Collier & Hoover, 1987; Joe & Malach, 1992; Levine, 1987; Rogler et al., 1991). Consequently, optimal models for delivering services and education may be ones that are implemented by professionals who are sensitive to the social, psychological, and philosophical values of minority groups. O'Connor (1993) noted that "to better understand the meaning of services to Indians, it is important to look not only at programs, but also at the cultural background of the people using the services" (p. 315). The National Indian Council on Aging (1981) stressed the need for culturally sensitive services as well as for planning and implementation that involved American Indians themselves. Recognition of clients' rights to participate in the planning of services that affect them can be extended to all individuals with disabilities, irrespective of their ethnic origin or the severity of their disabilities (Gerry & Minsky, 1992; Heumann, 1993).

There have been several models for providing culturally sensitive services to minority groups. For example, family based models have encouraged collaboration between the families of persons with disabilities and professionals from service and educational organizations (Cottone, Handelsman, & Walters, 1986; Emener, 1991; Joe & Malach, 1992; O'Connell, 1985). Some models have advocated progressive empowerment of persons from minority groups by training them to assume responsibilities that would be discharged typically by paraprofessionals (Runion & Gregory, 1984; Stuecher, Grossman, Hakala, & Kizlowski, 1985). Other models for delivering services have encouraged collaboration between persons receiving services and professionals who have been educated about the distinctive needs of minority populations (Martin, White, Saravanabhavan, & Carlise, 1993; Metoyer-Duran, 1993; Yukl, 1986).

Because the values and attitudes of persons from minority groups can be distinctive, sensitive response to these factors is a condition for delivering effective services. Kuehn and Imm-Thomas (1993) warned that programs developed for nonminority populations might have to be adapted before these programs could be extrapolated to minority groups. Adaptation would be required for programs that were not culturally appropriate or where the personnel associated with those programs were not culturally accommodated. Cultural accommodation, which refers to the interpersonal attitudes of staff, requires that professionals understand the backgrounds, values, and attitudes of persons from minority groups.

Competition is another factor that can influence responses to educational models by learners from different cultures; competition can be positive for some learners and negative for others. If adult learners respond suitably to competitive situations, these can be employed productively with them. When competition has detrimental effects on learning, these effects may be reduced through the use of small groups, cooperative learning, and shared responsibility for the completion of assignments. However, if such strategies were still not effective, there would be no intrinsic reason to maintain competitive learning activities.

Analogous to the different responses exhibited by learners to competition, there can be very different responses to the ways that learners are grouped for instruction. Whereas some persons learn best in isolation, others prefer group learning. Persons from certain cultures often respond best to learning tasks that mirror the cooperative patterns of social interaction that those persons employ to solve problems in their day to day routines (Baca & Cervantes, 1989; Bloome, 1987; Castaneda, 1976; Chan & Rueda, 1979; Field & Aebersold, 1990; Fillmore, 1981).

If instructors group persons for cooperative learning, they must justify their rationale for doing so. For example, if several learners exhibited deficiencies of the identical type, these learners might be grouped so that they could benefit from a single programmatic emphasis. Alternatively, persons with strengths and weaknesses in distinct areas could be grouped together, allowing learners with different profiles to compensate for the skills that any single member of the group lacked as an individual. However, even when grouping of learners for instructional purposes can be justified, instructors would still have to assess any potential social disadvantages of the grouping.

Another factor that instructors need to consider is the reaction that adults who are not proficient in English may exhibit to instruction in English. Such learners may be quiet, slow to respond, and reluctant to engage in activities. They may require repeated directions, continued reassurances, and ongoing support. Learners receiving formal instruction in a second language may exhibit responses that are indirectly related to factors such as their views of themselves as adult learners, values that are derived from their cultural groups, distinctive experiences related to their status as migrant workers or immigrants, or economic factors.

Linguistic Diversity

There is an extensive body of literature about multicultural literacy education in the schools (Edelsky, 1991; Freeman & Freeman, 1992; Hayes, Bahruth, & Kessler, 1991; Smallwood, 1991). However, despite a large multicultural adult population (U.S. Bureau of Census, 1991), only recently have suggestions been made about the special literacy needs of these adults. When adults are instructed with a language in which they are only partially proficient, they may not be able to develop skills at a level comparable to that which they would have achieved had that instruction been in their primary language. Given the value that society places on second-language acquisition, the methods that are employed to teach a second language are important because these can influence the learning of English as well as important corollary skills such as literacy (Casanova & Arias, 1993; Lambert, 1975).

Additionally, because of the length of time that can be required for effective comprehension of English, persons learning English as a second language can have difficulty understanding expressions that appear in special contexts such as workbooks or computerized materials. Cummins (1984) indicated that second-language learners can take years to acquire context-restricted conversational skills in English. If the linguistic requirements of instructional materials are not synchronized to the linguistic abilities of learners, the effectiveness of those materials will be reduced.

The specific language skills of individuals acquiring English as a second language must be examined in order to effectively match instructional demands with the skills of the learners. For example, individuals in the initial stages of acquiring English will have to rely primarily on literacy instruction in their native languages. They can benefit also from instruction in English as a second language, but this instruction would likely focus on the development of rudimentary literacy skills and vocabulary (Williams & Capizzi-Snipper, 1990). Additionally, instruction in native languages or in English will have the greatest impact if it is perceived by individuals as relevant to their personal experiences. When literacy programs are developed, instructors can determine the domains in which English will be used by the learners (e.g., employment, social interactions, classroom etiquette, home tasks, or supervision of children) to obtain clues about the vocabulary and language that the learners are likely to value.

Determining individuals' literacy levels in their primary languages can be critical for instructors. Individuals with disabilities from culturally and linguistically diverse backgrounds can have a variety of experiences that can affect their literacy development. For example, some learners with disabilities may be third or fourth generation Americans who had been placed in restrictive educational programs in which they were required to speak only English and were discouraged from communication in their native languages (Cummins, 1984; Skutnabb-Kangas, 1981; Williams & Capizzi-Snipper, 1990). Under these circumstances, their literacy development could have been influenced significantly by their disabilities as well as by the attempt to acquire literacy skills through a weaker language. These individuals present a great challenge to educators. Although at one time literacy skills might have been acquired with relative ease in the native languages of such learners, learning may subsequently require repeated reinforcement by a variety of instructional methods. Even when learners from this group have received previous instruction in English, the comprehensiveness of the skills they have developed cannot be taken for granted because the instruction may have been sporadic and unstable.

In contrast, individuals who are recent immigrants to the United States and who have been exposed to literacy instruction in their native languages may exhibit problems that are greater as a result of their disabilities rather than as a result of programmatic eccentricities in their previous instruction. Individuals who possess literacy skills in their native languages can build on these existing skills as they develop literacy in English (Williams & Capizzi-Snipper, 1990).

Language may be the most significant learning barrier encountered by persons who speak English as a second language. Literacy curricula that are sensitive to the languages, backgrounds, values, and goals of the learners can be critical to helping them pass beyond this barrier. The relevance of curricula with these characteristics can be further enhanced if learners themselves participate in the selection of materials, instructional techniques, and scheduling (Riggs & Allen, 1989).

Perez and Torres-Guzman (1992) recommended that Spanish-English bilingual learners be taught with instructional approaches that discouraged competition and that reflected the environments of the learners. They identified the whole language approach to literacy instruction as a program that had these characteristics. Their endorsement of whole language programs for bilingual and nonnative speakers of English has been supported by other experts in the field (Flores et al., 1985; Heald-Taylor, 1986; Peyton & Reed, 1990; Riggs & Allen, 1989; Smallwood, 1991). Whole language approaches have the additional benefit of promoting retention because learners associate instructional materials with familiar referents (Allen, 1986; Enright & McCloskey, 1985).

Rueda (1991) suggested that if reading activity were to increase among language minority students who had been placed in special education programs, instructors would need to develop optimal learning environments that allowed those students to read and write on familiar topics and that did not emphasize drilling, decoding, nor writing activities with a focus on mechanics and form.

Another approach to teaching students with different languages involves the restructuring of classroom discourse (McCollum, 1991). Cross-cultural comparisons of classroom discourse have shown that different learning environments can embody rights, obligations, values, and assumptions that influence the interactions of teachers and students. When persons who have been instructed in ethnically and culturally nonintegrated classes are subsequently placed in integrated settings, their diverse, previously established perceptions can influence their reactions to literacy experiences (Au & Jordan, 1981; Au & Mason, 1981; Barnhardt, 1982; Erickson & Mohatt, 1981, 1982; Heath, 1983; Michaels, 1981; Philips, 1972, 1983). A possible solution to this predictable problem can be provided when teachers act as facilitators for instructional conversations. Participants can have opportunities to learn from their peers during conversations that can be introduced in a mediated fashion and eventually become independent (Tharp & Gallimore, 1988).

Other solutions to this problem include the *reciprocal teaching approach* (Palincsar & David, 1991), and the *task and talk activities* (Hiebert & Fisher, 1991). The reciprocal teaching approach encourages learners to generate questions about text, relate their previous experiences to new information, summarize, identify what they perceive as confusing, and recommend strategies for making text more meaningful. The task and talk activities use dialogue between student and teacher as an essential element of the learning process by students. Additionally, task and talk activities enable instructors to form insights about why certain learning activities are successful or frustrating with specific learners.

Gaffney and Anderson (1991) proposed a two-pronged approach designed to help linguistically diverse learners acquire literacy skills and to help instructors develop their abilities to be effective with such learners. The presence of teacher education within this approach was viewed as a pivotal element that was linked to effective instruction for linguistically diverse learners.

Adults with disabilities are not addressed specifically in much of the extensive literature about the needs of culturally and linguistically diverse learners. Nonetheless, many of the insights that have been developed have implications for the instruction of adults with disabilities. For example, Banks (1989) identified goals for participants in multicultural learning programs. All learners in these programs should

- be academically successful
- develop positive attitudes about themselves
- form tolerant attitudes toward different groups
- understand the basis for the views of persons from different groups

Discussing reading instruction specifically, Richardson and Morgan (1994) suggested goals for the instructors of multicultural learners. Instructors in these programs should

- assess learners' linguistic abilities
- identify supplementary programs to help learners develop proficiency in English
- gather information about learners' languages and cultures
- emphasize oral language activities
- highlight instructional materials that reflect learners' cultures and backgrounds
- develop positive self-concepts among learners
- respect learners' views about the functions and value of reading

Although intended for implementation with youth in schools, these goals are equally appropriate for culturally diverse adult learners with disabilities.

Two themes that run through the literature on literacy programs for bilingual and nonnative speakers of English concern the need to incorporate learners' native language linguistic abilities and their distinctive background experiences. These themes are restated within the field of special education in the literature about multicultural education (Ada, 1986; Baca & Cervantes, 1989; Cardenas, 1986; Castaneda, 1976; Cummins, 1984; Ford & Jones, 1990; Ramirez, 1988; Salend, 1990). The activities reviewed in the following section reflect these two themes.

Literacy Activities for Multicultural Learners

The vocabulary, grammar, and format of materials within instructional programs can be different from that which learners have encountered outside of instructional programs. The eccentricity of learning materials can create problems for all learners, but these problems are accentuated for linguistically diverse learners. The following examples illustrate instructional activities that could increase the accessibility of learning materials to linguistically diverse learners.

Personalized Dictionaries

Academic workbooks and computerized materials can contain special vocabulary that learners are unlikely to have encountered in other situations. With assistance from the learners, instructors can devise a reference list of frequently encountered special vocabulary. Unlike the definitions of terms that might appear in a textbook, these definitions would be created by the learners themselves, using the learners' distinctive grammar, dialect, and language. If the learners required help writing the definitions, the instructors could assist them.

Entries for this reference list could be made in a notebook or on index cards. Not only vocabulary but even small passages could be photocopied, taped to index cards, and then paraphrased by learners in their own language. A benefit of using index cards is that the limited space encourages learners to paraphrase rather than translate the passages attached to them.

This activity can be adapted for learners working in groups. By collaborating with more advanced readers, learners who would otherwise be frustrated can successfully create a dictionary of specialized vocabulary to assist them when they use workbooks or computerized materials.

Adapted Passages

Personalized dictionaries can increase the meaningfulness of textbooks, workbooks, and computerized materials. In the same way, passages adapted by instructors can increase the relevance of the special materials that are employed in literacy instruction. If learners are to complete a set of drills, instructors can adapt the passages in those drills so that the problems are linked to referents that are meaningful to the learners.

An adaptation may simply entail the change of referents in a worksheet so that the context becomes relevant to learners and their communities. For example, the authors of a set of vocabulary drills might present random words and personally meaningless sentences as they tried to help the learners differentiate short vowels from long vowels. The worksheet could be adapted so that the same generalizations were still being covered, but using vocabulary and sentences extracted from meaningful passages that had been created by the learners.

Community-Staffed Learning Activities

The impact of learning activities can be increased if the activities involve familiar and meaningful referents. Instead of reading about academic topics that are abstract and impersonal, demonstrations might be arranged in which learners cooperate in the preparation of a meal, the planning of a field trip, or any motivating event. Community members can be invited to assist with these activities. Community-staffed activities can help learners establish a connection between literacy activities and persons in their communities who they may admire and respect. As a result of this connection, the relevance of literacy skills may be highlighted in an especially motivating fashion.

Illustrated Logs

Whenever a community-staffed activity is arranged, an illustration geared to that activity can be created. These illustrations can be drawings made by the learners themselves. Or the illustrations can be photographs. If one does use photographs, a single picture from a camera can be inexpensively photocopied so that each learner has a personal copy.

The learners can make notes and comments in the spaces surrounding the drawing or photograph. These illustrations can be compiled in a special log. Subsequently, when they have to employ information that had been highlighted in a specific activity, the learners can consult the page from the log that contains the appropriate illustration and notes. If learners lack the skills to take notes themselves, an instructor would help them.

Famous Authors

Although native English speaking authors have dominated the field of English literature, persons who have made literary contributions to other languages and cultures can be designated by instructors and learners. A bulletin board can be created on which items associated with these persons are exhibited for the learners. The learners themselves can be encouraged to select authors, draw pictures of them, locate appropriate illustrations, and write short statements for display on the bulletin board.

As with the other activities in this section, the famous authors activity could be presented in a way that encourages learners to develop positive concepts of themselves as readers. However, another goal of programs that promote diversity is to encourage participants to develop appropriate attitudes towards persons from other groups. The famous authors activity, as well as the following activity about interviews, is an opportunity to promote this objective.

Interviews

Although bulletin boards that highlight famous authors can be effective, visits by persons in the community who use reading and writing in their occupations or daily routines can be even more effective. Learners can be provided with cue sheets that help them attend to key points that visitors are stressing during their presentations. Exhibit 12–1, or any of the worksheets in Chapter 12, might be adapted readily into cue sheets that could help multicultural learners take notes. The information recorded by learners on these cue sheets could be written in their primary languages or in dialects. If learners were unable to complete the cue sheets independently, they could be assisted by instructors or they could complete the sheets in groups.

Home-Based Literacy Activities

There are opportunities to reinforce both reading and writing on a daily basis within learners' homes. Learners can use samples of print found in their homes as familiar referents to be listed in their personalized dictionaries. Examples of reading materials that might be available in homes would be mail, recipes, novels, magazines, containers for videos, covers of audiotapes and CDs, ingredients on foods, religious materials, personal letters, receipts, television listings, instructions on games, operating directions for appliances, warnings on tools, or the explanations included with home repair kits. Opportunities for home-based writing activities can include grocery lists, telephone messages, personal notes, checks, bills, game scores, measurements, or letters. To reinforce learning, persons could be encouraged to write unfamiliar words that they have encountered onto index cards or into notebooks. Problems that they encounter when attempting to write at home also can be noted. When these notes are brought to class, group discussions can enable the learners to recognize and employ the novel words and the appropriate contexts for those words.

Summary

Culture and language are factors that differentiate diverse learners with disabilities. A program that responds effectively to the needs of diverse learners is one in which the learners view themselves as capable of being successful and in which they achieve their full potential. Additionally, an optimal program encourages participants to develop sensitivity to persons from other groups.

Activities were described to illustrate instructional formats that might be effective for persons from minority groups. These activities have a high probability of being effective because they are built on the linguistic and cultural foundation that adult learners bring to literacy instruction. Additionally, these activities highlight the connection between adult learners with disabilities and their communities.

CHAPTER

12

Literacy and Transition

with
Bruno J. D'Alonzo, Michael Shaunessy, and Nile Stanley

*T*ransition has been defined as secondary school services leading to employment (Will, 1984). However, this definition has been criticized because of its exclusive emphasis on high school students and employment (Halpern, 1985). Halloran (1993) reviewed federal legislative initiatives as one indication that the scope of transition had expanded to include social interaction, community living, learner empowerment, and quality of life.

As an example of a holistic approach to transition, the Individuals with Disabilities Education Act of 1990 (P. L. 101-476) contained a definition of transition as:

> a coordinated set of activities . . . which promotes movement from school to postschool activities, including postsecondary education, vocational training, integrated employment . . . continuing and adult education, adult services, independent living, or community participation. The coordinated set of activities shall be based upon the individual student's needs, taking into account the student's preferences and interests, and shall include instruction, community experiences, the development of employment and other post-school adult living objectives. (29 U.S.C. § 1401 (a) (19) Supp. 1993)

The elements of the preceding definition were incorporated into a definition of transition adopted by the Division of Career Development and Transition within the Council for Exceptional Children. This definition began with an encapsulation of transition as "a change in status

233

from behaving primarily as a student to assuming emerging adult roles in the community" (Halpern, 1994, p. 117). Programs for persons with disabilities should enable them to interact with persons in the mainstream of society, make decisions about their lives, and prepare for employment. As a result of a successful transition program, persons with disabilities may obtain and maintain employment. Because the support that can enable persons to achieve these goals can begin before school (Wolery, 1993) and continue into the adult years (Weisgerber, 1991), some transition services have been referred to as lifespan transition programs.

Life-span approaches to transition emphasize that learning activities can be arranged functionally and taught in natural settings (Clark, Field, Patton, Brolin, & Sitlington, 1994). Such functionally organized learning can enhance retention and generalization of learning, and it can provide opportunities for learners with disabilities to interact with persons without disabilities (Dever, 1988; Falvey, 1986).

Career Education and Transition

Persons who remain in high school have a 40% greater probability of being employed than young people who withdraw from high school (Grubb, 1995). As an indication of the direct connection between a high school diploma and employment, the employment rate for black youth who did not graduate from high school during the mid 1980s was 47% (National Collaboration for Youth, 1989). Even those dropouts who were successful finding jobs could expect to earn only 60% of the salaries paid to high school graduates (Grubb, 1995). Over a lifetime, the amount earned by a typical high school graduate has been hundreds of thousands of dollars greater than that earned by nongraduates (Boyer-Stephens, 1991; Catterall, 1986; McDill, Natriello, & Pallas, 1986).

During the 1980s, the number of high school dropouts in the nation averaged one million youths each year (West, 1991). In 1988, nearly 13% of all persons between 16 and 24 years of age had not completed high school and were not at that time enrolled in school (Frase, 1989). Although the figures from 1988 represented a considerable decline from those tabulated twenty years earlier, the number of dropouts in 1988 still amounted to over 4 million persons. The number of students dropping out of high school has remained stable for the past decade. As evidence, dropout rates were substantially unchanged during the decade ending in 1994 (Children's Defense Fund, 1994).

Dropouts have not exhibited a homogeneous profile of backgrounds, characteristics, or behaviors (Frase, 1989). Nonetheless, there seem to be certain groups that have been particularly at-risk for dropping out of high school, such as young persons within inner cities. For this group the dropout rate has exceeded 50% (West, 1991). The dropout rate for Latinos was over 35% in 1991, nearly three times the national average of 12.1% (Children's Defense Fund, 1994). Gajar, Goodman, and McAfee (1993) reviewed studies in which the national dropout rate among learners with disabilities was estimated to be between 25 and 36%. Dropout rates were variable among persons with different types of disabilities. Persons with mild disabilities exhibited the greatest risk, accounting for as high as 90% of the dropouts among learners with disabilities. Although the link between dropping out of high school and unemployment is important for all persons of working age, it is critical for individuals with disabilities, among whom only 20% are employed (National Center for Youth with Disabilities, 1993).

The majority of high school students, aware of the dire consequences of high school dropout, have looked to high school education as a roadway to employment. This perception is in contrast to that of most parents, teachers, and administrators, who view the secondary curriculum as a conduit to advanced learning or as preparation for community and citizenship responsibilities (Gajar et al., 1993). As a consequence of the latter view, a curricular chasm has developed, with academically focused education on one side and vocational education on the other (Grubb, 1995). Not only has a split developed, but academic preparation has expanded and been emphasized while vocational preparation has diminished (Edgar, 1987). The restricted opportunities for vocational preparation that have resulted can be a significant factor leading to the alienation of learners from high schools (Boyer-Stephens, 1991; DeStefano & Wermuth, 1992; Miller & Schloss, 1982; West, 1991). Conversely, programs that have discouraged dropout by nurturing a sense of belonging among students have emphasized the link between learning and employment (Bearden, Spencer, Moracco, 1989; Gajar et al., 1993; Hamilton, 1986).

Writing instruction can offer an example of the curricular chasm that may separate students from the employment responsibilities for which high school education can be preparatory. Surveys of employers (Lovitt, 1991; Schloss, Smith, & Schloss, 1995) have identified specific writing skills that are critical for workers. Among the skills prioritized by employers were the ability to accurately compose or complete messages, forms, business letters, records, checks, receipts, schedules, assignment notes, and employment-related examinations.

Lovitt (1991) recommended that high school writing curricula reflect functional employment tasks as a means of preparing learners for work. Among the sample instructional tasks he identified were completion of application forms, recording phone messages, using writing to keep track of written assignments, and making written requests to businesses about employment opportunities. He recommended that learners be evaluated based on whether their writing assignments were completed in manners that were decipherable and accurate. Brolin (1992) provided numerous suggestions for instructional activities that incorporated writing into occupational guidance and preparation. Lessons and worksheets to supplement these activities were designed to help learners explore careers, choose an occupation, and apply for employment. Isaacson (1995) recommended that learning to write be incorporated into job tasks such as composing technical descriptions, résumés, contracts, advertisements, brochures, project proposals, and progress reports. Washburn (1994) described instructional activities to assist learners in filling out forms and writing letters of application for jobs, employment résumés, biographies, and vocational research papers.

These instructional recommendations were directed at teachers of learners with disabilities. Suggestions for learners with disabilities are particularly needed in view of data indicating that even youth who participate in secondary programs have a high rate of unemployment after they exit the schools (National Center for Youth with Disabilities, 1993). Those who do find employment are likely to receive minimal wages and not progress beyond positions at the entry levels of businesses (Benz & Halpern, 1987; Edgar, 1987; McAfee, 1988).

Sheltered employment has been and continues to be the prevalent type of employment for persons with developmental disabilities. Sheltered employment, which can include workshops as well as crews of persons who provide services in communities, centers about nonprofit rehabilitation facilities that provide managed care to workers with disabilities. Murphy and Rogan (1995) reviewed data indicating that only 18,000 individuals were employed at sheltered sites in 1968. As an indication of the growth in the number of sites, more than 20,000 individuals were receiving services in 1993 at sheltered workshops in New York alone. Nationally, more than 228,000 persons participated in sheltered workshops in 1993. These figures would more than triple if individuals at day programs were included.

The rationale for sheltered employment is that it is a therapeutic situation enabling individuals with developmental disabilities to safely achieve their full potential as learners and workers. However, critics have charged that sheltered workshops segregate persons with disabilities from their nondisabled peers and fail to meet vocational and reha-bilitation goals when persons with disabilities are placed at sites that lack current equipment, adequate training programs, and sound busi-ness practices (Murphy & Rogan, 1995).

Critics of sheltered employment believe that workshops are like greenhouses, creating dependents who may be successful in artificial environments but who do not generalize those skills to less restrictive sites (Murphy & Rogan, 1995). As an alternative, natural supports within communities can be used to train and later sustain persons with disabilities placed in integrated sites (Bradley, Ashbaugh, & Blaney, 1994). Integrated approaches to work can promote community access, independence, personal empowerment, vocational readiness, and suc-cessful employment. Integrated employment can reduce discrimina-tion against individuals with disabilities and it can inspire persons with disabilities to achieve goals that could seem unattainable in sheltered workshops (Murphy & Rogan, 1995).

Instructional suggestions of the type that have been reviewed can be effective at sheltered workshops as well as in many integrated employment sites. However, developments in the workplace may require more fundamental changes in education and training for employment (Bailey, 1995; U. S. Department of Labor, Education, and Commerce, 1988). Employers have agreed that there is a widening gap between their needs and the qualifications of entry-level workers (U. S. Department of Labor, Education, and Commerce, 1988). Specifically, traditional high school curricula may be preparing individuals for mass production models of employment that are becoming progressively obsolete. Bailey (1995) viewed traditional curricula as teacher-cen-tered approaches in which information was presented in fragmented, fact-based, and noncontextual fashions. The mass production models of employment to which Bailey linked traditional curricula have required workers to discharge routine, precisely defined tasks without an understanding of the bases for those tasks. Bailey contrasted tradi-tional curricula with integrated approaches to pedagogy in which stu-dent-centered learning can prepare individuals to solve meaningful problems encountered at work sites in their communities. Integrated approaches can facilitate the transition to increasingly prevalent high-performance work sites where workers are expected to show initiative solving problems for which they understand the origin.

Surveys of instructors in vocational training programs have indi-cated that reading as well as academic learning in mathematics and writing are necessary for successful learning by students with mild handicaps (Evers & Bursuck, 1994; Sitlington & Okolo, 1987). Not only prior to employment but even after employment, reading, writing, mathematics, and oral communication can empower individuals as well as enhance their work related skills (Gajar et al., 1993; Schloss et al., 1995). Even academic subjects such as literature and social studies can be suitable for learners in vocational programs when this study develops the moral, civic, and political sensitivities appropriate for all learners. Refocused views of the preparation required for the workplace constitute a rationale for a school to work curriculum in which academic and vocational education are integrated (Bailey, 1995). Such a curriculum may provide the optimal, inclusive transition environment for learners without disabilities as well as individuals with disabilities (Maddy-Bernstein & Coyle-Williams, 1995).

Lankard (1992) described eight models for integrating real world, job skills with academic skills. The models were based on strategies such as increased incorporation of academic content within vocational courses, use of teachers trained in vocational and academic areas, increased incorporation of vocational content within academic courses, curricular realignment to ensure an optimal balance of vocational and academic instruction, assignment of student projects such as a senior year research paper or an internship with a local business, team teaching by vocational and academic teachers, and alternative organization of high school programs using occupational clusters to ensure balanced learning.

Because of the link between high school curricula and transition, the differences between vocational education and career education have been highlighted in the professional literature (Gajar et al., 1993). In vocational education, learners are trained about an occupation in order to directly prepare them for employment within that occupation. It is an "example of a specialized, direct instruction program for teaching students with and without disabilities very specific life skills content in the area of employment" (Clark et al., 1994, p. 129). The subsequent employment could be paid or unpaid and the preparatory training would be in lieu of a baccalaureate degree or advanced degree (Schloss et al., 1995). Emphasizing that career and vocational programs were not based on a common set of assumptions, Clark and Kolstoe (1995) differentiated career education as a broader alternative for instruction than the "narrow job-preparation approach of vocational education" (p. 18). From a complementary vantage, Gajar, Goodman, and McAfee (1993) described the historical foundation for vocational education" as "a need to ensure that business and industry had access to a population that could perform the increasingly complex tasks that industrialization created" (p. 259).

Fuller and Whealon (1979) reviewed research on transition and concluded that optimal approaches rely on models of career learning that embrace individuals' full lives. The most popular model of life-span transition has been Brolin's *Life-Centered Career Education Competency-Based Curriculum Model* (1995) which focused on daily living and social skills as well as occupational skills. Life-span models can facilitate the progression of persons with disabilities from dependence to independence (Razeghi, Kokàska, Gruenhagen, & Fair 1987; Szymanski, Turner, & Hershenson, 1992; Weisgerber, 1991).

When applied to adolescents with disabilities, transition has been equated with the movement from school to employment (Will, 1984). Although transition is certainly linked inextricably to employment, it is tied also to "participating in post-secondary education, maintaining a home, becoming appropriately involved in the community, and experiencing satisfactory personal and social relationships" (Halpern, 1994, p. 117). Consequently, transition does not culminate until persons can live successfully in their communities (Clark, et al. 1994; Halpern, 1985, 1994).

When transition is viewed from this perspective, the relevance of high school experiences as well as experiences that precede high school becomes apparent (Razeghi et al., 1987). This point was anticipated by Super (1953), who was one of the first scholars to underscore the relationship between early learning experiences and employment. Also sensitive to a life-span approach to instruction, Bailey (1985) developed the outline for a curriculum of prevocational experiences that are synchronized to key events in learners' development. Weisgerber (1991) detailed a life-span curriculum that could begin at birth and extend into the senior years. Clark, Carlson, Fisher, Cook, and D'Alonzo (1991) detailed basic principles for providing career education and transition education to learners prior to high school. The principles they identified reinforced the appropriateness of extending these types of education to all learners with disabilities, beginning the process at birth, and continuing the education throughout individuals' lives.

Although transition programs should contain a component in which information about careers is disseminated, optimal transition programs should contain an intervention phase as well (Clark et al., 1991). In the intervention phase, learners actually develop the specific skills for precise jobs. Montague (1988) described a program to develop the following job-related social skills: understanding instructions, asking questions, asking for help, accepting criticism, arranging job responsibilities, accepting assistance, giving instructions, offering assistance, apologizing, and convincing others. Skills taught during the intervention phase have been grouped under categories such as decision making, punctuality, cooperation, hygiene, and adaptability (Baumgart, 1990; Chamberlain, 1988; Mithaug, Martin, & Agran, 1987; Weisgerber, 1991). Brolin's *Life-Centered Career Education* (1992) is an extensive curriculum of instructional activities, learning materials, and assessment tasks that comprises both the dissemination and intervention phases of career education. These materials span daily living, interpersonal relationships, and occupational skills. Skills within these categories would be individually designated for specific learners.

The designation of individual skills should be the responsibility of an interdisciplinary team of educators, professionals, and employers (Baumgart, 1990; Weisgerber, 1991). Though such collaborative approaches are desirable when planning programs for all learners (Smith & Edelen-Smith, 1993), collaboration is critical when planning for the complex needs of individuals with disabilities.

Although the unavailability of services certainly restricts adult learning, the lack of well-coordinated services can also be a significant obstacle. If service providers inadvertently compete with one another, adults seeking intervention can be confused about turning to a college, social agency, or volunteer group. A report about the federal government's involvement in adult literacy concluded that basic skills training was fragmented at all levels (Chisman, 1989). The report cautioned that adult literacy problems would not be solved by school reform or by private volunteers working in isolation.

Because services are provided under the auspices of multiple laws, agencies, and policies, the delivery of services has been problematic. Programmatic barriers have included lack of services, lack of coordination between agencies, duplication of services, and poor marketing. Ament (1987), citing examples of successful collaborative arrangements, noted that collaboration expands, organizes, and efficiently delivers services. Collaborations can develop among businesses, school, community institutions, professional groups, and social agencies. For example, universities have collaborated with local literacy groups by allowing tutors to receive credit within teacher training programs. Under such arrangements, the teacher interns benefited by exposure to community-based and functional education; and adult learners benefited by receiving supervised and systematic instruction.

Emerging technology has highlighted the need for interdisciplinary teams. For though computers, electronic devices, and robotics have created opportunities to assist individuals with disabilities, the transition of learners to maximum independence in home environments, community settings, and work sites that rely on technology can require extremely specific training and special adaptations. These problems are compounded when one considers the speed with which changes in technology itself have been occurring (Steinhoff & Lyons, 1993). Addressing the impact of changes in workplaces on persons with disabilities, Brown, Joseph, and Wotruba (1989) emphasized that successful responses to these changes could be contingent upon contributions from specialists in areas such as technology who could participate on teams that also included parents, teachers, agency workers, and employers.

Because of the increasing complexity of literacy demands in the workplace, the types of literacy required for success in the workplace have expanded as well. Fantini (1986) identified types of skills that could be required for success at some employment sites. Fantini argued that these skills could be equated with traditional concepts of literacy.

- technological literacy: ability to employ the skills associated with computerized technology and robotics
- telecommunications literacy: ability to transmit information through telecommunications and computers
- multicultural literacy: understanding of different cultures as components of a global society
- civic literacy: understanding of legal and community issues
- aesthetic literacy: ability to incorporate the enjoyment of various art forms into one's life
- career literacy: understanding of employment opportunities
- problem-solving literacy: ability to find, organize, analyze, synthesize, and apply information to problems

When assembling teams to respond to the literacy issues involved in transition, guidance counselors can provide invaluable assistance to other team members as well as to learners. An obvious contribution that they can make is advice about community resources and local vocational opportunities. However, counselors can also be valuable resources because they have the consultation skills to persuade parents and employers to increase their involvement in the vocational planning process.

In addition to being implemented by an interdisciplinary team, career education should be sensitive to the evolving roles that individuals with disabilities can occupy during their lives (Brolin & D'Alonzo, 1979; Brolin & Kokaska, 1979). This dimension of career education is evident in the following definition, developed within the Division on Career Development of the Council for Exceptional Children (1978):

Career education . . . provides the . . . academic, daily living, personal-social and occupational knowledge and specific vocational skills necessary for . . . pursuits as a student, citizen, volunteer, family member and participant in meaningful leisure time activities. (*[Official Actions of the Delegate Assembly of the 56th Annual Council for Exceptional Children International Convention in Kansas City*, 1978,]* p. 46)

If one compares the preceding definition of career education with the definition of transition cited at the beginning of this chapter (Individuals with Disabilities Education Act, 1990), career education, rather than vocational education, emerges as the complement to life-span approaches to transition. Table 12–1 defines several popular philosophies of transition that are, to different degrees, all compatible with career education.

Transition and Community Living

Within a life-span approach to transition, employment is viewed as only a single dimension of a multifaceted goal for the independence of persons with disabilities. Although rooted in employment, transition is connected to opportunities that are broader than employment (Clark et al., 1994; Halpern, 1985, 1994). Halpern (1993) proposed that transition programs be evaluated based on their success in promoting quality of life. He viewed quality of life as having three domains: physical well-being, performance of adult roles, and personal fulfillment. Within the physical domain were outcomes such as physical health, mental health, access to food, clothing, lodging, financial security, and safety. Within the second domain were outcomes such as access to the community, mobility, employment, access to recreation, opportunities for personal relationships, opportunities for social relationships, access to education, opportunities to discharge citizenship responsibilities, and opportunities for spiritual fulfillment. The personal fulfillment domain included happiness, satisfaction, and a sense of general well-being. Such holistic views of transition assume opportunities for independent living as a condition for being successful.

Chronicling the dramatic shift from institutional to community living among persons with developmental disabilities during the past 35 years, Larkin, Hayden, and Abery (1994) weighed the advantages and disadvantages of independent living. Thirty-three residential institutions closed during the 25-year period preceding 1986. However, more than double that amount of institutions will have closed during the 10-year span culminating in 1996. The number of persons in institutions will have decreased by more than 120,000 during the 35-year period that will end in 1996.

Table 12-1   Philosophies That Are a Basis for Transition Services

Womb to Tomb

The phrase "womb to tomb" emphasizes that the scope of transition exceeds the span of the school years. Proponents of the "womb to tomb" philosophy emphasize that transition is a continuous and planned set of activities that includes not only kindergarten through high school but the periods that precede and proceed schooling.

Occupational Clusters

This philosophy of transition is tied to the exploration of occupational clusters. Occupational or career clusters can help adult learners gather information about employment alternatives. Although the jobs within clusters could require different technical skills, there would be a common domain of knowledge that permeated all of the jobs in each cluster. In 1971, the United States Office of Education[*] identified occupational clusters such as agribusiness, natural resources, office employment, construction, environment, homemaking, tourism, communication, and media.

Collaboration

Because of the complex requirements of transition programs, persons from the community can assist school personnel with the programs. Even when specialized personnel are available within schools, the effectiveness of transition programs can be limited if the programs are sequestered from community sites. Collaborative approaches to transition not only take advantage of community resources but promote generalized learning through community integration.

Infusion

Infusion is the process through which academic skills are synchronized to the students' transition needs. In such programs, transition concepts are reinforced during a distinct type of instruction, such as literacy instruction. For example, understanding careers through the examination of pamphlets could be expanded to include the learning of word identification skills.

Separate Programs Approach

Advocates of this approach point out that transition planning, or at least a segment of transition planning, warrants a separate place in the instructional plan that is developed for individuals. Such an approach could be reconcilable with the provisions of the Individuals with Disabilities Education Act of 1990 and the Americans with Disabilities Act of 1990.

*U.S. Office of Education (1971). *Occupational Clusters*. Washington, DC: U.S. Government Printing Office.

Within states, there has been variability within these national trends (Larkin et al., 1994). For example, during the 10-year period ending in 1988, Michigan's population of institutionalized persons with developmental disabilities decreased by nearly 80%. But other states, such as Arkansas and Tennessee, had institutionalized populations that remained almost stable. And Nevada's institutionalized population increased by more than 50%. However, there has been an unprecedented change in residential situations at the national level. This change is evidenced by the fact that the number of persons with developmental disabilities living in community settings has increased from less than 60,000 to more than 250,000 individuals during the past 15 years alone.

What are the factors on which successful community living depends and how can community living be promoted? Although the results of research about residential alternatives are far from homogeneous, several corollaries about successful community living permeate this literature (Hayden & Abery, 1994):

- Persons with disabilities should be able to choose residential alternatives.
- Persons with disabilities should have financial support that would enable them to live in community residences.
- An essential goal of support service is to facilitate the transition to independence for individuals with disabilities.
- Natural supports for persons with disabilities are available from family, friends, and community members.
- Community living is tied inextricably to opportunities for health, safety, employment, education, leisure, and social interaction.
- Service providers should strive to not intrude into the lives of individuals receiving services.

Table 12–2 contains definitions of independent living and other residential models that could be appropriate for persons with disabilities. The table is organized from the most restrictive residential model (public residential facilities) to the least restrictive model (independent living).

Table 12–3 highlights different residential models and indicates the probable impact that types of residence will have on the development of specific transition skills (i.e., decision making, financial planning, interpersonal skills, and community involvement skills).

Table 12–2   Residential Alternatives for Persons With Disabilities

Residential Model	Characteristics
Public Residential Facilities	Institutionalized facilities with trained staff and full-time supervision for residents. Residents are segregated from the community.

Table 12-2 *(continued)*

Residential Model	Characteristics
Sheltered Villages	Institutionalized facilities with trained staff and full-time supervision for residents. Privately supported, the facilities are located often in rural areas where the residents are segregated from the community.
Public Community Facilities	Institutionalized facilities with trained staff and full-time supervision for residents. (These residences are also referred to as *Intermediate Care Facilities*.) Residents are segregated from the community for some activities but integrated for other activities.
Public Group Homes	Government-operated homes shared by groups of persons and supervised by a staff which may be part-time. Residents may be segregated from the community for some activities but integrated for other activities.
Private Group Homes	Privately operated homes that otherwise have the same characteristics as *public group homes*.
Cooperatively Owned Group Homes	Homes that are owned jointly by residents and for which a full-time or part-time staff may be employed. Residents may be segregated from the community for some activities but integrated for other activities.
Foster Care	Persons with disabilities live in the home and under the supervision of a caregiver. The caregiver may be paid a stipend for these services. The degree to which residents are integrated can vary according to the attitudes of caregivers.
Publicly Managed, Supervised Apartments	Government-operated apartments are leased to individuals. Persons are supervised or assisted by an apartment manager who may be part-time. Residents may be segregated from the community for some activities but integrated for other activities.
Privately Managed, Supervised Apartments	Privately managed apartments that have the same characteristics as *publicly managed, supervised apartments*.
Cooperatively Owned, Supervised Apartments	Cooperatively owned apartments or condominiums are leased to individuals. Otherwise, this type of residence has the same characteristic as *publicly or privately owned supervised apartments*.
Independent Living	A wide range of residential options that could include renting or purchasing a residence in ways similar to those by which residences are selected and maintained by persons without disabilities. Persons with disabilities would have unrestricted access to community activities and could request assistance from agency personnel as appropriate.

245

Table 12–3 Impact of Residential Models on the Goals of Transition Plans

Residential Models	Transition Goals			
	Decision Making	Financial Planning	Inter-personal Skills	Community Involve-ment Skills
Public Residential Facilities	−	−	−	−
Sheltered Villages	−	−	−	−
Public Community Facilities	−	−	−	−/+
Public Group Homes	−	−	−	−/+
Private Group Homes	−	−	−	−/+
Group Homes Owned Cooperatively by Residents	−/+	−/+	−/+	−/+
Foster Care	−	−	−	−/+
Publicly Managed Supervised Apartments	−/+	−/+	−/+	−/+
Privately Managed Supervised Apartments	−/+	−/+	−/+	−/+
Individually Leased Supervised Apartments	−/+	−/+	−/+	−/+
Independent Living	+	+	+	+

+ positive impact; − negative impact; −/+ positive and/or negative impact

Instructional Strategies That Complement Transition

Six models of literacy instruction have been reviewed in this book—approaches that are computer-assisted, skills-based, whole language-based, psychoeducational, functional, and children's literature-based. All of these models are compatible with life-span transition programs. As an indication of this compatibility, all six models could enable learners to meet reading objectives based on community demands. However, some instructional models, such as those that are skills-based, whole language-based, or functional, would complement community-based reading objectives more effectively than the others. Wiederholt and Dunn (1995) identified aspects of independent living that were linked to reading ability. These aspects included daily living skills, aptitude, interests, job-seeking skills, interpersonal skills, appearance, health, mobility, values, and attitudes.

Gartland (1995) developed a list of reading objectives based on community demands. The list was organized using the general categories of following directions, gaining information, understanding forms, and recreational reading. The following objectives were among those that she identified:

- follow directions by reading and complying with building signs
- follow directions by reading and complying with pedestrian signs or road signs
- follow directions by reading and complying with telephone procedures
- follow directions by reading and complying with labels on items such as food products, appliances, clothing, or medicine
- gain information from travel materials such as schedules, maps, guides, or printed emergency procedures
- gain information from financial materials such as contracts, bills, or monetary statements
- gain information from work-related materials such as manuals, memoranda, or safety information
- complete forms or applications for services such as social security, medical aid, insurance, employment, or banking
- complete forms or applications for items such as magazines, licenses, credit cards, or loans
- read recreational materials such as books, magazines, newspapers, television guides, movie schedules, music programs, restaurant listings, or sports information

Virtually any type of instructional activity can be adapted for learners with disabilities who are involved in a transition program. The term *accommodation* has been used to refer to simple educational changes that increase the likelihood of successful learning (Gajar, 1992; Polloway & Smith, 1991). These changes could characterize instruction, instructional materials, the learning environment, or tests. The following examples were among the multiple accommodations listed by Smith, Polloway, Patton, and Dowdy (1995):

- course outlines developed by instructors to assist learners
- supplements to course outlines that include questions, assignments, and evaluation criteria
- advance organizers that highlight key material
- audiovisual supplements
- variable instructional strategies that offer opportunities for persons with distinct learning styles
- variable grouping arrangements
- tape recorders as note-taking devices
- taped books and tests
- individualized time adjustments to help students complete assignments
- assignment notebooks
- manipulative learning devices
- highlighting of important passages in textbooks
- rewording of passages on tests using the reading vocabulary of individual learners
- altering features such as spacing, margins, length, instructions, or response format so that tests have a format familiar to learners

Ciborowski (1994, 1995) proposed a multistage set of accommodations to help learners read textbooks and other materials that could otherwise frustrate them. She recommended that instruction be broken into three phases that would comprise the times before, during, and after reading. The prereading phase would encourage learners to transfer knowledge they already possessed to the passage they were preparing to read. Additionally, the prereading phase would encourage learners to become motivated, to realize the purpose for which they were about to read, and to develop a general sense of the content within the passage they were preparing to read. The activities in phase one focused on comprehending vocabulary, making predictions, and forming visual images. Phase two, which centered on actual reading, relied on student-centered instructional techniques such as reciprocal teaching by instructors and learners, use of a varied repertoire of skills, and effective modeling of reading strategies by instructors. In phase three, readers consolidated and extended the knowledge gained from the materials they had read. Phase three included strategies such as revision of tasks begun in the prereading phase, written response to summary questions, and collaborative preparation for tests.

Ciborowski identified reciprocal teaching as a component of the multistage procedure she advocated. *Reciprocal teaching* is itself a multistage instructional procedure (Brown, Palincsar, & Armbruster, 1988) in which instructors and learners read and then analyze passages. The analysis requires summarization, questioning, clarification, and prediction. The instructor takes the lead, initially modeling these strategies. But the learners assume progressively greater responsibility and eventually control the instruction.

As part of reciprocal teaching, learners can be instructed about how to generate questions. Bartel (1995) developed strategies in which instructors provided models of effective questions that enabled learners to focus discussion, gather more information at a particular level of discussion, obtain additional information, or progress from factual to more abstract levels of understanding. The instructors eventually decreased the number of modeled questions that they were presenting, encouraging learners to use features of printed texts, such as pictures, headings, or topic sentences, as aids in forming their own questions. The resulting learner-generated questions could be used during the initial stage of reading to help individuals prepare for comprehension or during the final stage to reinforce comprehension and promote generalization. Questions generated as a result of such procedures could focus on information that was factual, interpretive, applied, or evaluative (Singer, 1978).

Strategies That Complement Career Education

The literacy strategies described in this chapter are not focused precisely and exclusively on community-based objectives. But neither are the strategies so general as to be appropriate for all reading materials. Instead, the strategies are directed toward career objectives. Despite this career focus, the strategies do not assume that instructors have developed extensive expertise about specific careers or career education. The activities do not even assume that instructors possess special expertise about literacy instruction. As such, the following strategies can be used by teachers with a wide range of expertise and experience.

Career Speakers

Persons representing different careers can address adult learners and discuss occupations with them. During these discussions, the literacy requirements of different jobs can be emphasized by the speakers.

The impact of these discussions may be increased if learners are provided with worksheets outlining the literacy demands of careers.

This type of worksheet can help learners ask questions, take notes, and make comparisons between occupations. Exhibit 12–1 is a sample of such a worksheet.

Exhibit 12–1
Worksheet for Use With Career Speakers or
During Job Site Visits

Name _____

Job _____

Related Reading Materials:

instructions	_____	manuals	_____
magazines	_____	checks	_____
messages	_____	letters	_____
bills	_____	reports	_____
signs	_____	directories	_____
tests	_____	computers	_____
application forms	_____	advertisements	_____
telephone books	_____		

Notes:

_____

_____

_____

_____

Job Site Visits

Visits by career speakers can be preceded by job site visits. Or a job site visit might follow a presentation by a career speaker. During the job site visits, learners can have opportunities to observe workers who may be occupied with different jobs at the same work site. A job site visit to a restaurant could highlight jobs in cooking, cleaning, waiting, sales, and management.

By adapting a worksheet such as that in Exhibit 12–1, awareness of work-related literacy expectations can be developed. This awareness can be reinforced when the learners subsequently visit other restaurants or banks, for they may be able to view these as workplaces, using the perspective formed during their field trips.

Career Note Exchange

After a presentation by a classroom speaker or a visit to a work site, a learner can address written questions to an individual worker. A structured form that suggests categories of questions to ask, such as Exhibit 12–2, can simplify the forming of questions. If individuals lack the skills to complete the form, they could be assisted by an instructor or by another adult.

Career Vocabulary

Learners can be involved in creative activities that reinforce their understanding of careers. Assembling collages with occupational pictures is an example of an art activity that can enable instructors to introduce novel, career vocabulary. If photographs are taken after a job site visit, the items, tools, or equipment in the photographs can be labeled or captioned. If materials, such as manuals, posters, or signs are brought back from a job site visit, the words in these materials can be highlighted. By such techniques, vocabulary related to specific careers can be taught in a contextual manner.

Almost any familiar item can be a simple pretext for learning vocabulary associated with careers. For example, learners can attempt to identify vocations connected with a product such as a carton of milk. Under the direction of the instructor, learners can create lists that might comprise individuals that nurture the cows, maintain the dairy, process, bottle, transport, advertise, and sell the milk.

Exhibit 12-2
Worksheet for Addressing Questions to Workers

Name _____

Job _____

Types of Questions:

how to apply	_____	training	_____
responsibilities	_____	age limits	_____
salary	_____	job demand	_____
work schedule	_____	safety	_____
gender limitations	_____	promotion schedule	_____
compatible with disabilities	_____		

Questions:

_____

_____

_____

_____

Career Books, Films, and Videotapes

Books that highlight careers can be effective for teaching reading as well as writing, spelling, and critical thinking. Occupational films or videotapes provide comparable opportunities to develop critical viewing skills and career knowledge simultaneously. Exhibit 12–3 is a worksheet that could assist readers or viewers as they examine these mate-

**Exhibit 12–3
Worksheet for Taking Notes About a
Career Book or Film**

Name _____

Job _____

Directions:

Highlight in *green* the items below that are *benefits* of this job.

Highlight in *red* the items below that are *drawbacks* of this job.

salary

application

safety

location

job demand

job mobility

training requirements

accessibility to persons from both genders

accessibility to persons of different ages

accessibility to persons with disabilities

Notes:

_____

_____

_____

_____

rials. If learners are unable to complete such a worksheet by themselves, an instructor or another adult would assist them.

Libraries of Career Pamphlets

Businesses, professional organizations, and trade schools may furnish occupational pamphlets. These occupational pamphlets, which are often illustrated, can be displayed on racks or shelves to entice learners into picking them up and examining them. Once learners become interested, the pamphlets can be used to inform learners about careers. Such a library of readable pamphlets could help learners prepare for career speakers or for visits to job sites.

Exhibit 12–4 is a worksheet that could help adult learners take notes while they investigate the literacy requirements associated with different jobs. If they filled out the worksheet initially with information from pamphlets, they might confirm the accuracy of their notes when they interact later with career speakers or examined job sites.

Career Bulletin Boards

As with displays of career pamphlets, career bulletin boards can be opportunities to engender interest about occupations. Career bulletin boards can help adult learners form receptive attitudes toward classroom visitors. And the bulletin board may reinforce some of the important concepts that were emphasized by career speakers.

Career-Day Fair

A career-day fair can overlap with career pamphlet activities. At a career-day fair, employers and exhibitors from vocational schools can display information about occupations. A worksheet such as Exhibit 12–4 could be filled out about jobs. Adult learners could assemble pamphlets and literature about various careers and subsequently visit appropriate work sites. If learners are unable to complete the worksheets, instructors or other adults could assist them.

Career Learning Centers

Learning centers enable adult learners at different ability levels in reading to work independently or in small groups. Often with minimal changes, centers that have already been established to assist with the development of reading or writing can be adapted to reflect career motifs.

Exhibit 12–4
Worksheet for Taking Notes From a Career Pamphlet

Name _____

Job _____

Types of Reading Required:

books

magazines

forms

letters

advertisements

manuals

directories

bills

instructions

warnings

maps

Notes:

_____

_____

_____

_____

For example, skills-based worksheets can be rephrased using occupational contexts. Or a career pamphlet can be the basis for a whole language activity. Job applications or job safety warnings could be used to supplement a functional reading program. Such adaptations provide meaningful backdrops for literacy learning while simultaneously building the awareness of careers that is linked to successful transition.

Simplified Career Aptitude Inventories

Career aptitude inventories are administered frequently to high school students. On the basis of their responses to questions in the inventories, learners can be advised that they display strengths for certain types of jobs. These inventories may contain hundreds of questions and result in complex analyses. Such lengthy inventories would be inappropriate for adults with limited literacy skills. However, such inventories are attractive as instructional materials that can develop learners' interest in careers.

As an alternative to a formal career aptitude inventory, instructors can create a personalized inventory with only a dozen or so statements. The statements can be tailored to careers that are accessible to the learners. For example, *yes* or *no* responses to the following items might be the basis for discussing careers as custodians, grounds keepers, or gardeners.

- I like to help with cleaning.
- I like to clean with water.
- I like to sweep.
- I like to be around people.
- I like to be outdoors.
- I like to cut grass with a lawn mower.
- I like to work alone.
- I like to take care of plants.

Different items could be devised to prod learners' interests in other types of careers.

Exhibit 12–5 is an example of a general inventory that could complement learning about a wide range of careers. The purpose of such inventories is not to assess career aptitude but to initiate dialogue that can raise learners' awareness about careers. Such dialogue could be the pretext for additional transition activities or literacy activities.

Employment Simulations

Functional literacy skills that could be crucial for individual learners might include the reading of classified employment advertisements,

---

Exhibit 12–5
Worksheet for Matching Characteristics of
Jobs With Characteristics of Learners

Name _____

Job _____

	Job Characteristics:	**Personal Characteristics:**
time	Flexible—Rigid	Flexible—Rigid
salary	need little—need much	need little—need much
access	don't need special access—need special access	don't need special access—need special access
strength	physical—nonphysical	physical—nonphysical
independence	independent—dependent	independent—dependent
reading skills	skilled—unskilled	skilled—unskilled
mobility	mobile—nonmobile	mobile—nonmobile

---

use of a sign to locate a personnel office, or completion of a job application form. Terms that could be important when locating or applying for a job might be *experience, work history, skills, abilities, part-time, full-time, confidential, recommendation, recruitment, seasonal, urban, rural, or limitations.*

Abbreviations used at work sites are another example of vocabulary of which learners need to be aware. OTR (over the road), MPH (miles per hour), and MPG (miles per gallon) are abbreviations that are likely to be recognized by truckers. WPM (words per minute), Mac (Macintosh), IBM (International Business Machines), RAM (random access memory), and HD (hard drive) are abbreviations that are more likely to be recognized by office workers. In addition, terms with meanings peculiar to certain work environments, such as *rotate the stock* or *police the area*, can be used at job sites.

Words that occur on signs at work sites are a third category of vocabulary of which learners need to be aware. Examples of such vocabulary and phrases could be *hazard, high voltage, danger, authorized personnel only, no smoking, flammable, hard hat area, construction area, no trespassing, slippery, emergency, wet paint, keep out, watch step, fire extinguisher,* or *alarm.*

Teachers can use simulated employment situations to prepare learners for encounters with vocational literacy tasks. In addition to helping learners recognize special vocational terms, simulations can incorporate training about the procedures through which workers can request assistance understanding unfamiliar terms from colleagues and supervisors.

Predeveloped Curricula

Instructional activities such as those that have been reviewed can be incorporated as units within transition curricula that have already been developed. Predeveloped curricula usually are accompanied by instructional manuals as well as materials that learners can use. An example would be *Expanding Horizons*, a program that used audiocassettes and filmstrips to instruct students about seven basic aspects of employment and life management (ACTV, 1995). The components of the curriculum included applying for a job, the first days on the job, co-worker relationships, honesty, dealing with pay checks, understanding payroll deductions, job advancement, and job changes. The use of video-recording technology is another avenue employed within curricula developed by ACTV. This technology allows instructors to monitor learners who may be interacting with several different units on specialized topics such as shop safety or general topics such as entry into the world of work. Another example of a predeveloped curriculum would be *Social Skills on the Job*, a videotape with accompanying computer disks and worksheets. The worksheet activities can enhance job literacy as well as job performance (Macro Systems, 1989). The following list contains some of the numerous published transition curricula:

- *Bridges: Making the Transition from School to Work* (Zeien & Anderson, 1993)
- *Career Education: A Curriculum Manual for Students with Handicaps* (Baumgart, 1990)

- *EBSCO Transitions Skills Centers* (EBSCO, 1990)
- *Life-Centered Career Education* (Brolin, 1992)
- *Prevocational Assessment and Curriculum Guide* (Mithaug, Martin, & Stewart, 1990)
- *Transition Skills Guide: An Integrated Curriculum with Reading and Math Materials* (Wircenski, 1992)
- *Social Competence and Employability Skills Curriculum* (Weisgerber, 1989)
- *Vocational Curriculum for Developmentally Disabled Persons* (Wehman & McLaughlin, 1990)
- *Vocational Entry-Skills for Secondary and Adult Students with Learning Disabilities: A Teacher's Guide to Implementing the ITP* (Washburn, 1994)

Several books contain extensive lists of curricular materials that can be incorporated into transition curricula. Three recent, comprehensive sources include *Life Skills Instruction for All Students with Special Needs: A Practical Guide for Integrating Real-life Content into the Curriculum* (Cronin & Patton, 1993), *Vocational Entry-Skills for Secondary and Adult Students with Learning Disabilities: A Teacher's Guide to Implementing the ITP* (Washburn, 1994), and *The Special Education Sourcebook: A Teacher's Guide to Programs, Materials, and Information Sources* (Rosenberg & Edmond-Rosenberg, 1994).

In addition to curricula that have been designed specifically for assisting persons with developmental disabilities, multiple curricula have been created by occupational therapists for adults with brain injury. Individual units and sometimes entire sections of these curricula can be adapted for learners with developmental disabilities. For example, *Community Living Skills Workbook for the Head Injured Adult* (Angle & Buxton, 1991) contains exercises on daily living skills as well as prevocational and vocational skills. *The Cognitive Rehabilitation Workbook: A Dynamic Approach for Adults with Brain Injury* (Dougherty & Radomski, 1993) contains information on a number of tasks that involve literacy skills such as reading maps, telephone directories, schedules, calendars, newspapers, and written instructions.

Community and Home-Based Programs

The preceding activities may be most appropriate for persons with mild and moderate disabilities. But persons with severe disabilities may benefit as well from programs that combine literacy instruction with preparation for transition. Persons with severe disabilities might require additional experiences to achieve the goals at which the preceding activities were aimed. These additional experiences, which can precede actual employment by many years, can be an opportunity to combine learning about careers with the development of literacy skills in community and home settings.

Functional, community-based experiences help persons acquire skills that they retain and generalize (Falvey, 1986). Falvey listed the following, desirable characteristics of skills taught in a functional curriculum:

- The skills should transfer to several environments.
- The skills should be employed frequently.
- The skills should be compatible with family needs.
- The skills should be compatible with community needs.
- The skills should promote independence.

Dever (1988) identified factors on the basis of which the skills taught in functional, community-based curricula can be modified. The factors included the individual learners themselves, the persons with whom they would be interacting, and the environments to which the skills would generalize. The opportunities for implementing both career education and literacy learning can extend beyond school to include home settings (Neel & Billingsley, 1989). Cronin and Patton (1993) provided examples for introducing real-life materials from outside the classroom into the curriculum. They reviewed instructional materials that could support life skills lessons about the community and one's residence and that could be implemented in school or in nonacademic environments.

Home Opportunities

There are opportunities for developing literacy skills in learners' homes. Such opportunities can be worthwhile because they involve families of the learners. Additionally, resources to support formal literacy programs can be limited, especially in rural areas (Richards & Smith, 1992). And even if formal literacy programs are available, the extension of literacy learning to nonacademic environments can enhance the overall learning.

Samples of literacy activities that have career motifs can be devised for the home. Examples of suitable career motifs could be cleaning, grooming pets, general maintenance, sorting items in pantries, gardening, recycling, cleaning a swimming pool, taking care of laundry, baby-sitting, cooking, organizing coupons, maintaining vehicles, and checking safety equipment.

The following example about cleaning laundry illustrates how literacy skills could be nurtured in an informal manner at learners' homes.

1. The adult learners sort laundry into piles of white and colored garments.
2. They load the white garments into a washing machine.
3. After reading directions on the box of detergent or the washer, they select the water temperature, set the washer to the correct cycle, and start the machine. (If learners cannot read the instructions, a parent, adult, or caregiver can read them while pointing to the directions.)
4. When the cycle has been completed, learners transfer the laundry to a dryer. They read the instructions on a box of fabric softener sheets and insert the correct number of sheets. They set the timer on the dryer, set the temperature on the dryer, and start the dryer. (If learners cannot read the instructions, a parent, adult, or caregiver can read them while pointing to the directions.)
5. While the white load is drying, learners repeat the washing procedure with the colored laundry.
6. When the drying cycle has been completed, the clothing is removed, folded, and sorted.
7   The drying procedure is repeated with the colored clothing.

This laundering example combines learning about reading as well as the development of prevocational skills that may eventually transfer to paid employment. Adults could supervise this laundering procedure at the learners' homes, the homes of acquaintances, or commercial laundries. Satisfactory performance could be evaluated by observation. The criterion for successful learning could be several consecutive trials washing the laundry.

In addition to developing literacy skills and specific job skills, such activities can develop a wide range of general career skills such as remaining on task, attending to instructions, responding to verbal feedback, following a sequence, sorting, comprehending measures of quantity, and comprehending time. Table 12–4 identifies other examples of functional, pre-employment activities for which there may be opportunities in learners' homes.

Table 12–4 Clerical Activities at Home That Can Be Opportunities for Developing Literacy and Career Transition Skills

Activity	Opportunities					
	House	**Garage**	**Yard**	**Kitchen**	**Animals**	**Laundry**
clean	X	X	X	X	X	X
groom					X	
watch and care for	X		X		X	
cook				X		
garden			X			
sort tools	X		X	X		
operate appliances	X	X		X		X
prepare for tasks	X	X	X	X	X	X
repair items	X	X	X	X	X	X

Summary

Transition is a life-long process that helps persons with disabilities change their situations from ones where they are receiving care to ones where they can work, interact with the mainstream of society, and live with maximum independence. Programs have been designed to prepare adult learners for transition to employment while simultaneously developing their literacy skills. Literacy skills can be developed well in advance of the stage at which learners assume employment at precise job sites. The literacy skills should be developed through strategies that are varied, motivating, able to be implemented by interdisciplinary teams of personnel, and that complement learning about diverse careers.

Examples were reviewed to indicate that literacy skills could be combined with home- and community-based training of functional, prevocational skills. Persons with developmental disabilities who are maintaining or seeking employment can be successful while living in a full range of residential settings. However, independent living and other residential models that encourage unrestricted access to communities have the highest probability of developing the personal traits that complement both the goals of transition and adult literacy programs.

CHAPTER

13

Literacy Programs for Persons With Severe Disabilities

with
Sheela Stuart

During the past 25 years, society's attitude toward individuals with severe disabilities has changed. One indication of this change is the dramatic increase in the number of adults with disabilities living in community settings. There were less than 60,000 persons with developmental disabilities living in community settings 15 years ago; today there are more than 250,000 persons (Larkin et al., 1994).

Although all individuals with disabilities do not have to choose to live in environments where they can interact regularly with nondisabled persons, all individuals with disabilities should have the right to make this choice (Heumann, 1993; Parent, 1992; Turnbull, Bateman, & Turnbull, 1993). Taylor and Bogdan (1993) documented the reactions of some individuals with disabilities and their families, as well as professionals and public employees, who misunderstood the objective of the deinstitutionalization movement as the coerced displacement of all individuals with disabilities into integrated settings. This reaction may have been based on a misperception that independence was an absolute rather than relative goal. As Clees (1992) pointed out, the degree of independence that should characterize community living for an individual with a disability depends on three variable factors: the extent of the individual's community living skills, the resources required to develop and maintain those skills, and the availability of required resources in the individual's community.

If coercion was an aspect of the deinstitutionalization movement, it was directed not at persons with disabilities but at institutions that had prevented individuals' from developing independence and interaction with their nondisabled peers. Such nonvoluntarily segregated environments were criticized as residential Devil's Islands, places to which individuals' with disabilities could be sent but from which they might never emerge. Examples of prejudice and discrimination against individuals with disabilities are well documented and these "continue to be a serious and pervasive social problem" (Americans with Disabilities Act, 1990, Section 2). There have been reports of prejudice and discrimination in the treatment of persons with disabilities who live in residential institutions (West, 1993). But even if one disregards examples of prejudice and discrimination, individuals with disabilities who reside at professionally managed facilities staffed with caring personnel can be segregated inadvertently from beneficial community experiences (Klein, 1992; Taylor & Bogdan, 1993).

Parallel to this reassessment of residential opportunities, there has been a reassessment of the learning programs available to persons with severe disabilities. These programs, traditionally referred to as *compensatory programs*, are intended to substitute for the learning that would take place in the programs of persons with mild or moderate disabilities or persons without disabilities. The rationale for compensatory programs that are applied exclusively to individuals with severe disabilities is that these programs can best meet the needs of learners who would be frustrated by more demanding learning tasks. Although this logic seems self-evident, a case can be made that compensatory programs, like restrictive residential facilities, can constitute Devil's Islands from which learners may never return.

For example, learners with severe disabilities may be exposed to environments where they are surrounded by colored lights, shimmering visual displays, and enticing sounds. If learners who formerly were distracted and uncomfortable exhibit pleasure and attention during such experiences, educators, parents, and caregivers would likely support the continuation of those experiences.

However, one would still need to assess the goal of such experiences. If the sole goal were to increase attention and elicit a favorable mood from the learners, such compensatory learning tasks could be adequate. However, if educators, parents, caregivers, advocates, and persons with disabilities themselves set more sophisticated goals for learning, what are the prospects that light and sound displays would achieve those goals? What are the prospects that such displays would develop skills that generalize to other experiences, environments, and contexts? More specifically, what are the prospects that literacy, progress toward literacy, or even positive attitudes toward literacy would be engendered by compensatory learning tasks that neither resembled reading nor had communication as their goal?

Just as residential institutions for persons with disabilities should be criticized if those arrangements do not incorporate opportunities for the residents to progress to less restrictive settings, so instructional programs for individuals with disabilities should be criticized if those programs are not linked to opportunities for less restrictive types of learning and self-determination (Wehman, 1994).

Less restrictive programs are referred to often under the heading of community-based instruction. Community-based instruction comprises skills that are relevant to learners' environments and that are taught in those environments (Duran, 1992). Community-based instruction is only one component of a larger initiative that is directed at community inclusion, participation, and empowerment (Nisbet, Covert, & Schuh, 1992).

Less restrictive programs are referred to also as functional programs. Although the terms *community-based instruction* and *functional learning* can have similar connotations, functional learning programs can have a distinctive set of characteristics that distinguish them from other programs intended for learners with severe disabilities. Learning programs for adults with severe disabilities are functional if they incorporate, to the extent possible, three characteristics:

- Learning tasks within the programs should resemble the less restrictive learning for which those tasks are a substitute.
- Learning within the programs should be aimed at the same goal as the less restrictive learning for which those programs substitute.
- Learning that results from the programs should generalize to diverse contexts.

If these three characteristics are present, then literacy programs for persons with severe disabilities become functional, comprising a position on a learning continuum that is linked to remedial literacy programs for adults with moderate or mild disabilities. The programs would be linked potentially to mainstream literacy programs for adults with mild disabilities (Figure 13–1).

Speaking specifically about transition programs for persons with severe disabilities, Berkell (1992) identified three barriers to effective programs: cost, confusion about responsibility for programs, and an underassessment by society about the potential for community learning by individuals with severe disabilities. She pointed out that this third factor, stereotypes of persons with disabilities as feeble and nonadaptable, can be reinforced by compensatory programs that are implemented in segregated settings. Szymanski, Turner, and Hershenson (1992) reviewed research indicating that the instructional programs of learners with severe disabilities were frequently other directed, nonresponsive to the wishes of learners, and characterized by limited learning choices.

Academic Versus Nonacademic Learning

Among programs intended for adult learners with severe disabilities, some approaches focus learning solely on nonacademic learning. Typically, these programs emphasize preparation for tasks associated with jobs. There are also programmatic approaches that focus exclusively on academic learning. The development of this chasm among approaches to instruction for adolescents with disabilities in secondary schools was chronicled by Browning, Dunn, and Brown (1994). When programs are dichotomized in this fashion, approaches on both sides of this artificial chasm seem inadequate.

Clark and Kolstoe's (1995) model of career education for adolescents with disabilities is an example of a program that avoided this dichotomous classification. This model explicitly recognized the relevance of academic learning for all persons, even persons with severe and profound learning disabilities. Although other models are less explicit about the role of reading and academic skills in ensuring success, several educational models have defined critical career skills for which reading is the implicit base (Brolin & D'Alonzo, 1979; Hoyt, 1979; Kokaska & Brolin, 1985).

If learners have demonstrated even modest gains in reading, they can be instructed using strategies drawn from a large selection of individualized programs that incorporate word recognition and comprehension (Trapani, 1990). However, how does one nurture academic

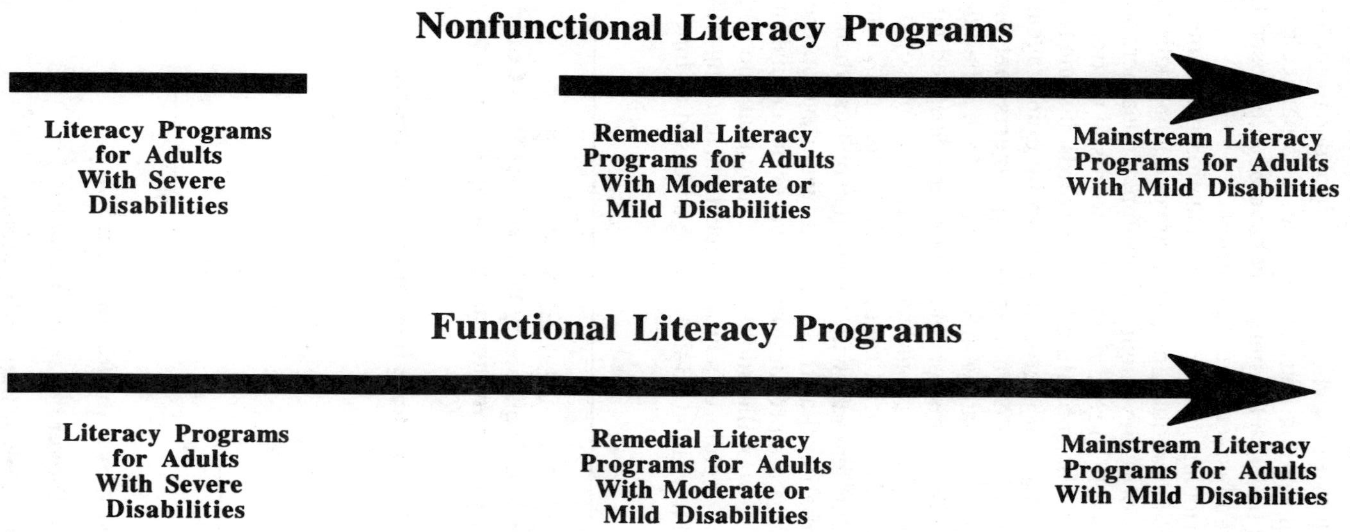

Nonfunctional Literacy Programs

Literacy Programs
for Adults
With Severe
Disabilities

Remedial Literacy
Programs for Adults
With Moderate or
Mild Disabilities

Mainstream Literacy
Programs for Adults
With Mild Disabilities

Functional Literacy Programs

Literacy Programs
for Adults
With Severe
Disabilities

Remedial Literacy
Programs for Adults
With Moderate or
Mild Disabilities

Mainstream Literacy
Programs for Adults
With Mild Disabilities

Figure 13–1. Continuum of educational opportunities within literacy programs that are nonfunctional and programs that are functional.

skills among adult learners who have not responded to such individualized programs of reading instruction? This is a particularly difficult issue to address because learners may have been exposed to literacy programs recurrently over extended periods.

Within a curriculum for vocational education programs, Baumgart (1990) illustrated techniques for adapting vocational skills to learners at different levels of achievement. For example, if learners with severe disabilities are unable to read the printed words in written schedules, pictorial cues might be substituted for the words. If some learners find a schedule composed of pictorial cues to be unmanageable, those learners might manipulate small models of objects that the learners had been taught to associate with key events in their schedules.

Most literacy programs for nonreaders are designed for young or remedial learners. These programs are intended to prepare children for the acquisition of initial reading skills. Such programs may be unsuitable for adult learners with severe disabilities when there is no immediate expectation that these learners will develop the skills for which the activities are preparatory. However, functionalism is a relative concept. In view of the additional learning that one might expect during the course of children's future education, learning tasks such as those illustrated in Exhibit 13–1 might be assessed as functional liter-

---

Exhibit 13–1
Example of a Preliteracy Worksheet That Could Be Judged as Nonfunctional for Many Adult Learners

1. **Follow the directions beneath this illustration.**

1. **Place an X over the larger square.**

2. **Place an O over the smaller square.**

3. **Color the area within each square.**

acy tasks for children. But it is less likely that the same worksheet could be incorporated into functional literacy programs for adult learners with severe disabilities.

In contrast, there are functional reading activities that can be more appropriate for adults than lessons aimed at children. These functional reading activities, which are not intended as a gateway to subsequent learning with traditional educational materials, are distinct from reading activities for persons without disabilities. Nonetheless, these alternative literacy activities could be aimed at the same general goals and, to a limited extent, resemble the traditional reading instruction for which they would substitute.

In Figure 13–2, alternative reading activities are identified and arranged hierarchically. Most of these activities can complement learning programs in which the functional, on-site development of skills is emphasized. By viewing the activities along a hierarchical continuum, such as that displayed in Figure 13–2, instructors can perceive opportunities for placing learners in individualized programs that can be adapted to meet the changing needs of those learners.

The range of activities includes rudimentary learning tasks, such as the exhibition of patterned literacy behaviors. Other activities require progressively more complex degrees of attention. These more complex activities can direct the attention of learners to graphic illustrations, to global features of printed material, to print in the environment, to rebus symbols, or to items that have been selected and labeled for individual learners. Opportunities for using alternative or augmentative communication devices can also constitute an alternative path to literacy for persons with severe disabilities.

Rebus Programs

Within fields such as special education and communication disorders, there is a tradition of employing instructional techniques using pictorial communication. These systems were devised initially to assist the communication of nonspeaking individuals with unimpaired language aptitude (Archer, 1977; McDonald, 1977; McLean & McLean, 1974; McNaughton & Kates, 1980; Silverman, McNaughton, & Kates, 1978; Woolman, 1980). In such programs, persons who were physically impaired, such as persons with cerebral palsy, might simulate oral communication by arranging plastic or cardboard symbols to represent the elements of speech. If persons lacked the physical dexterity to manipulate symbols, mechanical or electronic devices might be employed to adapt learning tasks to the learners' abilities (Allaire &

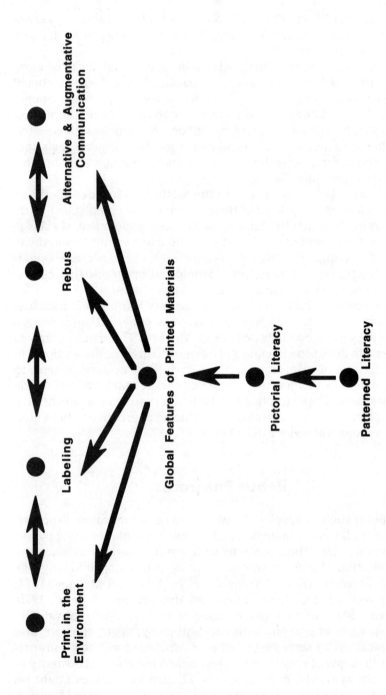

Figure 13–2. Progressive literacy programs for adult learners with severe disabilities.

Print in the
Environment

Labeling

Rebus

Alternative & Augmentative
Communication

Global Features of Printed Materials

Pictorial Literacy

Patterned Literacy

Miller, 1982; Silverman, 1980). Even though these programs were designed to assist persons with physical disabilities and unimpaired language aptitude, the programs also have been employed with persons who are mentally retarded (Harris-Vanderheiden, 1977).

Although pictorially based communication can be a substitute for speech, it can be an expedient instructional technique as well. When used as an instructional technique, pictorially based communication can prepare persons for learning to read and write. And in the cases of some persons with severe disabilities, pictorially based communication may be an effective substitute for traditional literacy.

Rebus systems may be the most popular pictographic communication techniques for teaching readinglike skills (Clark, Davies, & Woodcock, 1974; Clark & Woodcock, 1976; Moores, 1980). In rebus programs, words in a line of print are replaced with symbols. When appropriate, a representative symbol is devised. In a sentence such as, "a screwdriver is in the yellow toolbox," it would require little ingenuity to devise an appropriate, representative symbol for the word *screwdriver* or the word *toolbox*. Assuming that the symbols could be developed in colors, a surrogate symbol for the adjective *yellow* would be simple to create. Though more abstract, even a preposition such as *on* could be accommodated. However, there would be words that would defy representative, pictorial substitutes. Nonexperiential words, such as *a* or *the* would have to be omitted, represented in standard alphabetical form, or replaced with nonrepresentative symbols.

Though persons with unimpaired language aptitude might respond well to literacy programs that rely on pictorial communication, persons with severe learning problems could be frustrated if activities assumed a degree of language structure that was advanced beyond their levels of development (Chapman & Miller, 1980). Not only among persons with severe disabilities, but even among persons with mild and moderate mental retardation, the incidence of language disability is significantly higher than in the general population (Langone, 1992). Consequently, the use of rebus programs with persons with mild and moderate disabilities would have to be approached cautiously. Additionally, pictographic systems, because they are artificial, distinct from real life print, and found only in instructional settings, are not reinforced by the print that occurs in the learners' noninstructional environments (Moores, 1980).

Alternative Pictorial Literacy Programs

There are pictorial literacy programs that do not use rebus symbols and that encourage learners to extract information from pictures.

These alternative programs make less assumptions about learners' language development than the rebus programs. Additionally, the probability can be increased that skills developed in these alternative pictorial literacy programs will transfer beyond the classroom.

As an example, persons can be taught to solve simple literacy problems with the illustrations in books or magazines. The following list contains a hypothetical set of skills that might be suitable for some learners (Giordano, 1984).

1. Identify persons in illustrations.
2. Identify familiar objects in illustrations.
3. Identify characteristics of persons (e.g., gender, height, or weight).
4. Assign objects to categories (e.g., edibility, shape, or texture).
5. Group persons into categories (e.g., firefighters or children).
6. Group objects into categories (e.g., tools, utensils, or appliances).
7. Identify actions of persons (e.g., bending over, running, or sitting).
8. Identify actions associated with objects (e.g., falling, tilting, or spilling).
9. Identify emotions associated with facial expressions, body posture, or the general mood of a scene.
10. Supply words that explain an interrelated set of illustrations.

The set of pictorial literacy skills with which adult learners would be instructed should be tailored to the individual needs and aptitudes of those learners. When one compares alternative pictorial literacy programs with rebus programs, an immediate disadvantage becomes apparent. Alternative pictorial literacy programs, which are less structured than rebus programs, may not be suitable for learners who respond well to highly structured learning routines. Nonetheless, pictorial literacy programs have several benefits. For example, even though the programs are comparatively informal, they can still encompass a comprehensive set of reading skills. The following additional advantages might persuade some instructors to employ alternative pictorial literacy programs:

- Any printed materials that contain illustrations can be used.
- Any illustrated materials that learners find motivating can be used.
- Adult learners who cannot read the actual words in books, magazines, or manuals could develop enhanced self-esteem

after using printed materials for which they have positive associations.

- As a result of developing sensitivity to illustrations, learners might become responsive to pictorial signs in work environments, such as safety warnings or procedural directions.
- Skills can be fostered that generalize to the illustrated materials that surround adult learners in their communities.

Programs That Emphasize Global Features of Printed Materials

If learners respond positively to pictorial literacy programs, the programs might be expanded to encompass skills based on simple and straightforward features of books, magazines, or manuals. For example, without being able to read the titles of books, adult learners could still become aware that there are titles and that these titles occur in predictable positions within books. The following list contains a hypothetical scope and sequence of skills based on global features of printed materials. These skills could supplement or follow a pictorial literacy program (Giordano, 1984).

1. Learners examine a book (or manual or magazine), holding the book right side up.
2. Learners recognize the occurrences of irregularities in a book (e.g., they recognize that a portion of a page has been ripped away or that an inkblot occurs prominently on a page).
3. Learners turn pages from right to left.
4. Learners demonstrate awareness of major sections of a book (e.g., they recognize the beginning, middle, and end).
5. Learners demonstrate awareness of page numbers.
6. Learners locate the title of a book.
7. Learners locate the author's name on the cover or title sheet of a book.
8. Learners locate a page on which an illustration occurs.
9. Learners differentiate realistic illustrations from abstract representations (e.g., they differentiate photographs or realistic drawings from maps or technical schemata.)
10. Learners locate the letter with which their name begins when this letter occurs in a prominent position on a page.

Programs that develop sensitivity to global features of printed materials can have benefits comparable to those of pictorial literacy programs. Additionally, such programs can be used with any type of material, irrespective of whether that material contains illustrations. Programs based on global features of printed materials can complement pictorial literacy programs or be bridges to more advanced literacy programs, such as rebus programs or programs that help learners recognize and comprehend words.

Programs That Emphasize Patterned Literacy

If learners are successful in pictorial literacy programs, one can supplement those programs with more challenging activities, such as activities that direct learners' attention to global features of printed materials. But if learners are frustrated by pictorial literacy programs, or if they are marginally successful in such programs, are there less challenging literacy programs available?

Discussing language and literacy development, Pflaum (1986) reviewed research indicating that young, preliterate children pass though stages in which they exhibit the overt actions of readers. Somewhat analogously, nonvocal learners pass frequently through developmental stages in which they devise techniques to substitute for speech (Harris, 1976). Patterned literacy activities, in which learners are encouraged to manifest the overt behaviors associated with reading, can occupy a comparable position in the literacy learning of persons with severe disabilities.

For example, when learners with different levels of abilities are grouped together for vocational training, the readers in the group may be given books. These learners will be expected to complete activities with those books. But the nonreaders can also be given books. As the readers interact with the materials, they will exhibit specific behaviors, such as intermittently opening and closing their books, turning pages, pointing to words, or examining illustrations. In patterned literacy programs, the nonreaders would be encouraged to pattern these overt behaviors that are associated with reading.

When interactions with printed materials take place in meaningful contexts, seemingly superficial interactions can form a base on which subsequent functional reading skills may be built. But even when programs do not lead to functional reading skills, patterned literacy programs can have other benefits.

- Patterned literacy programs develop generalization skills by exposing learners to printed materials in novel locations.

- Patterned literacy activities call the attention of learners to the functional problems for which printed materials can be solutions.
- Patterned literacy activities enhance the self-concepts of learners with severe disabilities.
- Patterned literacy activities promote social interaction among learners with severe disabilities.
- Patterned literacy activities promote social interaction between learners with severe disabilities and those with less severe disabilities.

Programs That Emphasize Print in the Environment

Literacy programs for persons with severe disabilities may attempt to focus learners' attention to print that appears with high frequency in the environment. These programs are patterned after a "milieu approach" to oral language instruction in which the generalization of oral language skills to functional situations is emphasized (Hart & Rogers-Warren, 1978). Woolcock (1990) illustrated strategies to promote the generalization of career skills among persons with traumatic brain injury. He reviewed literature about learners' ability to generalize after on-site and simulated vocational training. He concluded that both instructional models could be effective if they encompassed aspects of the learners' environments that were functional and recurring.

Examples of focal words for programs that emphasize print in the environment might include *MEN, WOMEN, STOP, EXIT*, and *DANGER*. Other focal words could be drawn from food products, restaurants, buildings, or stores with which learners were familiar. The precise words that were designated for instruction with specific learners would vary, based on the personal experiences of those learners, their interests, and the print that they encountered in their surroundings. The assumption of this approach is that print in the environment will reinforce the learning of the words with which students are instructed.

A program based on this approach can help adult learners perceive the functional purposes of print and the functional goals of reading. Additionally, it may result in awareness of the meaning of specific printed words. For example, learners with severe disabilities who are unable to recognize the 26 letters of the alphabet may still be able to recognize 26 high-frequency words in their environments. The learning of high-frequency words is facilitated by the recurrent exposure to the words and by the association of those words with distinctive contextual features.

As an example of a distinctive contextual feature, the association of *STOP* with a red octagon facilitates recognition of that word. The same would be true for the word *POISON* when it is linked with a skull and crossed bones. Because of the distinctive manner in which some words are formed, the names of fast food restaurants (such as *McDonalds*) or packaged cereals (such as *Cheerios*) can be recognized holistically by adult learners who cannot recognize letters presented in isolated, non-meaningful contexts.

Labeling Programs

If adults begin to recognize distinctively printed and formatted words from their environments, the words they have learned can be rewritten without the distinctive contextual clues. The distinctively printed words can then be paired with the rewritten version of those words in a learning exercise.

For example, the word *STOP*, displayed against a red octagon, could be paired with the same word, composed of nondistinctive letters and excluding the contextual clues. The goal of such activities would be to help learners discriminate words presented without contextual cues.

If learners were successful with this type of activity, one might label items not linked with signs. For example, large cards with the words *DESK* and *DOOR* can be attached to those items. These cards can be incorporated into activities intended to develop learners' awareness of the words. The immediate goal of such activities would be for learners to demonstrate awareness of the signs fixed to items. A more advanced goal might be for learners to solve problems in which they had to discriminate the words on the signs. For example, they might be challenged to match a sign that they were given with the appropriate sign from a set of several that had been placed on items about a room. Long-range instructional goals might be to recognize, verbalize, and comprehend the words on the signs. In vocational oriented literacy programs, labeling activities of this sort might enable learners to develop new capacities for accessing tools, appliances, or physical facilities related to their jobs.

Augmentative and Alternative Communication

When individuals with disabilities fail at learning tasks, there may be a tendency among some educators to dismiss those tasks as beyond the aptitudes of those learners. Sharpton and West (1992) proposed a three-tier approach to instruction. The first tier is direct instruction of the learning task. If the learners are not successful, the second tier is the adaptation of the learning task. In the third tier, learners are assisted with those portions of the task that are responsible for their frustration. One would progress through the final two tiers of instruction only if learners were not successful at the direct learning in the first tier.

All of the approaches that have been described in this chapter can be thought of as adaptations of traditional literacy instruction for learners who have not responded to such instruction. However, augmentative and alternative communication can be a distinct avenue for assisting learners to communicate. If one views alternative and augmentative communication as a type of artificial intelligence, then the depiction of technology-facilitated learning as the exemplar of assisted learning seems plausible (Maddux, 1993).

Augmentative and alternative communication systems can be viewed along a spectrum that spans high technology to instructor-created devices (Alliance for Technology Access, 1994; Church & Glennen, 1992). As such, augmentative and alternative communication devices can be thought of as distinct formats for instruction that can complement the instructional goals of literacy programs for learners with severe disabilities.

An unsophisticated device might be a lap tray with pictures on it. Learners with limited language ability could point to the pictures to communicate. High technology systems employ microcomputers with software that enable the user to produce printed words or electronically synthesized speech. Although the computerized devices can require proficiency with a keyboard, the technology that is most appropriate for learners with severe disabilities employs pictures, symbols, or single letters.

Since these devices are designed to develop or enhance conversational abilities, the selection of pictures, symbols, or letters is determined by this goal. However, just as writing instruction nurtures the development of emerging reading skills, these devices can provide an opportunity for nurturing reading skills.

For example, persons may be using pictorial, communication boards on which there are symbols and matched letters. The symbols are usually abbreviated, line drawings with a letter, word, or phrase next to each. A picture of hands reaching for a block could be associated with the word *get*. But this pictorial symbol and word could be manipulated to emphasize literacy skills as well as oral communication skills. For example, the instructor might initially pair pictures that are large with words that are smaller. The ratio of the size of the picture to the size of the word could be manipulated progressively so as to channel the learners' attention to the words.

There are other ways that the design of an augmentative and alternative communication system can reinforce literacy learning. The writing of messages can incorporate the sequencing of two key strokes on a computerized device. The first key stroke could be a picture and the second key stroke could be a single letter associated with that picture. For example to send the message that *I want to wear my belt*, the first key stroke could be a picture indicating clothing. The next stroke could be the letter *b*. As a result of such activities, learners may associate the initial letters of written words with those actual words.

There are many opportunities to design interactive, literacy rich activities through augmentative and alternative communication devices. For example, persons using these devices could choose a symbol to complete a phrase or sentence in a book. As a long-range goal, learners might begin to "write" by pointing to symbols that would be transcribed by a listener or that would be recorded by a computer. Table 13–1 contains an explanation of opportunities for developing ini-

Table 13–1   Literacy Programs for Adult Learners With Severe Disabilities

Patterned Literacy	Adult learners pattern behaviors associated with reading (such as holding a book or newspaper, turning pages, or writing responses).
Pictorial Literacy	Adult learners gather information and solve problems using the illustrations in printed materials (such as magazines, books, newspapers, and pamphlets).
Global Features of Printed Materials	Adult learners gather information and solve problems using predictable features or sections of printed materials (such as table of contents, index, pagination, or captions for illustrations).
Print in the Environment	Adult learners recognize words that are linked to predictable situations or items in their surroundings (such as *STOP, EXIT, POISON*, or names of packaged products).
Rebus	Adult learners recognize pictorial symbols that have replaced the words in sentences.
Augmentative and Alternative Communication	Adult learners associate pictorial images with letters, using simple devices (such as pictures matched with their beginning letters) or technologically sophisticated devices (such as key boards linked to computers that produce simulated speech).

tial literacy skills with augmentative and alternative communication devices. The table also identifies the opportunities associated with other literacy programs for persons with severe disabilities. Table 13-2 contains information about assistive technology that could be the basis for literacy instruction as well as speech and language assistance.

Table 13-2   Examples of Augmentative and Alternative Communication Devices That Can Be the Pretext for Developing Limited Literacy Skills

ALPHA TALKER

Description: A low-cost communication aid that is easy to use.

Technical information: 4, 8, and 32 key location overlay options; digitized speech; weighs 2.14 lbs.; dimensions 13 3/4" × 8 1/4" × 2 1/4"; rechargeable battery.

Manufacturer: Prentke Romich; 1-800-262-1990; approximate cost: $1095.00

CANON COMMUNICATOR

Description: Reasonably priced, small alphanumeric keyboard that produces printed output on a built-in strip tape printer.

Technical information: 26 alphabet keys; digitized speech; built-in written output; controllable volume; weighs approximately 1 lb.; 5" × 7" dimensions; rechargeable battery.

Manufacturer: Canon; 1-214-830-9600; approximate price range: $850.00-1,100.00.

DIGIVOX

Description: Portable computer with programmable keyboard layout.

Technical information: 1-48 key layout variations; digitized speech; message accessed by topic, spell patterns, or pictures; ability to be connected to larger computers, ability to store speech to a disk; weighs 3.8 lbs.; dimensions 11.625" × 8.875" × 1.87"; rechargeable battery.

Manufacturer: Sentient Systems Technology; 1-800-344-1778; approximate price range: $2,150.00-2,995.00.

DYNAVOX

Description: A portable augmentative communication device with changeable picture symbol screens.

Technical information: 1-60 key layout variations; synthesized speech; variety of voice options; printer may be connected for written output; weighs 10.5 lbs.; dimensions 13 3/4" × 10 3/8" × 3 3/4"; rechargeable battery.

Manufacturer: Sentient Systems Technology; 1-800-344-1778; approximate price range: $4,495.00-5,540.00.

LIBERATOR

Description: A portable system with speech and a small paper printer. The system can be accessed through direct selection, head master, joysticks, and single switches. It includes a calculator, notebook, and scratch pad.

(continued)

Table 13–2 *(continued)*

Technical information: 8, 32, or 128 key overlay options; synthesized speech; several voice options; built-in printer; includes notebook, scratch pad, and calculator; weighs 7 lbs. 14 oz.; dimensions; 13.2" × 10.9" × 3"; volume control; rechargeable battery.

Manufacturer: Prentke Romich; 1–800–262–1990; approximate price range: $7,345.00–8,390.00.

LIGHT TALKER

Description: Portable communication aid with 26 different access methods including light pointer, Morse code, and joystick. It can access any computer through a keyboard emulator. Recent models feature digitized speech output.

Technical information: 8, 32, or 128 key location overlay options; different models can use synthesized speech or digitized speech; weighs approximately 6 lbs.; dimensions 13" × 8 7/8" × 3 1/2"; rechargeable battery.

Manufacturer: Prentke Romich; 1–800–262–1990; approximate price range: $5,170.00–5,895.00.

MACAW

Description: A small system with 2 minutes of digitized speech output.

Technical information: 2, 4, 8, 16, or 32 key location overlay options; 32 symbols can be customized for the user; digitized speech output; weighs 2.7 lbs.; dimensions 11 1/2" × 7 3/4" × 2 1/2"; rechargeable battery.

Manufacturer: Zygo; 1–800–234–6006; approximate price range: $1,150.00–1,795.00.

MESSAGEMATE 20 or 40

Description: A small, reasonably priced, lightweight device with recording capability. Since the messages are recorded, it can incorporate any language, sound, or voice.

Technical information: Model 20 has 1, 2, 5, or 20 key overlay options; Model 40 has 1, 2, 4, 10, or 40 key overlay options; digitized speech; weighs 1 3/4 lbs.; dimensions 11 3/4" × 3" × 1 1/4"; rechargeable battery.

Manufacturer: Words+; 1–800–869–8521; approximate price range: $499.00–999.00.

PARROT

Description: A small, reasonably priced, portable communication system than allows up to 16 brief messages to be recorded.

Technical information: 16 keys; digitized speech output; weighs 3 lbs.; dimensions 5 1/4" × 4" × 1 1/2"; rechargeable battery.

Manufacturer: Zygo; 1–800–234–6006; approximate price range: $750.00–850.00.

REAL VOICE

Description: A portable communication aid that has human-voice-quality and a built-in printer.

(continued)

Table 13–2 *(continued)*

Technical information: Digitized speech; weighs 12 lbs.; dimensions 15 1/2" × 10" × 3"; rechargeable battery.

Manufacturer: Adaptive Communication Systems; 1–800–262–1990; approximate price range: $ 5,170.00–5,895.00.

SPEAKEASY

Description: A low-cost communication device that stores up to 12 messages with a total recording time of 2 minutes.

Technical information: 12 keys with 2 minutes recording time for each key; weighs approximately 3 lbs.; dimensions 8" × 6" × 3"; rechargeable battery.

Manufacturer: Able Net; 1–800–322–0956; approximate cost is $365.00.

SYSTEM 2000

Description: A comprehensive communication system including computer, voice synthesizer, and input device.

Technical information: 1–32 key overlay variations; synthesized speech; weighs 10.7 lbs; dimensions 11 3/4" × 9 1/2" × 2 1/4"; rechargeable battery.

Manufacturer: Words+; 1–800–869–8521; approximate price range: $5,873.00–8,435.00.

TOUCH TALKER

Description: A portable communication system that can encode words, phrases, and sentences that have been customized for the user. Printed output appears on an LCD screen.

Technical information: 8, 32, or 128 key location overlay options; synthesized speech; weighs approximately 6 lbs.; dimensions 13" × 8 7/8" × 3 1/2"; rechargeable battery.

Manufacturer: Prentke Romich; 1–800–262–1990; approximate price range: $5,170.00–5,895.00.

VOIS 160

Description: A communication system with customized text. A two-line LCD display shows all text entries.

Technical information: 8, 24, or 104 key location options; synthesized speech; standard keyboard; contains pre-stored vocabulary and opportunity for storing user-created messages; printer may be connected for written output; weighs 5 lbs. 8 oz.; dimensions 16 1/2" × 8 3/4" × 3 1/4"; rechargeable battery.

Manufacturer: Phonic Ear; 1–800–227–0735; approximate cost: $4,352.00.

WOLF

Description: A low-cost communication aid built into a "Touch and Tell" case. It can be programmed by the user with up to 800 words. Preprogrammed vocabulary is also available.

Technical information: 1 to 36 key options; synthesized speech; weighs 6 lbs.; dimensions 10" × 14" × 2"; rechargeable battery.

Manufacturer: Wayne County RESA; 1–313–467–1610; approximate price range: $400.00–450.00

Summary

Literacy activities can be adapted for adult learners with severe problems. Several types of programs were reviewed: patterned literacy, pictorial literacy, global features of printed materials, print in the environment, and labeling. Pictorially based literacy programs, which may involve illustrations or rebus symbols, can be formatted to assist persons who are using augmentative and alternative communication devices.

These programs can be viewed progressively as a ladder of literacy opportunities for persons with severe disabilities. Another attractive feature of these programs is that, with the exception of the rebus program, they do not assume that adult learners have extensive language development. As such, the programs can be appropriate for many persons with severe learning disabilities who would be unsuccessful in other literacy programs. And because these activities do not require extremely structured drills or restrictive materials, they can be implemented in the context of functional, on-site, field-based instruction. Finally, these literacy activities, because they rely on stimuli that surround learners in their environments, foster generalized learning.

References

ACTV (1995). *Entering the world of work*. New York: Author.

Ada, A. F. (1986). Creative education for bilingual teachers. *Harvard Education Review, 56*, 386–394.

Aiken, L. R. (1985). *Psychological testing and assessment*. Boston, MA: Allyn & Bacon.

Alexis-Ford, B. (1995). African American community involvement processes and special education: Essential networks for effective education. In B. A. Ford, F. E. Obiakor, & J. M. Patton (Eds.), *Effective education of African American exceptional learners: New perspectives* (pp. 235–272). Austin, TX: PRO-ED.

Algozzine, B. (1991). Decision making and curriculum-based assessment. In B. Y. L. Wong (Ed.), *Learning about learning disabilities* (pp. 39–58). San Diego, CA: Academic Press.

Allaire, J. H., & Miller, J. M. (1983). Nonspeech communication. In M. E. Snell (Ed.), *Systematic instruction of the moderately and severely handicapped* (2nd ed., pp. 289–313). Columbus, OH: Merrill.

Allen, R. V. (1986). Developing contexts to support second language acquisition. *Language Arts, 63*, 61–66.

Alliance for Technology Access. (1994). *Computer resources for people with disabilities: A guide to exploring today's assistive technology*. Alameda, CA: Hunter House.

Alpern, G. D. (1967). Measurement of "untestable" autistic children. *Journal of Abnormal Psychology, 72*, 478–486.

Alvermann, D. E., & Phelps, S. F. (1994). *Content reading and literacy: Succeeding in today's diverse classrooms*. Needham Heights, MA: Allyn & Bacon.

Ament, R. R. (1987). *Collaboration in adult education: Overview.* Columbus, OH: Clearinghouse on Adult, Career, and Vocational Education. (ERIC Document Reproduction Service No. ED 282 091)

American Guidance Service. (1985). *Kaufman test of educational achievement.* Circle Pines, MN: American Guidance Service.

American Library Association (1990). *First steps to literacy—Library programs for parents, teachers, and caregivers.* Chicago: Author.

Americans with Disabilities Act of 1990, Pub. L. No. 101-336, (Codified at 42 U. S. C. A. Sec. 12101), 104 stat. 328 (1991).

Anastasi, A. (1981). Coaching, test sophistication, and developed abilities. *American Psychologist, 36,* 1086–1093.

Anastasi, A. (1982). *Psychological testing* (5th ed.). New York: Macmillan.

Anders, P. L. (1981). Test review: Tests of Functional Literacy. *Journal of Reading, 24,* 612–619.

Anderson, B. V, & Barnitz, J. G. (1984). Cross-cultural schemata and reading comprehension instruction. *Journal of Reading, 28,* 102–108.

Anderson, D. J. (1993). Health Issues. In E. Sutton, A. R. Factor, B. A. Hawkins, T. Heller, & G. B. Seltzer (Eds.), *Older adults with developmental disabilities: Optimizing choice and change* (pp. 29–48). Baltimore: Brookes.

Anderson, J. (1991). *Technology and adult literacy.* New York: Routledge.

Anderson, J. A. (1988, January-February). Cognitive styles and multicultural populations. *Journal of Teacher Education,* 2–9.

Angle, D. K., & Buxton, J. M. (1991). *Community living skills workbook for the head injured adult.* Gaithersburg, MD: Aspen.

Archer, L. (1977) Blissymbols—A nonverbal communication system. *Journal of Speech and Hearing Disorders, 42,* 568–579.

Aronowitz, S. (1981). Toward redefining literacy. *Social Policy, 12,* 53–55.

Artensani, A. J., Itkonen, T., Fryxell, D., & Woolcock, W. W. (1995). Community instruction. In W. W. Woolcock & J. W. Domaracki (Eds.), *Instructional strategies in the community: A resource guide for community instruction for persons with disabilities* (pp. 1–16). Austin, TX: PRO-ED.

Askov, E. N., & Turner, B. C. (1989, Winter). Using technology for teaching basic skills to adults. *Adult Literacy Special Interest Group Newsletter,* pp. 2–5.

Au, K. H., & Jordan, C. (1981). Teaching reading to Hawaiian children: Analysis of a culturally appropriate instructional event. *Anthropology and Education Quarterly, 11,* 91–115.

Au, K. H., & Mason, J. (1981). Social organizational factors in learning to read: The balance of rights hypothesis. *Reading Research Quarterly, 17*(1), 115–152.

Azarnoff, P. (1983). *Health, illness, and disability: A guide to books for children and young adults.* New York: Bowker.

Baca, L. M., & Cervantes, H. T. (1989). *The bilingual special education interface* (2nd ed.). Columbus, OH: Merrill.

Bailey, L. J. (1985). *Career education for teachers and counselors: A practical approach* (2nd ed.). Cranston, RI: Carroll Press.

Bailey, T. R. (1995). The integration of work and school: Education and the changing workplace. In W. N. Grubb (Ed.), *Education through occupations in American high schools: Approaches to integrating academic and vocational education* (Vol. 1; pp. 26–38). New York: Teachers College Press.

Ballard, L. (1992). Portfolios and self-assessment. *English Journal, 81*(2), 46–48.

Balow, I. H., Farr, R. C., & Hogan, T. P. (1992). *Metropolitan Achievement Test 7.* San Antonio, TX: Psychological Corp.

Banks, J. A. (1989). Multicultural education: Characteristics and goals. In J. A. Banks and C. A. M. Banks (Eds.), *Multicultural education: Issues and perspectives* (pp. 2–26). Boston: Allyn & Bacon.

Banks, J. A. (1994). *An introduction to multicultural education.* Needham Heights, MA: Allyn & Bacon.

Barasovska, J. (1988). *Getting started with experience stories.* Syracuse, NY: New Readers Press.

Barnhardt, C. (1982). Tuning-in: Athabaskan teachers and Athabaskan students. In R. Barnhardt (Ed.), *Cross-cultural issues in Alaskan education* (Vol. 2, pp. 152-158). Fairbanks: Centers for Cross-Cultural Studies, University of Alaska.

Barrs, M. (1990). The Primary Language Record: Reflection of issues in evaluation. *Language Arts, 67,* 244–253.

Barrs, M., Ellis, S., Hester, H., & Thomas, A. (1990). *Patterns of learning: The Primary Language Record and the national curriculum.* London, England: Center for Language in Primary Education.

Bartel, N. R. (1995). Teaching students who have reading problems. In D. D. Hammill & N. R. Bartel (Eds.), *Teaching students with learning and behavior problems: Managing mild-to-moderate difficulties in resource and inclusive settings* (6th ed., pp. 83–150). Austin, TX: PRO-ED.

Baskin, B. H., & Harris, K. H. (1984). *More notes from a different drummer: A guide to juvenile fiction portraying the disabled.* New York: Bowker.

Baskwill, J., & Whitman, P. (1988). *Evaluation: Whole language, whole child.* New York: Scholastic.

Baston, T., & Bergman, E. (Eds.). (1985). *Angels and outcasts: An anthology of deaf characters in literature* (3rd ed.). Washington, DC: Gallaudet.

Bates, P. (1990). Appendix: Best practices and quality transition indicators. In Wehman, P. (Ed.), *Life beyond the classroom: Transition strategies for young people with disabilities* (pp. 91–98). Baltimore: Brookes.

Baumann, J. F. (1988). *Reading assessment: An instructional decision-making perspective.* Columbus, OH: Merrill.

Baumgart, D. (1990). *Career education: A curriculum manual for students with handicaps.* Rockville, MD: Aspen.

Bearden, L. J., Spencer, W. A., & Moracco, J. C. (1989). A study of high school dropouts. *The School Counselor, 37,* 113–120.

Bender, W. N. (1991). *Introduction to learning disabilities: Identification, assessment, and teaching strategies.* Needham Heights, MA: Allyn & Bacon.

Bengtson, V. L., & Schaie, K. W. (Eds.). (1989). *The course of later life: Research and reflections.* New York: Springer.

Benz, M. R., & Halpern, A. S. (1987). Transition services for secondary students with mild disabilities: A statewide perspective. *Exceptional Children, 53,* 507–514.

Berkell, D. E. (1992). Transition issues for secondary school students with autism and developmental disabilities. In F. R. Rusch, L. Destefano, J. Chadsey-Rusch, L. A. Phelps, & E. Szymanski (Eds.), *Transition from school to adult life: Models, linkages, and policy* (pp. 459–472). Sycamore, IL: Sycamore.

Bernazza-Haase, A. M., Robinson, R. D., & Beach, R. (1979). Teaching the aged reader: Issues and strategies. *Educational Gerontology, 4,* 229–237.

Betts, E. A. (1946). *Foundations of reading instruction.* New York: American.

Biniakunu, B. D. (1991). Regenerating African decayed land: Can reading contribute? *Journal of Reading, 35,* 104–107.

Birren, J. E. (1989). My perspective on research on aging. In V. L. Bengtson & K. W. Schaie (Eds.), *The course of later life: Research and reflections* (pp. 135–149). New York: Springer.

Birren, J. E., & Birren, B. A. (1990). The concepts, models, and history of the psychology of aging. In J. E. Birren & K. W. Schaie (Eds.), *Handbook of the psychology of aging* (3rd ed., pp. 3–20). San Diego, CA: Academic Press.

Birren, J. E., & Schaie, K. W. (1990). *Handbook of the psychology of aging* (3rd ed.). San Diego, CA: Academic Press.

Birren, J. E., Woods, A. M., & Williams, M. V. (1980). Behavioral slowing with age: Causes, organization, and consequences. In L. W. Poon (Ed.), *Aging in the 1980s: Psychological issues* (pp. 293–308). Washington, DC: American Psychological Association.

Bishop, M. (1988). Why Johnny's dad can't read. *Policy Review, 40,* 19–25.

Blake, R. (1981, October/November). Disabled older persons: A demographic analysis. *Journal of Rehabilitation,* 19–27.

Bloome, D. (1987). Reading as a social process in a middle school classroom. In D. Bloome (Ed.), *Literacy and schooling* (pp. 123–149). Norwood, NJ: Ablex.

Boyer-Stephens, A. (1991). The vocational connection. In L. L. West (Ed.), *Effective strategies for dropout prevention of at-risk youth* (pp. 99–124), Austin, TX: PRO-ED.

Bradley, V. J., Ashbaugh, J. W., & Blaney, B. C. (Eds.). (1994). *Creating individual supports for people with developmental disabilities: A mandate for change at many levels* . Baltimore: Brookes.

Bratcher, S. (1994). *Evaluating children's writing: A handbook of communication choices for classroom teachers.* New York: St. Martin's.

Brolin, D. (1992). *Life-centered career education.* Reston, VA: Council for Exceptional Children.

Brolin, D. E. (1995). *Career education: A functional life skills approach* (3rd ed.). Englewood Cliffs, NJ: Merrill.

Brolin, D. E., & D'Alonzo B. J. (1979). Critical issues in career education for handicapped students. *Exceptional Children, 45,* 246–253.

Brolin, D. E., & Kokaska, C. J. (1979). *Career education for exceptional children and youth.* Columbus, OH: Merrill.

Brown, A. L. (1980). Metacognitive development and reading. In R. J. Sporo, B. C. Bruce, & W. F. Brewer (Eds.), *Theoretical issues in reading comprehension* (pp. 453–481). Hillsdale, NJ: Erlbaum.

Brown, A. L., Palincsar, A., & Armbruster, B. (1988). Instructing comprehension: Fostering activities in interactive learning situations. In H. Mandl, N. Stein, & T. Trabasso (Eds.), *Learning from texts.* Hillsdale, NJ: Erlbaum.

Brown, F. (1987). Meaningful assessment of people with severe and profound handicaps. In M. E. Snell (Ed.), *Systematic instruction of persons with severe handicaps* (pp. 39–63). Columbus, OH: Merrill.

Brown, F. G. (1983). *Principles of educational and psychological testing* (3rd ed.). New York: Holt, Rinehart, & Winston.

Brown, J. I., Bennett, J. M., & Hanna, G. S. (1981). *The Nelson-Denny Reading Test.* Chicago: Riverside.

Brown, J. M., Joseph, D. F., & Wotruba, J. W. (1989). Factors affecting employers' roles in the school-to-work transition of persons with disabilities. In D. E. Berkell & J. M. Brown (Eds.), *Transition from school to work for persons with disabilities* (pp. 187–226). New York: Longman.

Brown, V. L., Hammill, D. D., & Wiederholt, J. L. (1986). *Test of Reading Comprehension—Revised.* Austin, TX: PRO-ED.

Browning, P., Dunn, C., & Brown, C. (1994). *School to community transition for youth with disabilities.* In R. C. Eaves & P. J. McLaughlin (Eds.), *Recent advances in special education and rehabilitation* (pp. 193–209). Stoneham, MA: Andover.

Buckley, S. (1995). Teaching children with Down syndrome to read and write. In L. Nadel & D. Rosenthal (Eds.), *Down syndrome: Living and learning in the community* (pp. 158–169). New York: Wiley-Liss.

Burke, E. M. (1986). *Early childhood literature: For love of child and book.* Needham Heights, MA: Allyn & Bacon.

Burkhead, E. J. (1992). Computer applications in rehabilitation. In R. Parker & E. Szymanski (Eds.), *Rehabilitation counseling: Basics and beyond* (2nd ed., pp. 365–400). Austin: TX: PRO-ED.

Butler, R. N. (1989). Productive aging. In V. L. Bengtson & K. W. Schaie (Eds.), *The course of later life: Research and reflections* (pp. 55–64). New York: Springer.

Byrd, H. B. (1995). Curricular and pedagogical procedures for African American learners with academic and cognitive disabilities. In B. A. Ford, F. E. Obiakor, & J. M. Patton (Eds.), *Effective education of African American exceptional learners: New perspectives* (pp. 123–150). Austin, TX: PRO-ED.

Cardenas, J. A. (1986). The role of native-language instruction in bilingual education. *Phi Delta Kappan, 67,* 359–363.

Carnine, D., Silbert, J., & Kameenui, E. J. (1990). *Direct instruction reading* (2nd ed.). Columbus, OH: Merrill.

Casanova, U., & Arias, M. B. (1993). Contextualizing bilingual education. In M.B. Arias & U. Casanova (Eds.), *Bilingual education: politics, practice, research* (pp. 1–35). Chicago: University of Chicago Press.

Castaneda, A. (1976). Cultural democracy and the educational needs of Mexican American children. In R. L. Jones (Ed.), *Mainstreaming and the minority child* (pp. 181–214). Reston, VA: Council for Exceptional Children.

Cattell, R. B. (1971). *Abilities: Their structure, growth, and action.* Boston, MA: Houghton Mifflin.

Catterall, J. S. (1986). An intensive group counseling dropout prevention intervention: Some cautions on isolating at–risk adolescents within high schools. *American Educational Research Journal, 24,* 521–540.

Cervero, R. M. (1985). Is a common definition of adult literacy possible? *Adult Education Quarterly, 36,* 50–54.

Chadsey-Rusch, J., & O'Reilly, M. (1992). Social integration in employment and postsecondary educational setting: outcomes and process variables. In F. Rusch, L. Destefano, J. Chadsey-Rusch, L. A. Phelps, & E. Szymanski (Eds.), *Transition from school to adult life: Models, linkages, and policy* (pp. 245–264). Sycamore, IL: Sycamore.

Chall, J. S. (1984). *New views on developing basic skills with adults.* Paper presented at the National Adult Literacy Conference, Washington, DC. (ERIC Document Reproduction Service No. ED 240 299)

Chamberlain, M. A. (1988). Employers' rankings of factors judged critical to job success for individuals with severe disabilities. *Career Development for Exceptional Individuals, 11,* 141–147.

Chan, K. S., & Rueda, R. (1979). Poverty and culture in education: Separate but equal. *Exceptional Children, 45,* 421–428.

Chandler, S. K., Czerlinsky, T., & Wehman, P. (1993). Provisions of assistive technology: Bridging the gap to accessibility. In P. Wehman (Ed.), *The ADA mandate for social change.* (pp. 117–133). Baltimore: Brookes.

Chapman, R. S., & Miller, J. F. (1980). Analyzing language and communication in the child. In R. Schiefelbusch (Ed.), *Nonspeech language and communication: Analysis and intervention* (pp. 159–196). Austin, TX: PRO-ED.

Children's Defense Fund. (1994). *The state of America's children yearbook: 1994.* Washington, DC: Author.

Chisman, F. P. (1989). *Jump start: The federal role in adult literacy* (Final Report of the Project on Adult Literacy). Washington, DC: The Southport Institute for Policy Analysis.

Chisman, F. P. (1990a). Solving the literacy problem in the 1990s: The leadership agenda. In F. P. Chisman (Ed.), *Leadership for literacy: The agenda for the 1990s* (pp. 246–264). San Francisco: Jossey-Bass.

Chisman, F. P. (1990b). Toward a literate America: The leadership challenge. In F. P. Chisman (Ed.), *Leadership for literacy: The agenda for the 1990s* (pp. 1–24). San Francisco: Jossey-Bass.

Chisman, F. P., & Campbell, W. L. (1990). Narrowing the job-skills gap: A focus on workforce literacy. In F. P. Chisman (Ed.), *Leadership for literacy: The agenda for the 1990s* (pp. 1–24). San Francisco: Jossey-Bass.

Christensen, C. P. (1989). Cross-cultural awareness development: A conceptual model. *Counselor Education and Supervision, 28,* 270–287.

Church, G., & Bender, M. (1989). *Teaching with computers: A curriculum for special educators.* Boston, MA: College-Hill.

Church, G., & Glennen, S. (1992). *The handbook of assistive technology.* San Diego, CA: Singular.

Ciborowski, J. (1994). *Textbooks and the students who can't read them: A guide to teaching content.* Cambridge, MA: Brookline.

Ciborowski, J. (1995). Using textbooks with students who cannot read them. *Remedial and special education, 16*(2), 90–101.

Clark, C., Davies, M., & Woodcock, R. (1974). *Standard rebus glossary.* Circle Pines, MN: American Guidance Service.

Clark, C., & Woodcock, R. (1976). Graphic systems of communication. In L. L. Loyd (Ed.), *Communication assessment and intervention strategies* (pp. 549–607). Baltimore: University Park.

Clark, G. M. (1994). Is a functional curriculum approach compatible with an inclusive education model? *Teaching Exceptional Children, 26*(2), 36–39.

Clark, G. M., Carlson, B. C., Fisher, S., Cook, I. D., & D'Alonzo, B. J. (1991). Career development for students with disabilities in elementary schools: A position statement of the Division on Career Development. *Career Education for Exceptional Individuals, 14,* 109–120.

Clark, G. M., Field, S., Patton, J. R., Brolin, D. E., Sitlington, P. L. (1994). Life skills instruction: A necessary component for all students with disabilities—A position statement of the Division on Career Development and Transition. *Career Development for Exceptional Individuals, 17,* 125–134.

Clark, G. M., & Kolstoe, O. P. (1995). *Career development and transition education for adolescents with disabilities* (2nd ed.). Newton, MA: Allyn & Bacon.

Clees, T. (1992). Community living. In P. J. McLauglin & P. Wehman (Eds.), *Developmental disabilities: A handbook for best practices* (pp. 228–267). Stoneham, MA: Andover.

Cloud, N., & Medeiros-Landurand, P. (1989). *Multisystem: Systematic instructional planning for exceptional bilingual students.* Reston, VA: Council for Exceptional Children.

Cochran, P. S., & Bull, G. L. (1993). Computers and individuals with speech and language disorders. In J. D. Lindsey (Ed.), *Computers and exceptional individuals* (2nd ed., pp. 143–158). Austin, TX: PRO-ED.

Collier, C., & Hoover, J. J. (1987). Sociocultural considerations when referring minority children for learning disabilities. *Learning Disabilities Focus, 3*(1), 39–45.

Collins, M. D., & Cheek, E. H. (1993). *Diagnostic-prescriptive reading instruction: A guide for classroom teachers* (4th ed.). Madison, WI: Brown & Benchmark.

Collins, V. L. (1990). *Reader development bibliography* (4th ed.). Philadelphia, PA: Free Library.

Cooper, W., & Brown, B. J. (1992). Using portfolios to empower student writers. *English Journal, 81*(2), 40–45.

Cottone, R., Handelsman, M., & Walters, N. (1986). Understanding the influence of family systems on the rehabilitation process. *Journal of Applied Rehabilitation Counseling, 78*(2), 37–40.

Cronin, M. E., & Patton, J. R. (1993). *Life skills instruction for all students with special needs: A practical guide for integrating real-life content into the curriculum.* Austin, TX: PRO-ED.

Crowley-Weibel, C. (1992). *The library as literacy classroom: A program for teaching.* Chicago: American Library Association.

Cuban, L. (1986). *Teachers and machines: The classroom use of technology since 1920.* New York: Teachers College Press.

Cummins, J. (1984). *Bilingualism and special education: Issues in assessment and pedagogy.* San Diego, CA: College-Hill.

Cunningham, W. R. (1989). Intellectual abilities, speed of response, and aging. In V. L. Bengtson & K. W. Schaie (Eds.), *The course of later life: Research and reflections* (pp. 93–106). New York: Springer.

Dagostino, L., & Carifio, J. (1994). *Evaluative reading and literacy: A cognitive view.* Needham Heights, MA: Allyn & Bacon.

Davey, B. (1983). Think aloud: Modeling the cognitive process of reading comprehension. *Journal of Reading, 37,* 104–112.

Davidson, J., & Koppenhaver, D. (1993). *Adolescent literacy: What works and why* (2nd ed.). New York: Garland.

Deegan, J., & Brooks, N. A. (Eds.). (1985). *Women and disability: The double handicap.* New Brunswick, NJ: Transaction.

De Fina, A. A., Anstendig, L. L., & De Lawter, K. (1991). Alternative integrated reading/writing assessment and curriculum design. *Journal of Reading, 34,* 354–359.

DeSanti, R. J. (1979). Cue system utilization among older readers. *Educational Gerontology, 4,* 271–279.

DeStefano, L., & Wermuth, T. R. (1992). IDEA (P.L.101-476): Defining a second generation of transition services. In F. R. Rusch, L. DeStefano, J. Chadsey-Rusch, L. A. Phelps, & E. Szymanski (Eds.), *Transition from school to adult life: Models, linkages, and policy* (pp. 537–549). Sycamore, IL: Sycamore.

Dever, R. B. (1988). *Community living skills.* Washington, DC : American Association of Mental Retardation.

Dever, R. B. (1989). A taxonomy of community living skills. *Exceptional Children, 55,* 395–404.

Diaz-Lefebvre, R. (1990). The Hispanic adult learner in a rural community college. In B. B. Cassara (Ed.), *Adult education in a multicultural society* (pp. 211–231). New York: Routledge.

Dittmann-Kohli, F., & Baltes, P. B. (1986). Towards a neo-functionalist conception of adult intellectual development: Wisdom as a prototypical case of intellectual growth. In C. Alexander & E. Langer (Eds.), *Beyond formal operations: Alternative endpoints to human development* (pp. 107–156). New York: Oxford.

Dougherty, P. M., & Radomski, M. V. (1993). *The cognitive rehabilitation workbook: A dynamic assessment approach for adults with brain injury.* Gaithersburg, MD: Aspen.

Dubin, F., & Kuhlman, N. A. (1992). The dimensions of cross-cultural literacy: What is cross-cultural literacy? In F. Dubin & N. A. Kuhlman (Eds.). *Cross-cultural literacy: Global perspectives on reading and writing* (pp. v–x). Englewood Cliffs, NJ: Regents.

Dubois, R., Langley, M., & Stass, V. (1977). Assessing severely handicapped children. *Focus on Exceptional Children, 9,* 1–13.

DuBose, R. F. (1978). Assessment of behavioral repertoires of severely impaired persons. *International perspectives on future special education.* Reston, VA: Council for Exceptional Children.

Duran, E. (1992). *Vocational training and employment of the moderately and severely handicapped and autistic adolescent with particular emphasis to bilingual special education.* Springfield, IL: Thomas.

Dutton, D. B. (1985). Socioeconomic status and children's health. *Medical Care, 23,* 142–156.

EBSCO (1990). *EBSCO transition skills centers.* Birmingham, AL: Author.

Edelsky, C. (1991). *With literacy and justice for all.* Philadelphia. PA: Falmer.

Edgar, E. (1987). Secondary programs in special education: Are many of them justifiable? *Exceptional Children, 53,* 555–561.

Eggington, W. (1992). From oral to literature culture: An Australian aboriginal experience. In F. Dubin & N. A. Kuhlman (Eds.), *Cross-cultural literacy: Global perspectives on reading and writing* (pp. 81–98), Englewood Cliffs, NJ: Prentice Hall.

Elbow, P., & Belanoff, P. (1986). Portfolios as a substitute for proficiency examinations. *College Composition and Communication, 37,* 336–339.

Emener, W. (1991). An empowerment philosophy for rehabilitation in the 20th century. *Journal of Rehabilitation, 57*(4), 7–12.

Enright, D. S., & McCloskey, M. (1985). Yes talking!: Organizing the classroom to promote second language acquisition. *TESOL Quarterly, 19,* 431–453.

Erickson, E. H. (1968). *Identity: Youth and crisis.* New York: Norton.

Erickson, F., & Mohatt, G. (1981). Cultural differences in teaching styles in an Odawa school: A sociolinguistic approach. In H. T. Trueba, G. P. Gutherie, & K. H. Au (Eds.), *Culture in the bilingual classroom: Studies in classroom ethnography* (pp. 105–119). Rowley, MA: Newbury House.

Erickson, F., & Mohatt, G. (1982). Cultural organization of participant structures in two classrooms of Indian students. In G. D. Spindler (Ed.), *Doing the ethnography of schooling: Educational anthropology in action* (pp. 132–174). New York: Hold, Rinehart and Winston.

Evers, R. B., & Bursuck, W. (1994). Literacy demands in secondary technical vocational education programs: Teacher interviews. *Career Development for Exceptional Individuals, 17,* 135–143.

Everson, J. M., Burwell, J., & Killam, S. G. (1995). Working and contributing to one's community: Strategies for including young adults who are deaf-blind. In J. M. Everson (Ed.), *Supporting young adults who are deaf-blind in their communities: A transition planning guide for service providers, families, and friends* (pp. 131–158). Baltimore: Brookes.

Eyman, R. K., Grossman, H. J., Tarjan, G., & Miller, C. R. (1987). *Life expectancy and mental retardation.* Washington, DC: American Association on Mental Retardation.

Fabian, E. S., Luecking, R. G., & Tilson, G. P. (1994). *A working relationship: The job development specialist's guide to successful partnerships with business.* Baltimore: Brookes.

Falvey, M. (1986). *Community based curriculum: Educational strategies for students with severe handicaps,* Baltimore: Brookes.

Fantini, M. D. (1986). *Regaining excellence in education.* Columbus, OH: Merrill.

Farr, R., & Carey, R. (1986). *Reading: What can be measured?* Newark, DE: International Reading Association.

Feldblum, C. R. (1991). Employment protections. In J. West (Ed.), *The Americans with Disabilities Act: From policy to practice* (pp. 81–110). New York: Milbank.

Ferguson, P. M., Ferguson, D. L., & Taylor, S. J. (Eds.). (1992). *Interpreting disability: A qualitative reader.* New York: Teachers College Press.

Field, M. L., & Aebersold, J. A. (1990). Cultural attitudes toward reading: implications for teacher of ESL/bilingual readers. *Journal of Reading, 33,* 406–410.

Fillmore, L. W. (1981). Cultural perspectives on second language learning. *TESOL Reporter, 14,* 23–31.

Fine, J. F. (1991). Going high tech: Computerized literacy instruction. *Adult Learning, 1,* 11–14.

Fingeret, H. A. (1990). Changing literacy instruction: Moving beyond the status quo. In F. P. Chisman (Ed.), *Leadership for literacy: The agenda for the 1990s* (pp. 25–50). San Francisco: Jossey-Bass.

Finnegan, R., & Sinatra, R. (1991). Interactive computer-assisted instruction with adults. *Journal of Reading, 35,* 108–116.

Fitzgerald, J. H. (1983). Helping readers gain self-control over reading comprehension. *Reading Teacher, 37,* 249–253.

Flavell, J. H. (1987). Speculations about the nature and development of metacognition. In R. H. Kluwe & F. E. Weinert (Eds.), *Perspective on the development of memory and cognition* (pp. 21–39). Hillsdale, NJ: Erlbaum.

Flores, B., Garcia, E., Gonzalez, S., Hidalgo, G., Kaczmarek, K., & Romero, T. (1985). *Bilingual instructional strategies.* Caramel, CA: Hampton-Brown.

Ford, B. A., & Jones, C. (1990). An ethnic feelings book: Created by students with developmental handicaps. *Teaching Exceptional Children, 22*(4), 36–39.

Foster, S. E. (1990). Upgrading the skills of literacy professionals: The profession matures. In F. P. Chisman (Ed.), *Leadership for literacy: The agenda for the 1990s* (pp. 73–95). San Francisco: Jossey-Bass.

Fowler, A. E., Doherty, B. J., & Boynton, L. (1995). Basis of reading skill in young adults with Down syndrome. In L. Nadel & D. Rosenthal (Eds.), *Down syndrome: Living and learning in the community* (pp. 182–196). New York: Wiley-Liss.

Fox, B. J., & Fingeret, A. (1984). Test review: Reading Evaluation Adult Diagnosis (revised). *Journal of Reading, 28,* 258–261.

Fox, L. C., & Weaver, F. L. (1981). Minimal competency testing: Issues & options. *Academic Therapy, 16,* 425–434.

Frase, M. J. (1989). *Dropout rates in the United States: 1988.* Washington, DC: National Center for Educational Statistics.

Freeman, Y., & Freeman, D. (1992). *Whole language for second language learners.* Portsmouth, NH: Heinemann.

French, J. (1987). *Adult literacy: A source book and guide.* New York: Garland.

Friedberg, J. B., Mullins, J. B., & Weir-Sudiennik, A. (1992). *Portraying persons with disabilities: An annotated bibliography of nonfiction for children and teenagers.* New Providence, NJ: Bowker.

Friere, P., & Macedo, D. (1988) *Literacy: Reading the word and the world.* New York: Routledge.

Froese, V. (1991). Assessment: Form and function. In V. Froese (Ed.), *Whole-language: Practice and theory* (pp. 283–311). Needham Heights, MA: Allyn & Bacon.

Fuchs, L. S., & Fuchs, D. (1990). Traditional academic assessment: An overview. In R. A. Gable & J. M. Hendrickson (Eds.), *Assessing students with special needs: A sourcebook for analyzing and correcting errors in academics* (pp. 1–13). White Plains, NY: Longman.

Fuller, J. W., & Whealon, T. O. (1979). *Career education: A lifelong process.* Chicago: Nelson-Hall.

Gaffney, J. S., & Anderson, R. C. (1991). Two-tiered scaffolding: Congruent processes of teaching and learning. In E. H. Hiebert (Ed.), *Literacy for a diverse society* (pp. 184–198). New York: Teachers College Press.

Gajar, A. H. (1992). University-based models. In F. R. Rusch, L. Destefano, J. Chadsey-Rusch, L. A. Phelps, & E. Szymanski (Eds.), *Transition from school to adult life: Models, linkages, and policy* (pp. 51–70). Sycamore, IL: Sycamore.

Gajar, A., Goodman, L., & McAfee, J. (1993). *Secondary schools and beyond: Transition of Individuals with mild disabilities.* New York: Merrill.

Garner, R., Alexander, P. A., & Hare, V. C. (1991). Reading comprehension failure in children. In B. Y. L. Wong (Ed.), *Learning about learning disabilities* (pp. 283–307). San Diego, CA: Academic Press.

Gartland, D. (1995). Reading instruction. In P. J. Schloss, M. A. Smith, & C. N. Schloss (Eds.), *Instructional methods for adolescents with learning and behavior problems* (2nd ed., pp. 225–254). Needham Heights, MA: Allyn & Bacon.

Gerber, P. J., & Reiff, H. B. (1994). *Learning disabilities in adulthood: Persisting problems and evolving issues.* Stoneham, MA: Andover.

Gerry, M. H., & Minsky, A. J. (1992). Guiding principles for public policy on natural supports. In J. Nisbet (Ed.), *Natural supports in school, at work, and in the community for people with severe disabilities* (pp. 341–346). Baltimore: Brookes.

Gillespie, E. B., & Lieberman, L. M. (1983). Individualizing minimum competency testing for learning disabled students. *Journal of Learning Disabilities, 16,* 565–566.

Gilligan, C. (1982). *In a different voice: Psychological theory and women's development.* Cambridge, MA: Harvard.

Gilligan, C., Murphy, J. M., & Tappan, M. B. (1990). Moral development beyond adolescence. In C. N. Alexander & E. J. Langer (Eds.), *Higher stages of human development: Perspectives on adult growth* (pp. 235–286). New York: Oxford.

Giordano, G. (1984). *Teaching writing to learning disabled students.* Austin, TX: PRO-ED.

Giordano, G. (1988). *Reading Comprehension Inventory.* Bensenville, IL: Scholastic Testing Service.

Giordano, G. (1993). *Diagnostic and remedial mathematics in special education.* Springfield, IL: C. C. Thomas.

Glazer, J. I. (1986). *Literature for young children* (2nd ed.). Columbus, OH: Merrill.

Glazer, S. M. (1992). *Reading comprehension: Self-monitoring strategies to develop independent readers.* New York: Scholastic.

Glazer, S. M., & Burke, E. M. (1994). *An integrated approach to early literacy: Literature to language.* Needham Heights, MA: Allyn & Bacon.

Gollnick, D. M., & Chinn, P. C. (1990). *Multicultural education in a pluralistic society* (3rd ed.). New York: Macmillan.

Goodman, K., Goodman, Y., & Hood, W. (1988). *The whole language evaluation book.* Portsmouth, NH: Heinemann.

Gould, R. L. (1978). *Transformations: Growth and change in adult life.* New York: Simon & Schuster.

Graham, C. R., & Cookson, P. S. (1990). Linguistic minorities and adult education in the United States. In B. B. Cassara (Ed.), *Adult education in a multicultural society* (pp. 45–62). New York: Routledge.

Green, M. L. (1989). Methods for teaching non-English speaking adults. *Adult Learning, 10,* 25–26.

Greenfield, L., & Noguiera, F. (1980). Reading should be functional: The APL approach. In L. Johnson (Ed.), *Reading and the adult learner* (pp. 37–52). Newark, DE: International Reading Association.

Grubb, W. N. (1995). Resolving the paradox of the high school. In W. N. Grubb (Ed.), *Education through occupations in American high schools: Approaches to integrating academic and vocational education* (Volume 1; pp. 1–10). New York: Teachers College Press.

Guendelman, S. (1985). At risk: Health needs of Hispanic children. *Health and Social Work, 10,* 183–190.

Guthrie, J. T., & Kirsch, I. S. (1984). The emergent perspective on literacy. *Phi Delta Kappan, 65,* 351–355.

Gutkin, T. B., & Curtis, M. J. (1982). School-based consultation: Theory and techniques. In C. R. Reynolds & T. B. Gutkin (Eds.), *The handbook of school psychology* (pp. 796–828). New York: Wiley.

Hagerty, P. (1992). *Readers' workshop: Real reading.* New York: Scholastic.

Halloran, W. D. (1993). Transition services requirement: Issues, implications, challenge. In R. D. Eaves & P. J. McLaughlin (Eds.), *Recent advances in special education and rehabilitation* (pp. 210–224). Stoneham, MA: Andover.

Halpern, A. S. (1985). Transition: A look at the foundations. *Exceptional Children, 51,* 479–486.

Halpern, A. S. (1993). Quality of life as a conceptual framework for evaluating transition outcomes. *Exceptional Children, 59,* 486–498.

Halpern, A. S. (1994). The transition of youth with disabilities to adult life: A position statement of the Division on Career Development and Transition, the Council for Exceptional Children. *Career Development for Exceptional Individuals, 17,* 115–124.

Hamilton, S. F. (1986). Raising standards and reducing dropout rates. *Teachers College Record, 87,* 410–429.

Hammill, D. D., Brown, L., Bryant, B. R. (1992). *A consumer's guide to tests in print* (2nd ed.). Austin, TX: PRO-ED.

Hannaford, A. E. (1993). Computers and exceptional individuals. In J. D. Lindsey (Ed.), *Computers and exceptional individuals* (2nd ed., pp. 3–26). Austin, TX: PRO-ED.

Harman, D. (1986). If everyone can read, why are there so many illiterates? In A. Skagen (Ed.), *Workplace literacy* (pp. 13–21). New York: American Management Association.

Harris, S. L. (1976). Teaching language to nonverbal children—with emphasis on problems of generalization. *Psychological Bulletin, 82,* 565–580.

Harris-Vanderheiden, D. (1977). Blissymbols and the mentally retarded. In G. Vanderheiden & K. Grilley (Eds.), *Non-vocal communication techniques and aids for the severely physically handicapped* (pp. 120–131). Baltimore: University Park.

Harry, B. (1992). *Cultural diversity, families, and the special education system.* New York: Teacher College Press.

Harry, B. (1994). *The disproportionate representation of minority students in special education: Theories and recommendations.* Alexandria, VA: National Association of State Directors of Special Education.

Harry, B. (1995). African American families. In B. A. Ford, F. E. Obiakor, & J. M. Patton (Eds.), *Effective education of African American exceptional learners: New perspectives* (pp. 211–214). Austin, TX: PRO-ED.

Hart, B., & Rogers-Warren, L. (1978). A milieu approach to teaching language. In R. Schiefelbusch (Ed.), *Language intervention strategies* (pp. 193–236). Baltimore: University Park.

Hart, M. U. (1992). *Working and educating for life: Feminist and international perspectives on adult education.* New York: Routledge.

Hasselbring, T. S., & Moore, P. (1990). Computer-based assessment and error analysis. In R. A. Gable & J. M. Hendrickson (Eds.), *Assessing students with special needs: A sourcebook for analyzing and correcting errors in academics* (pp. 102–116). New York: Longman.

Havighurst, R. J. (1961). *Developmental tasks and education.* New York: McKay.

Hawkins, B. A. (1993). Leisure participation and life satisfaction of older adults with mental retardation and Down syndrome. In E. Sutton, A. R. Factor, B. A. Hawkins, T. Heller, & G. B. Seltzer (Eds.), *Older adults with developmental disabilities: Optimizing choice and change* (pp. 141–156). Baltimore: Brookes.

Hayden, M. F., & Abery, B. H. (Eds.). (1994). *Challenges for a service system in transition: Ensuring quality community experiences for persons with developmental disabilities.* Baltimore: Brookes.

Hayes, C., Bahruth, R., & Kessler, C. (1991). *Literacy con carino.* Portsmouth, NH: Heinemann.

Hayes, M. L. (1993). *You don't outgrow it: Living with learning disabilities.* Novato, CA: Academic Therapy.

Heald-Taylor, G. (1986). *Whole language strategies for ESL primary students.* Toronto, Canada: Ontario Institute for Studies in Education.

Heath, S. B. (1983). *Ways with words.* New York: Cambridge University Press.

Heilsel, M., & Gordon, L. (1984). Literacy and social milieu: Reading behavior of the black elderly. *Adult Education Quarterly, 34,* 63–70.

Herber, H. L., & Herber, J. N. (1993). *Teaching in content areas with reading, writing, and reasoning.* Needham Heights, MA: Allyn & Bacon.

Hernstein, R. J. (1982). IQ testing and the media. *The Atlantic Monthly, 16,* 68–74.

Hess, C. (1992). Applications for youth with severe disabilities. In Wehman, P. (Ed.), *Life beyond the classroom: Transition strategies for young people with disabilities* (pp. 261–275). Baltimore: Brookes.

Heumann, J. E. (1993a). A disabled woman's reflections: Myths and realities of integration. In J. A. Racino, P. Walker, S. O'Connor, & S. J. Taylor (Eds.), *Housing, support and community: Choices and strategies for adults with disabilities* (Volume 2, pp. 233–249). Baltimore: Brookes.

Heumann, J. E. (1993b). Social implications for disabled and nondisabled people. In J. L. Crispen (Ed.), *The Americans with Disabilities Act: Its impact on libraries* (pp. 23–26), Chicago: American Library Association.

Hiebert, E. H., & Fisher, C. W. (1991). Task and talk structures that foster literacy. In E. H. Hiebert (Ed.), *Literacy for a diverse society* (pp. 141–156). New York: Teachers College Press.

Higgins, P. C. (1992). *Making disability: Exploring the social transformation of human variation.* Springfield, IL: Thomas.

Hispanic Americans Council on Scientific Affairs. (1991). Hispanic health in the United States. *Journal of the American Medical Association, 265,* 248–252.

Holcomb, C. A. (1981). Reading difficulty of informational materials from a health maintenance organization. *Journal of Reading, 25,* 130–133.

Hooks, B. (1990). *Yearning: Race, gender, and cultural politics.* Boston: South End.

Hoover, H. D., Hieronymous, A. N., Frisbie, D. A., & Dunbar, S. B. (1993). *Iowa test of basic skills.* Chicago: Riverside.

Hopkins, K. D., & Stanley, J. C. (1981). *Educational and psychological measurement and evaluation* (6th ed.). Englewood Cliffs, NJ: Prentice-Hall.

Horn, J. L., & Donaldson, G. (1976). On the myth of intellectual decline in adulthood. *American Psychologist, 31,* 701–719.

Horn, J. L., & Donaldson, G. (1980). Cognitive development II: Adulthood development of human abilities. In O. G. Brim & J. Kagan (Eds.), *Constancy and change in human development* (pp. 445–529). Cambridge, MA: Harvard.

Howell, K. W., Fox, S. L., & Morehead, M. K. (1993). *Curriculum-based evaluation: Teaching and decision making* (2nd ed.). Pacific Grove, CA: Brooks-Cole.

Hoy, C., & Gregg, N. (1994). *Assessment: The special educator's role.* Pacific Grove, CA: Brooks-Cole.

Hoyt, K. B. (1979). Career education for exceptional individuals: Challenges for the future. In C. J. Kokaska (Ed.), *Career futures for exceptional individuals* (pp. 37–43). Reston, VA: Council for Exceptional Children.

Hughes, M. A. (1989). *Poverty in cities.* Washington, DC: National League of Cities.

Hughes, T., & Wehman, P. (1992). Supported employment. In P. J. McLaughlin & P. Wehman (Eds.), *Developmental disabilities: A handbook for best practice* (pp. 184–205). Boston: Andover.

Hultsch, D. F., & Dixon, R. A. (1990). Learning and memory in aging. In J. E. Birren & K. W. Schaie (Eds.), *Handbook of the psychology of aging* (3rd ed., pp. 258–274). San Diego, CA: Academic Press.

Hummel, J. W., & Archer, P. (1993). Implementing the computer concept. In J. D. Lindsey (Ed.), *Computers and exceptional individuals* (2nd ed., pp. 227–249). Austin, TX: PRO-ED.

Hunter, C. S., & Harman, D. (1985). *Adult illiteracy in the United States.* New York: McGraw-Hill.

Huyck, M. H. (1990). Gender differences in aging. In J. E. Birren & K. W. Schaie (Eds.), *Handbook of the psychology of aging* (3rd ed., pp. 124–134). San Diego, CA: Academic Press.

Individuals with Disabilities Education Act of 1990, P.L. 101-476 (1990). Education for All Handicapped Children Act. (EHA), 20 U.S.C. Sections 1400 et seq. and amendments.

Inge, K. J., & Shepherd, J. (1995). Assistive technology applications and strategies for school system personnel. In K. F. Flippo, K. J. Inge, & J. M. Barcus (Eds.), *Assistive technology: A resource for school, work, and community* (pp. 133–166). Baltimore: Brookes.

Irwin, J. W. (1991). *Teaching reading comprehension processes* (2nd ed.). Englewood Cliffs, NJ: Prentice-Hall.

Issacson, S. (1995). Written language. In P. J. Schloss, M. A. Smith, & C. N. Schloss (Eds.), *Instructional methods for adolescents with learning and behavior problems* (2nd ed., pp. 200–224). Needham Heights, MA: Allyn & Bacon.

Jackson, J. S., Antonucci, T. C., & Gibson, R. C. (1990). Cultural, racial, and ethnic minority influences on aging. In J. E. Birren & K. W. Schaie (Eds.), *Handbook of the psychology of aging* (3rd ed., pp. 103–123). San Diego, CA: Academic Press.

Jacobson, R. L. (1993). Computers' role in fight for adult literacy may be stymied by professional problems. *Chronicle of Higher Education, 39*(48), A16–A17.

Jarvis, P. (1983). *Adult and continuing education: theory and practice.* New York: Nichols.

Joe, J. R., & Malach, R. S. (1992). Families with Native American Roots. In E. W. Lynch & M. J. Hanson (Eds.), *Developing cross-cultural competence* (pp. 89–119). Baltimore: Brookes.

Johnson, J. E. (1988). Administrative data management for special education. In J. D. Lindsey (Ed.), *Computers and exceptional individuals* (pp. 229–248). Columbus OH: Merrill.

Jones, E. V. (1981). *Reading instruction for the adult illiterate.* Chicago: American Library Association.

Karlsen, B., & Gardner, E. F. (1985) *Stanford Diagnostic Reading Test.* New York: Harcourt, Brace, Jovanovich.

Kazemac, F. E. (1988). Women and adult literacy: Considering the other half of the house. *Lifelong Learning, 11*, 23–24.

Kearsley, G., Hunter, B., & Furlong, M. (1992). *We teach with technology: New visions for education.* Wilsonville, OR: Franklin-Beedle.

Keefe, D., & Meyer, V. (1991). Teaching adult new readers the whole language way. *Journal of Reading, 35,* 180–183.

Kelly, R. E. (1993). Computers and individuals with sensory impairments. In J. D. Lindsey (Ed.), *Computers and exceptional individuals* (2nd ed., pp. 179–201). Austin, TX: PRO-ED.

Kennedy, K., & Roeder, S. (1975). *Using language experience with adults: A guide for teachers.* Syracuse, NY: New Readers Press.

Kiernan, W. E. (1995). Creative job options: A chance to work. In L. Nadel & D. Rosenthal (Eds.), *Down syndrome: Living and learning in the community* (pp. 276–288). New York: Wiley-Liss.

Kierner, D., & DuBose, R. F. (1974). Assessing the cognitive development of pre-school deaf-blind children. *Education of the Visually Handicapped, 6,* 103–105.

Kingston, A. J. (1979). Reading and the aged: A statement of the problem. *Educational Gerontology, 4,* 205–207.

Kinney, M. A., & Harry, A. L. (1991). An informal inventory for adolescents that assesses the reader, the text, and the task. *Journal of Reading, 34,* 643–647.

Kirsch, I. S., Jungeblut, A, Jenkins, L., & Kolstad, A. (1993). *Adult literacy in America: A first look at the results of the national adult literacy survey.* Washington, DC: National Center for Educational Statistics.

Kivlahan, D. R., Walker, R. D., Donovan, D. M., & Mischke, H. D. (1985). Detoxification recidivism among urban American Indian alcoholics. *American Journal of Psychiatry, 142,* 1467–1470.

Klein, J. (1992). Get me the hell out of here: Supporting people with disabilities to live in their own homes. In J. Nisbet (Ed.), *Natural supports in school, at work, and in the community for people with severe disabilities* (pp. 277–339). Baltimore: Brookes.

Knoll, J. A., & Racino, J. A. (1994). Field in search of a home: The need for support personnel to develop a new identity. In V. J. Bradley, J. W. Ashbaugh, & B. C. Blaney (Eds.), *Creating individual supports for people with developmental disabilities: A mandate for change at many levels* (pp. 299–324). Baltimore: Brookes.

Kokaska, C. J., & Brolin, D. E. (1985). *Career education for handicapped individuals* (2nd ed.). Columbus, OH: Merrill.

Kozol, J. (1985). *Illiterate America.* New York: Doubleday.

Kramer, D. (1983). Post-formal operations? A need for further conceptualization. *Human Development, 26,* 91–105.

Kramer, J. J., & Mitchell, J. V., Jr. (1985). Computer-based assessment and test interpretation: Promises, prospects, and pitfalls. *Computers in Human Behavior, 3 & 4* (special issue).

Kuehn, M. L., & Imm-Thomas, P. (1993). A multicultural context. In E. Sutton, A. R. Factor, B. A. Hawkins, T. Heller, & G. B. Seltzer (Eds.), *Older adults with developmental disabilities: Optimizing choice and change* (pp. 327–343). Baltimore: Brookes.

Lachman, M. E., Steinberg, E. S., & Trotter. S. D. (1987). Effects of control beliefs and attributions on memory self-assessments and performance. *Psychology and Aging, 2,* 266–271.

Lambert, W. E. (1975). Culture and language as factors in learning and education. In A. Wolfgang (Ed.), *Education of immigrant students* (pp. 87-93). Toronto, Canada: Ontario Institute for Studies in Education.

Laminack, L. L. (1989). *Reading with children.* Syracuse, NY: Literacy Volunteers of America.

Landow, G. P. (1992). Hypertext, metatext, and the electronic canon. In M. C. Tuman (Ed.), *Literacy Online: The promise (and peril) of reading and writing with computers* (pp. 67–94). Pittsburgh, PA: University of Pittsburgh.

Langdon, H. W., & Clark, L. W. (1993). Profile of Hispanic/Latino American students. In L. W. Clark & D. E. Waltzman (Eds.), *Faculty and student challenges in facing cultural and linguistic diversity* (pp. 88–113). Springfield, IL: Thomas.

Langone, J. (1992). Mild to moderate mental retardation. In P. J. McLauglin & P. Wehman (Eds.), *Developmental disabilities: A handbook for best practices* (pp. 1–15). Stoneham, MA: Andover.

Lankard, B. A. (1992). *Integrating academic and vocational education: Strategies for implementation.* Columbus, OH: Clearinghouse on Adult, Career, and Vocational Education. (ERIC Document Reproduction Service No. ED 346 317)

Larkin, K. C., Hayden, M. F., & Abery, B. H. (1994). An overview of the community living concept. In M. F. Hayden & B. H. Abery (Eds.), *Challenges for a service system in transition: Ensuring quality community experiences for persons with developmental disabilities* (pp. 3–22). Baltimore: Brookes.

Laslett, P. (1991). *A fresh map of life: The emergence of the third age.* Cambridge, MA: Harvard.

Lengyel, L., & Evans, B. (1995). Measuring behavior. In W. W. Woolcock & J. W. Domaracki (Eds.), *Instructional strategies in the community: A resource guide for community instruction for persons with disabilities* (pp. 137–156). Austin, TX: PRO-ED.

Levine, R. E. (1987). Culture: A factor influencing the outcomes of occupational therapy. *Occupational Therapy in Health Care, 4*(1), 3–16.

Levinson, D., Darrow, C., Klein, E., Levinson, M., & McKee, B. (1978). *The seasons of a man's life.* New York: Ballantine.

LiBretto, E. V. (Ed.). (1990). *High/low handbook: Encouraging literacy in the 1990s* (3rd ed.). New York: Bowker.

Lipson, M. Y., & Wixson, K. K. (1991). *Assessment and instruction of reading disability: An interpretive approach.* New York: Harper-Collins.

Literacy Volunteers of America (1991) *How to add family literacy to your program.* Syracuse, NY: Author.

Loevinger, J. (1976). *Ego development: Conceptions and theories.* San Francisco: Jossey-Bass.

Logue, B. J. (1990). Race differences in long-term disability: Middle-aged and older American Indians, backs and whites in Oklahoma. *The Social Science Journal, 27*, 253–272.

Lombana, J. H. (1992). *Guidance for students with disabilities* (2nd ed.). Springfield, IL: Thomas.

Lovitt, T. (1991). *Preventing school dropouts: Tactics for at-risk, remedial, and mildly handicapped adolescents.* Austin, TX: PRO-ED.

Lubin, R. A., & Kiely, M. (1985). Epidemiology of aging in developmental disabilities. In M. P. Janicki & H. M. Wisniewski (Eds.), *Aging and developmental disabilities: Issues and approaches* (pp. 95–113). Baltimore: Brookes.

Lynch, P. (1986). *Using big books and predictable books.* New York: Scholastic.

Macro Systems (1989). *Social skills on the job.* Circle Pines, MN: American Guidance Service.

Maddux, C. D. (1993). Artificial intelligence and expert systems: What have we learned? In R. C. Eaves & P. J. McLaughlin (Eds.), *Recent advances in special education and rehabilitation* (pp. 142–164). Stoneham, MA: Andover.

Maddy-Bernstein, C., & Coyle-Williams, M. (1995). Addressing diversity in the classroom. In W. N. Grubb (Ed.), *Education through occupations in American high schools: The challenges of implementing curriculum integration* (Vol. 2; pp. 156–170). New York: Teachers College Press.

Majsterek, D. J., & Wilson, R. (1989). Computer-assisted instruction for students with learning disabilities: Considerations for practitioners. *Learning Disabilities Focus, 5*(1), 18–27.

Markwardt, F. C. (1989). *Peabody individual achievement test—Revised.* Circle Pines, MN: American Guidance Service.

Martin, W. E., White, K., Saravanabhavan, R. C., & Carlise, K. (1993). Training programs for working with older American Indians who are visually impaired. *American Rehabilitation, 19*(1), 2–6, 37.

Marzano, R. J., Hargerty, P. J., Valencia, S. W., & DeStefano, P. P. (1987). *Reading diagnosis and instruction: Theory into practice.* Englewood Cliffs, NJ: Prentice-Hall.

Masters, L. F., Mori, B. A., & Mori, A. A. (1993). *Teaching secondary students with mild learning and behavior problems: Methods, materials, strategies* (2nd ed.). Austin, TX: PRO-ED

May, P. A. (1986). Alcohol and drug misuse prevention programs for American Indians: Needs and opportunities. *Journal of Studies on Alcohol, 47,* 187–195.

May, P. A. (1987). Suicide and self-destruction among American Indian youths. *American Indian and Alaska Native Mental Health Research, 1*(1), 52–69.

May, P. A. (1988). Mental health and alcohol abuse indicators in the Albuquerque area of Indian Health Service: An exploratory chart review. *American Indian and Alaska Native Mental Health Research, 2*(1), 33–46.

McAfee, J. (1988). Adult adjustment of individuals with mental retardation. In P. J. Schloss, C. A. Hughes, & M. A. Smith (Eds.), *Mental retardation: Community transition* (pp. 115–162). Boston, MA: College-Hill.

McCleod, J., & Cropley, A. (1989). *Fostering academic excellence.* New York: Pergamon.

McCollum, P. (1991). Cross-cultural perspectives on classroom discourse and literacy. In E. H. Hiebert (Ed.), *Literacy for a diverse society* (pp. 108–121). New York: Teachers College Press.

McDill, E. L., Natriello, G., & Pallas, A. M. (1986). A population at risk: Potential consequences of tougher school standards for student dropouts. *American Journal of Education, 94,* 135–181.

McDonald, E. T. (1977). Design and application of communication boards. In G. Vanderheiden & K. Grilley (Eds.), *Non-vocal communication techniques and aids for the severely physically handicapped* (pp. 105–119). Baltimore: University Park.

McDonnell, J., Wilcox, B., & Hardman, M. L. (1991). *Secondary programs for students with developmental disabilities.* Boston: Allyn & Bacon.

McGraw-Hill. (1993). *The California Achievement Tests: 5.* New York: McGraw-Hill.

McIvor, M. C. (Ed.). (1990). *Family literacy in action: A survey of successful programs.* Syracuse, NY: New Readers Press.

McKee, N. C. (1987). *The depiction of the physically disabled in preadolescent contemporary realistic fiction: A content analysis.* Ann Arbor, MI: University Microfilms International.

McKenna, M. C., & Robinson, R. D. (1993). *Teaching through text.* New York: Longman.

McKinney, J. D. (1983). Performance of handicapped students on the North Carolina minimum competency test. *Exceptional Children, 49,* 547–550.

McLean, L., & McLean, J. (1974). A language training program for nonverbal autistic children. *Journal of Speech and Hearing Disorders, 39,* 186–193.

McNaughton, S., & Kates, B. (1980). The application of Blissymbols. In R. Schiefelbusch (Ed.), *Nonspeech language and communication: Analysis and interpretation* (pp. 303–321). Baltimore: University Park.

McNeil, J. D. (1984). *Reading comprehension: New directions for classroom practice.* Glenview, IL: Scott-Foresman.

McShane, D. (1988). An analysis of mental health research with American Indian youth. *Journal of Adolescence, 11,* 87–116.

Mehrens, W. A., & Lehmann, I. J. (1987). *Using standardized tests in education* (4th ed.). New York: Longman.

Mercado, C., & Romero, M. (1993). Assessment of students in bilingual education. In M. B. Arias & U. Casanova (Eds.), *Bilingual education: Politics, practice, research* (pp. 144–170). Chicago, IL: University of Chicago Press.

Metoyer-Duran, C. (1993). *Gatekeepers in ethnolinguistic communities.* Norwood, NJ: Ablex.

Metz, E. (1989, October). The issue: Adult literacy assessment. *Clearinghouse on Reading and Communication Skills Digest,* 1–3.

Michaels, S. (1981). "Sharing time": Children's narrative styles and differential access to literacy. *Language in Society, 10,* 423–442.

Mikulicky, L. (1990). National adult literacy and lifelong learning goals. *Phi Delta Kappan, 12,* 304–309.

Miller, S. R., & Schloss, P. J. (1982). *Career-vocational education for handicapped youth.* Rockville, MD: Aspen.

Mitchell, R. (1992). *Testing for learning: How new approaches to evaluation can improve American schools.* New York: Free Press.

Mithaug, D. E., Martin, J., & Stewart, J. (1990). *The prevocational assessment and curriculum guide.* Seattle, WA: Exceptional Education.

Mithaug, D. E., Martin, J., & Agran, M. (1987). Adaptability instruction: The goal of transition programming. *Exceptional Children, 53,* 500–505.

Mohanty, C., Russo, A., & Torres. L. (1991). *Third world women and the politics of feminism.* Bloomington, IN: University of Indiana Press.

Monsour, M., & Talan, C. (1993). *Library-based family literacy projects.* New York: American Library Association.

Montague, M. (1988). Job-related social skills training for adolescents with handicaps. *Career Development for Exceptional Individuals, 11,* 26–41.

Monteith, M. K. (1980). How well does the average American read? Some facts figures and opinions. *Journal of Reading, 23,* 460–464.

Montero-Sieburth, M. (1990). The education of Hispanic adults: Pedagogical strands and cultural meanings. In B. B. Cassara (Ed.), *Adult education in a multicultural society* (pp. 96–118). New York: Routledge.

Moore, D. W., Moore, S. A., Cunningham, P. M., & Cunningham, J. W. (1994). *Developing readers and writers in the content areas* (2nd ed.). New York: Longman.

Moores, D. F. (1980). Alternative communication modes: Visual-motor systems. In R. Schiefelbusch (Ed.), *Nonspeech language and communication: Analysis and intervention* (pp. 27–47). Austin, TX: PRO-ED.

Morgan, C. T. (1990). More than the three 'R's': The development of Black adult education in Manhattan. In B. Benner Cassara (Ed.), *Adult education in a multicultural society* (pp. 63–77). New York: Routledge.

Murphy, S. T., & Rogan, P. M. (1995). *Closing the shop: Conversion from sheltered to integrated work.* Baltimore: Brookes.

Nakanishi, D. T. (1990). Asian Pacific Americans and adult education: The social and political resocialization of a diverse immigrant and refugee population. In B. Benner Cassara (Ed.), *Adult education in a multicultural society* (pp. 119–146). New York: Routledge.

Naslund, R. A., Thorpe, L. P., & Lefever, D. W. (1981). *SRA achievement series.* Chicago: Science Research.

National Advisory Council on Adult Literacy. (1986). *Illiteracy in America: Extent, causes and suggested solutions.* Washington, DC: U. S. Government Printing Office.

National Center for Youth with Disabilities. (1993). *Teenagers at risk: A national perspective for state level services for adolescents with chronic illness or disability.* Minneapolis, MN: University of Minnesota.

National Collaboration for Youth. (1989). *Making the grade: A report card on American Youth.* Albany NY: Boyd.

National Indian Council on Aging. (1981). *American Indian elderly: A national profile.* Albuquerque: Author.

Neel, R. S., & Billingsley, R. E. (1989). IMPACT: *A functional curriculum handbook for students with moderate to severe disabilities.* Baltimore: Brookes.

Negrin, G. A., & Drugler, D. (1980). Essential literacy skills for functioning in an urban community. *Journal of Reading, 24,* 109–115.

Newman, A. P., & Beverstock, C. (1990). *Adult literacy.* Newark, DE: International Reading Association.

Newman, S., Vander Ver, D., & Ward, C. (1991). *Guidelines for the productive employment of older adults in child care.* Pittsburgh, PA: University of Pittsburgh Press.

Newton, E. S. (1980). Understanding the adult as a learner. In L. Johnson (Ed.), *Reading and the adult learner* (pp. 3–6). Newark, DE: International Reading Association.

Nickse, R. S. (1990). Family literacy programs: Ideas for action. *Adult Learning, 1*, 9–13.

Nisbet, J., Covert, S., & Schuh, M. (1992). Family involvement in the transition from school to adult life. In F. R. Rusch, L. Destefano, J. Chadsey-Rusch, L. A. Phelps, & E. Szymanski (Eds.), *Transition from school to adult life: Models, linkages, and policy* (pp. 407–424). Sycamore, IL: Sycamore.

Nolan, T. E. (1991). Self-questioning and prediction: Combining metacognitive strategies. *Journal of Reading, 35,* 132–138.

Nutt, L. M., & Malone, M. (1992). Gerontology. In P. J. McLaughlin & P. Wehman (Eds.), *Developmental disabilities: A handbook for best practices* (pp. 277–297). Stoneham, MA: Andover.

O'Connell, J. C. (1985). A family systems approach for serving rural, reservation Native American communities. *Journal of American Indian Education, 24*(2), 1–6.

O'Connell, J. C. (Ed.). (1987). *A study of the special problems and needs of American Indians with handicaps both on and off the reservation: Vol. 1. Executive summary.* Flagstaff, AZ: Native American Research and Training Center.

O'Connor, S. (1993). "I'm not Indian anymore": The challenge of providing culturally sensitive services to American Indians. In J. A. Racino, P. Walker, S. O'Connor, & S. J. Taylor (Eds.), *Housing, Support, and Community: Choices and strategies for adults with disabilities* (Vol. 2, pp. 313–331). Baltimore: Brookes.

Older American Act of 1965 as Amended through 12/88. (1989). *(U. S. House of Representatives Committee Print Serial No. 101A & U.S. Senate Special Committee on Aging Serial No. 101-B).* Washington, DC: U.S. Government Printing Office.

Orlich, D. C., Harder, R. J., Callahan, R. C., Kravas, C. H., Kauchak, D. P., Pendergrass, R. A., & Keogh, A J. (1985). *Teaching strategies* (2nd ed.). Lexington, MA: Heath.

Packer, A. H., & Campbell, W. L. (1990). Using computer technology for adult literacy instruction: Realizing the potential. In F. P. Chisman (Ed.), *Leadership for literacy: The agenda for the 1990s* (pp. 122–143). San Francisco: Jossey-Bass.

Pai, Y. (1990). Cultural pluralism, democracy and multicultural education. In B. B. Cassara (Ed.), *Adult Education in a multicultural society* (pp. 11–27). New York: Routledge.

Palincsar, A. S., & David, Y. M. (1991). Promoting literacy through classroom dialogue. In E. H. Hiebert (Ed.), *Literacy for a diverse society* (pp. 122–140). New York: Teachers College Press.

Parent, W. (1992). Quality of life and consumer choice. In Paul Wehman (Ed.), *The ADA mandate for social change* (pp. 19–41). Baltimore: Brookes.

Parent, W. S., Sherron, P., & Groah, C., (1992). Consumer assessment, job development, and job placement. In P. Wehman, P. Sale, & W. Parent (Eds.), *Supported employment: Strategies for integration of workers with disabilities* (pp. 105–148). Boston: Andover.

Parry, J. (1993). Title I—Employment. In L. O. Gostin & H. A. Beyer (Eds.), *Implementing the Americans with Disabilities Act: Rights and responsibilities of all Americans* (pp. 57–74). Baltimore: Brookes.

Paul, M. (1986). Reading after survival literacy: Language immersion and an idea from Confucius. *Journal of Reading, 29,* 423–427.

Paulson, F. L., Paulson, P. R., & Meyer, C. A. (1991). What makes a portfolio a portfolio? *Educational Leadership, 48,* 590–591.

Peraino, J. M. (1992). Post-21 follow-up studies: How do special education graduates fare? In Wehman, P. (Ed.), *Life beyond the classroom: Transition strategies for young people with disabilities* (pp. 21–70). Baltimore: Brookes.

Perez, B., & Torres-Guzman, M. E. (1992). *Learning in two worlds: An integrated Spanish/English biliteracy approach.* New York: Longman.

Perry, W. B. (1968). *Forms of intellectual and ethical development in the college years: A scheme.* New York: Holt, Rinehart, & Winston.

Pesta, J. (1994). Assistive, adaptive, amazing technologies. *Technos, 3*(2), 10–12.

Peterson, R., & Eeds, M. (1990). *Grand conversations: Literature groups in action.* New York: Scholastic.

Peyton, J., & Reed, L (1990). *Dialogue journal writing with nonnative English speakers: A handbook for teachers.* Alexandria, VA: Teachers of English to Speakers of Other Languages.

Pflaum, S. W. (1896). *The development of language and literacy in young children* (3rd ed.). Columbus, OH: Merrill.

Philips, S. U. (1972). Participant structures and communicative competence: Warm Springs children in community and classroom. In C. B. Cazden, V. P. John, & D. Hymes (Eds.), *Functions of language in the classroom* (pp. 370–394). New York: Teachers College Press.

Philips, S. U. (1983). *The invisible culture: Communication in the classroom and community on the Warm Springs Indian Reservation.* New York: Longman.

Piaget, J. (1970). Piaget's theory. In P. H. Mussen (Ed.), *Carmichael's manual of child psychology* (3rd ed., Vol. 1, pp. 703–732). New York: Wiley.

Piaget, J. (1972). Intellectual evolution from adolescence to adulthood. *Human Development, 15,* 1–12.

Pipes, M. A., Westby, C. E., & Ingelbret, E. (1993). Profile of Native American students. In L. W. Clark & D. E. Waltzman (Eds.), *Faculty and student challenges in facing cultural and linguistic diversity* (pp. 137–172). Springfield, IL: Thomas.

Polloway, E. A., & Smith, T. E. C. (1992). *Language instruction for students with disabilities.* Denver, CO: Love.

Porter, K. H. (1989). *Poverty in rural America: A national overview.* Washington, DC: Center on Budget and Policy Priorities.

Powell, T. H., Pancsofor, E. L., Steere, D. E., Butterworth, J., Itzkowitz, J. S., & Rainforth, B. (1991). *Supported employment: Providing integrated employment opportunities for persons with disabilities.* White Plains, NY: Longman.

Psychological Corporation (1992a). *Stanford Achievement Test.* San Antonio, TX: Psychological Corp.

Psychological Corporation (1992b). *Test of Academic Skills* (3rd ed.). San Antonio, TX: Psychological Corp.

Quicke, J. (1985). *Disability in modern children's fiction.* Brookline, MA: Brookline.

Ramirez, B. A. (1988). Culturally and linguistically diverse children. *Teaching Exceptional Children, 20*(4), 45.

Rankin, J. L., & Allen, J. L. (1991). Investigating the relationship between cognition and social thinking in adulthood: Stereotyping and attributional processes. In J. D. Sinnott & J. C. Cavanaugh (Eds.), *Bridging paradigms: Positive development in adulthood and cognitive aging* (pp. 137–172). New York: Praeger.

Raskind, M. H. (1994). Assistive technology for adults with learning disabilities: A rationale for use. In P. J. Gerber & H. B. Reiff (Eds.), *Learning disabilities in adulthood: Persisting problems and evolving issues* (pp. 152–167). Stoneham, MA: Andover.

Razeghi, J., Kokaska, C., Gruenhagen, K., & Fair, G. (1987). *The transition of youth with disabilities to adult life: A position statement of the Division on Career Development: The Council for Exceptional Children*, Reston, VA: Council for Exceptional Children.

Readence, J. E., Bean, T. W., & Baldwin, R. S. (1992). *Content area reading: An integrated approach* (4th ed.). Dubuque, IA: Kendall-Hunt.

Reid, R. C., Allard, K. E., & Hofmeister, A. M. (1993). The SECTOR courseware evaluation form. In J. D. Lindsey (Ed.), *Computers and exceptional individuals* (2nd ed., pp. 389–393). Austin, TX: PRO-ED.

Retish, P., Hitchings, W., Horvath, M., & Schmalle, B. (1991). *Students with mild disabilities in the secondary school.* New York: Longman.

Rhodes, L. K. & Natehson-Mejia, S. (1992). Anecdotal records: A powerful tool for ongoing literacy assessment. *The Reading Teacher, 45*, 502–509.

Rice, P. R., & Feldman, J. F. (1983). Living longer in the United States: Demographic changes and health needs of the elderly. *Health and Society, 61*, 362–396.

Richards, L., & Smith, Q. (1992). Independent living centers in rural communities. *Rural Special Education Quarterly, 11*(1), 5–10.

Richardson, J. S., & Morgan, R. F. (1994). *Reading to learn in the content areas* (2nd ed.). Belmont CA: Wadsworth.

Riches, V. C. (1993). *Standards of work performance: A functional assessment and training manual for training people with disabilities for employment.* Sydney, Australia: Maclennan & Petty.

Rigg, P., & Kazemek, F. (1983). Literacy and elders: What we know and what we need to know. *Educational Gerontology, 9*, 417–424.

Riggs, P., & Allen, V. (1989). *When they don't all speak English: Integrating the ESL student into the regular classroom.* Urbana, IL: National Council of Teachers of English.

Rinsky, L. A. (1993). *Teaching word recognition skills.* Scottsdale, AZ: Gorsuch Scarisbrick.

Robeck, M. C., & Wallace, R. R. (1990). *The psychology of reading: An interdisciplinary approach* (2nd ed.). Hillsdale, NJ: Erlbaum.

Robinson, R. D., & Bernazza-Haase, A. M. (1979). The reading process and the elderly. *Educational Gerontology, 4*, 223–228.

Rogler, L. H., Cortes, D. E., & Malady, R. G. (1991). Acculturation and mental health status among Hispanics. *American Psychologist, 46*, 585–597.

Rosenberg, M. S., & Edmond-Rosenberg, I. (1994). *The special education sourcebook: A teacher's guide to programs, materials, and information sources.* Bethesda, MD: Woodbine.

Rosow, L. V. (1990). Consumer advocacy, empowerment, and adult literacy. *Journal of Reading, 34,* 258–261.

Ross, E. P. (1989). How to use the whole language approach. *Adult Learning, 10,* 23–24.

Rothwell, W. J., & Brandenburg, D. C. (1990). *The workplace literacy primer: An action manual for training and development professionals.* Amherst, MA: HRD.

Rousculp, E. E., & Maring, G. H. (1992). Portfolios for a community of learners. *Journal of Reading, 35,* 378–385.

Rueda, R. (1991). Characteristics of literacy programs for language-minority students. In E. H. Hiebert (Ed.), *Literacy for a diverse society* (pp. 93–107). New York: Teachers College Press.

Runion, K., & Gregory, H. (1984). Special populations: Training Native Americans to deliver mental health services to their own people. *Counselor Education and Supervision, 23,* 225–233.

Rybash, J. M., Hoyer, W. J., & Roodin, P. A. (1986). *Adult cognition and aging: Developmental changes in processing, knowing, and thinking.* New York: Pergamon.

Salend, S. J. (1990). A migrant education guide for special education. *Teaching Exceptional Children, 22*(2), 18–21.

Salthouse, T. A. (1990). Cognitive competence and expertise in aging. In J. E. Birren & K. W. Schaie (Eds.), *Handbook of the psychology of aging* (3rd ed., pp. 310–319). San Diego, CA: Academic Press.

Salvia, J., & Ysseldyke, J. E. (1995). *Assessment* (6th ed.). Boston, MA: Houghton Mifflin.

Sattler, J. M. (1988). *Assessment of children* (3rd ed.). San Diego, CA: Sattler.

Schaafsma, D. (1993). *Eating on the street: Teaching literacy in a multicultural society.* Pittsburgh, PA: University of Pittsburgh.

Schaie, K. W. (1990). Intellectual development in adulthood. In J. E. Birren & K. W. Schaie (Eds.), *Handbook of the psychology of aging* (3rd ed., pp. 291–309). San Diego, CA: Academic Press.

Schloss, P. J., Smith, M. A., & Schloss, C. N. (1995). *Instructional methods for adolescents with learning and behavior problems* (2nd ed.). Needham Heights, MA: Allyn & Bacon.

Schwartz, H. J. (1992). "Dominion everywhere": Computers as cultural artifacts. In M. C. Tuman (Ed.), *Literacy Online: The promise (and peril) of reading and writing with computers* (pp. 95–108). Pittsburgh, PA: University of Pittsburgh Press.

Scully, M. J., & Johnston, C. L. (1991). The use of an educational therapy model with an illiterate adult. *Journal of Reading, 35,* 126–131.

Searfoss, L. W., & Readence, J. E. (1994). *Helping children learn to read* (3rd ed.), Needham Heights, MA: Allyn & Bacon.

Shapiro, J. P., Loed, P., Bouermaster, D., Wright, A., Headden, S., & Toch, T. (1993, December 13). Separate and unequal: Examining special education. *U.S. News and World Report,* 46–60.

Sharp, P. (1991). Picture books in the adult literacy curriculum. *Journal of Reading, 35,* 216–219.

Sharp, Q. Q. (1989). *Evaluation: Whole language checklists for evaluating your children for grades K to 6.* New York: Scholastic.

Sharpton, W. R., & West, M. D. (1992). Severe and profound mental retardation. In P. J. McLauglin & P. Wehman (Eds.), *Developmental disabilities: A handbook for best practices* (pp. 16–29). Stoneham, MA: Andover.

Sheehy, G. (1976). *Passages: Predictable crises of adult life.* New York: Dutton.

Silverman, F. (1980). *Communication for the speechless.* Englewood Cliffs, NJ: Prentice-Hall.

Silverman, H., McNaughton, S., & Kates, B. (1978). *Handbook of Blissymbolics for instructors, Bliss symbol users, parents and administrators.* Toronto, Canada: Blissymbolics Communication Institute.

Simmons, J. (1990). Portfolios as large-scale assessment. *Language Arts, 67,* 262–268.

Simonton, K. S. (1988). *Scientific genius: A psychology of science.* Cambridge, MA: Cambridge University.

Simonton, K. S. (1990). Creativity and wisdom in aging. In J. E. Birren & K. W. Schaie (Eds.), *Handbook of the psychology of aging* (3rd ed., pp. 320–329). San Diego, CA: Academic Press.

Simpson, J. M. (1990). Service to the handicapped. In K. M. Heim & D. P. Wallace (Eds.), *Adult services: An enduring focus for public libraries* (pp. 372–406). Chicago: American Library Association.

Singer, H. (1978, May). Active comprehension: From answering to asking questions, *The Reading Teacher, 32,* 903.

Sitlington, P. L., & Okolo, C. (1987). Statewide survey of vocational educators: Attitudes, training, and involvement with handicapped learners. *Journal of Career Development, 13,* 21–29.

Skagen, A. (Ed.). (1986). *Workplace literacy.* New York: American Management Association.

Skutnabb-Kangas, T. (1981). *Bilingualism or not: The education of minorities.* Clevedon, England: Multilingual Matters.

Slavin, R. E., Madden, N. A., Karweit, N. L., Dolan, L. J., & Wasik, B. A. (1994). Success for all: Getting reading right the first time. In E. H. Hiebert & B. M Taylor (Eds.), *Getting reading right from the start: Effective early literacy interventions* (pp. 125–147). Needham Heights, MA: Allyn & Bacon.

Sleeter, C. E., & Grant, C. A. (1987). An analysis of multicultural education in the United States. *Harvard Educational Review, 57,* 421–444.

Smallwood, B. (1991). *The literature connection: A read-aloud guide from multicultural classrooms.* Reading, MA: Addison-Wesley.

Smith, G. J., & Edelen-Smith, P. J. (1993). Restructuring secondary special education Hawaiian style. *Intervention in School and Clinic, 28,* 248–252, 256.

Smith, J., & Dauer, V. L. (1984). A comprehension monitoring strategy for reading content area materials. *Journal of Reading, 28,* 144–147.

Smith, T. E. C., Polloway, E. A., Patton, J. R., & Dowdy, C. A. (1995). *Teaching students with special needs in inclusive settings.* Needham Heights, MA: Allyn & Bacon.

Smull, M. W., & Danehey, A. J. (1994). Increasing quality while reducing costs: The challenge of the 1990s. In V. J. Bradley, J. W. Ashbaugh, & B. C. Blaney (Eds.), *Creating individual supports for people with developmental disabilities: A mandate for change at many levels* (pp. 59–78). Baltimore: Brookes.

Soifer, R., Irwin, M. E., Crumrine, B. M., Honzaki, E., Simmons, B. K., & Young, D. L. (1990). *The Complete theory-to-practice handbook of adult literacy: Curriculum design and teaching approaches.* New York: Teachers College Press.

Sowers, J., & Powers, L. (1991). *Vocational preparation and employment of students with physical and multiple disabilities.* Baltimore: Brookes.

Spache, G. D. (1981). *Diagnostic Reading Scales.* New York: McGraw-Hill.

Sparrow, S. S., & Cicchetti, D. V. (1978). Behavior rating scale inventory for moderately, severely, and profoundly retarded persons. *American Journal of Mental Deficiency, 82,* 365–374.

Stasz, B. B., Schwartz, R. G., & Weeden, J. C. (1991). Writing our lives: An adult basic skills program. *Journal of Reading, 35,* 30–33.

Stedman, L. C., & Kaestle, C. F. (1991). Literacy and reading performance in the United States from 1880 to the present. In L. C. Stedman & C. F. Kaestle (Eds.), *Literacy in the United States: Readers and reading since 1880* (pp. 75–128). New Haven, CT: Yale University Press.

Steinhoff, C. R., & Lyons, T. S. (1993). The hardware domain. In J. D. Lindsey (Ed.), *Computers and exceptional individuals* (2nd ed., pp. 27–44). Austin, TX: PRO-ED.

Stuecher, U., Grossman, E., Hakala, N., & Kizlowski, G. (1985). Training project for Indian school liaison and support personnel in special education. *Journal of American Indian Education, 24,* 9–19.

Sullivan, P. M., & Vernon, M. (1979). Psychological assessment of hearing impaired children. *School Psychology Review, 8,* 271–290.

Super, D. E. (1953). A theory of vocational development. *American Psychologist, 8,* 185–190.

Szymanski, E. M., Turner, K. D., & Hershenson, D. B. (1992). Career development and work adjustment of persons with disabilities: Theoretical perspectives and implications for transition. In F. R. Rusch, L. Destefano, J. Chadsey-Rusch, L. A. Phelps, & E. Szymanski (Eds.), *Transition from school to adult life: Models, linkages, and policy* (pp. 391–406). Sycamore, IL: Sycamore.

Taylor, S. J., & Bogdan, R. (1993). Promises made and promises to be broken. In Paul Wehman (Ed.), *The ADA mandate for social change* (pp. 255–268). Baltimore: Brookes.

Tesconi, C. A. (1990). Multiculturalism in education: The importance of meaning. In B. B. Cassara (Ed.), *Adult Education in a multicultural society* (pp. 28–44). New York: Routledge.

Tharp, R., & Gallimore, R. (1988). *Rousing minds to life: Teaching learning and schooling in social context.* New York: Cambridge University Press.

Thielke, H. M., & Shriberg, L. D. (1990). Effects of recurrent Otitis Media on language, speech, and educational achievement in Menominee Indian children. *Journal of American Indian Education, 29* (2), 25–35.

Thousand, J. S., & Villa, R. A. (1993). Strategies for educating learners with severe disabilities within their local home schools and communities. In E. L. Meyen, G. A. Vergason, & R. J. Whelan (Eds.), *Challenges facing special education* (pp. 285–322). Denver, CO: Love.

Thurman, E. (1986). Maintaining dignity in later years. In J. A. Summers (Ed.), *The right to grow up: An introduction to adults with developmental disabilities* (pp. 91–115). Baltimore: Brookes.

Tippeconnic, J. W. (1990). Adult education and the American Indian. In B. Benner Cassara (Ed.), *Adult education in a multicultural society* (pp. 78–95). New York: Routledge.

Trapani, C. (1990). *Transition goals for adolescents with learning disabilities.* Austin, TX: PRO-ED.

Traustadottir, R., Lutfiyya, Z. M., & Shoultz, B. (1994). Community living: A multicultural perspective. In M. F. Hayden & B. H. Abery (Eds.), *Challenges for a service system in transition: Ensuring quality community experiences for persons with developmental disabilities* (pp. 405–426). Baltimore: Brookes.

Troll, L. (1982). *Continuations: Adult development and aging.* Monterey, CA: Brookes-Cole.

Tuman, M. C. (1992). First thoughts. In M. C. Tuman (Ed.), *Literacy Online: The promise (and peril) of reading and writing with computers* (pp. 3–15). Pittsburgh, PA: University of Pittsburgh Press.

Turnbull, H. R., Bateman, D. F., & Turnbull, A. P. (1993). Family empowerment. In Paul Wehman (Ed.), *The ADA mandate for social change* (pp. 157–173). Baltimore: Brookes.

Turock, B. J. (1982). *Serving the older adult: A guide to library programs and information sources.* New York: Bowker.

U. S. Bureau of Census (1991). *1990 census of the population.* Washington, DC: Author.

U. S. Department of Labor, Department of Education, & Commerce (1988). *Building a quality workforce.* Washington, DC: U. S. Government Printing Office.

Usher, R., & Bryant I. (1989). *Adult education as theory, practice, and research: The captive triangle.* New York: Routledge.

Vacca, J. L., & Sparks, C. (1981). The evaluation of adults seeking improvement in reading. *Reading World, 20,* 197–200.

Vaillant, G. (1977). *Adaption to life.* Boston, MA: Little, Brown.

Valeri-Gold, M., Olson, J. R., & Deming, M. P. (1991). Portfolios: Collaborative authentic assessment opportunities for college developmental learners. *Journal of Reading, 35,* 298–305.

Van Fleet, C. (1990). Lifelong learning theory and the provision of adult services. In K. M. Heim & D. P Wallace (Eds.), *Adult services: An enduring focus for public libraries* (pp. 166–211). Chicago: American Library Association.

Wallace, G. L. (1993). Profile of African American students. In L. W. Clark & D. E. Waltzman (Eds.), *Faculty and student challenges in facing cultural and linguistic diversity* (pp. 63–87). Springfield, IL: Thomas.

Wallace, G., Larsen, S. C., & Elksnin, L. K. (1992). *Educational assessment of learning problems: Testing for Teaching* (2nd ed.). Needham Heights, MA: Allyn & Bacon.

Walz, T., Harper, D., & Wilson, J. (1986). The aging developmentally disabled person: A review. *The Gerontologist, 26*(6), 622–629.

Wangberg, E. G. (1986). An interactive, language experienced based microcomputer approach to reduce adult illiteracy. *Lifelong Learning, 9,* 8–12.

Washburn, W. (1994). *Vocational entry-skills for secondary and adult students with learning disabilities: A teacher's guide to implementing the ITP.* Novato, CA: Academic Therapy.

Wehman, P. (1992). *Life beyond the classroom: Transition strategies for young people with disabilities.* Baltimore: Brookes.

Wehman, P. (1993). Employment opportunities and career development. In P. Wehman (Ed.), *The ADA mandate for social change* (pp. 45–68). Baltimore: Brookes.

Wehman, P. (1994). Transition from school to adulthood for young people with disabilities: Critical issues and policies. In R. C. Eaves & P. J. McLaughlin (Eds.), *Recent advances in special education and rehabilitation* (pp. 178–192). Stoneham, MA: Andover.

Wehman, P., & McLaughlin, P. J. (1990). *Vocational curriculum for developmentally disabled persons.* Austin, TX: PRO-ED.

Wehman, P., Sale, P., & Parent, W. (1992). Vocational integration. In P. Wehman, P. Sale, & W. Parent (Eds.), *Supported employment: Strategies for integration of workers with disabilities* (pp. 215–240). Boston: Andover.

Weisgerber, R. A. (1989). *Social competence and employability skills curriculum.* Rockville, MD: Aspen.

Weisgerber, R. A. (1991). *Quality of life for persons with disabilities: Skill development and transitions across life stages.* Gaithersburg, MD: Aspen.

Welch, A. R., & Freebody, P. (1993). Introduction: Explanations of the current international "literacy crises." In P. Freebody & A. R. Welch (Eds.), *Knowledge, culture and power: International perspectives on literacy as policy and practice* (pp. 6–22). Pittsburgh, PA: University of Pittsburgh Press.

Werner, P. H. (1992). Integrated assessment system. *Journal of Reading, 35,* 416–418.

West, J. (1993). The evolution of disability rights. In L. O. Gostin & H. A. Beyer (Eds.), *Implementing the Americans with Disabilities Act: Rights and responsibilities of all Americans* (pp. 3–15). Baltimore: Brookes.

West, L. L., (1991) Introduction. In L. L. West (Ed.), *Effective strategies for dropout prevention of at-risk youth* (pp. 1–42), Austin, TX: PRO-ED.

Wiederholt, J. L., & Bryant, B. R. (1993). *Gray Oral Reading Tests—3.* Austin. TX: PRO-ED.

Wiederholt, J. L., & Dunn, C. (1995). Transition from school to independent living. In D. D. Hammill & N. R. Bartel (Eds.), *Teaching students with learning and behavior problems: Managing mild-to-moderate difficulties in resource and inclusive settings* (6th ed., pp. 381–417). Austin, TX: PRO-ED.

Wilkinson, G. S. (1993). *Wide Range Achievement Test—3.* Wilmington, DE: Jastak Associates.

Will, M. (1984). *OSERS programming for the transition of youth with disabilities: Bridges from school to working life.* Washington, DC: Office of Special Education and Rehabilitative Services.

Williams, J. D., & Capizzi-Snipper, G. (1990). *Literacy and bilingualism.* New York: Longman.

Willinsky, J. (1990). *The new literacy: Redefining reading and writing in the schools.* New York: Routledge.

Willis, S. L., & Schaie, K. W. (1986). Practical intelligence in later adulthood. In R. J. Sternberg & R. K. Wagner (Eds.), *Practical intelligence: Origins of competence in the everyday world* (pp. 236–268). London: Cambridge.

Wilson, W. J. (1989). *The truly disadvantaged: The inner city, the underclass, and public policy.* Chicago: University of Chicago Press.

Wircenski, J. (1992). *The transitions skills guide: An integrated curriculum with reading and math materials.* Gaithersburg, MD: Aspen.

Witt, J. C., Elliott, S. N., Kramer, J. J., & Gresham, F. M. (1994). *Assessment of children: Fundamental methods and practices.* Madison, WI: Brown & Benchmark.

Wolery, M. (1993). Transitions in early childhood special education: Issues and procedures. In E. L. Meyen, G. A. Vergason, & R. J. Whelan (Eds.), *Challenges facing special education* (pp. 5–25). Denver, CO: Love.

Wolfe, P. A. (1992). Challenges for service providers. In P. J. McLaughlin & P. Wehman (Eds.), *Developmental disabilities: A handbook for best practice* (pp. 124–141). Boston: Andover.

Wollman-Bonilla, J. (1991). *Response journals.* New York: Scholastic.

Wong, B. Y. L. (1991).The relevance of metacognition to learning disabilities. In B. Y. L. Wong (Ed.), *Learning about learning disabilities* (pp. 231–258). San Diego, CA: Academic Press.

Woodcock, R. W. (1987). *Woodcock Reading Mastery Tests—Revised.* Circle Pines, MN: American Guidance Service.

Woodcock, R. W., & Johnson, M. B. (1989). *Woodcock-Johnson Psychological Battery—Revised.* Allen, TX: DLM.

Woodward, J., & Gersten, R. (1992). Innovative technology for secondary students with learning disabilities. *Exceptional Children, 59,* 407–421.

Woolcock, W. W. (1990). Generalization strategies. In P. Wehman & J. S. Kreutzer (Eds.), *Vocational rehabilitation for persons with traumatic brain injury* (pp. 243–268). Rockville, MD: Aspen.

Woolman, D. H. (1980). A presymbolic training program. In R. Schiefelbusch (Ed.), *Nonspeech language and communication: Analysis and intervention* (pp. 67–103). Austin, TX: PRO-ED.

Workplace illiteracy: Economic time bomb? (1989, July). *Compressed Air Magazine,* pp. 24–28.

Ylvisaker, M., Szekeres, S. F., Harwick, P., & Tworek, P. (1994). Cognitive intervention. In R. C. Savage & G. F. Wolcott (Eds.) *Educational dimensions of acquired brain injury* (pp. 121–184). Austin, TX: PRO-ED.

Yukl, T. (1986). Cultural responsiveness and social work practice: An Indian clinic's success. *Health and Social Work, 11,* 223–229.

Zeien, K., & Anderson, B. (1993). *Bridges: Making the transition from school to work.* Portland, MA: Walch.

Ziegler, C. R. (1980). *The image of the physically handicapped in children's literature.* New York: Arno.

A

Materials for a Functional Reading Inventory

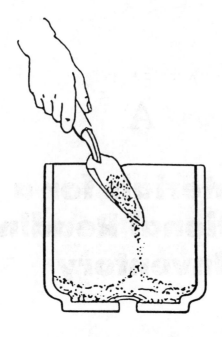

Repotting a House Plant

1. **Remove the plant from the original container.**
2. **Use a hammer to break an old pot into shards.**
3. **Cover the drainage hole with the pot shards. Add some soil. (See illustration.)**
4. **Place the plant in the center of the pot and fill around the sides with soil.**

Figure A-1. Instructions: How are pot shards used during transplanting? *(to cover the drainage hole)*

Oven Drying of Vegetables and Fruits

1. Vegetables and fruits can be dried in the oven of an ordinary kitchen range. But the oven's door must be left ajar. For electric ovens, leave the door ajar by placing a folded pot holder in a top corner to create an opening. Prop open the door of a gas oven with a twelve inch ruler. The opening lets out moist air.

2. Set the temperature regulator to 150 degrees for vegetables. During the last half of the drying period, reduce the temperature to 140 degrees. Most vegetables require at least four hours to dry.

3. Set the temperature regulator to 160 degrees for fruits. During the last half of the drying period, reduce the temperature to 150 degrees. Most fruits require at least six hours to dry.

Figure A–2. Instructions: At what temperature would one set the oven to begin drying an apple? *(160 degrees)*

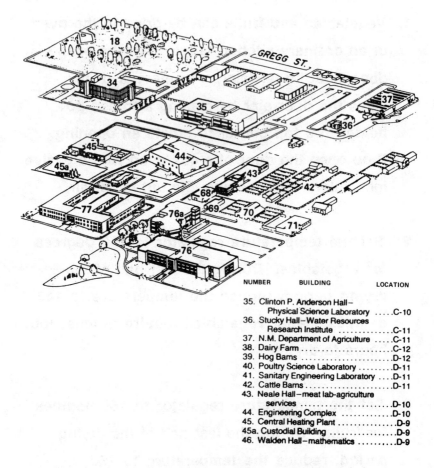

NUMBER	BUILDING	LOCATION

35. Clinton P. Anderson Hall –
    Physical Science Laboratory C-10
36. Stucky Hall – Water Resources
    Research Institute C-11
37. N.M. Department of Agriculture C-11
38. Dairy Farm C-12
39. Hog Barns D-12
40. Poultry Science Laboratory D-11
41. Sanitary Engineering Laboratory D-11
42. Cattle Barns D-11
43. Neale Hall – meat lab-agriculture
    services D-10
44. Engineering Complex D-10
45. Central Heating Plant D-9
45a. Custodial Building D-9
46. Walden Hall – mathematics D-9

Figure A-3.   Maps: How is building *42* used? *(cattle barns)*

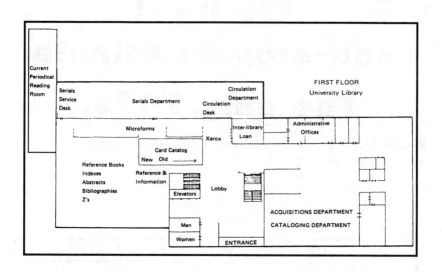

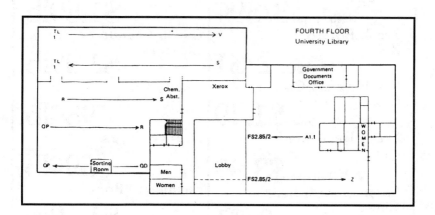

Figure A–4. Maps: On which floor are more departments located? *(first)*

Fly PELT
non-stop to Atlanta.
The only 747s.

Figure A–5. Advertisements: For what reason should one fly on this airline to Atlanta? *(nonstop flights or exclusive use of 747s)*

IN-STORE BAKERY	BULK FOODS
Fresh French Bread 1lb. Loaf 3/89¢	Tropical Mix $1.89lb.
Fresh Potato Rolls 12Ct. 2/$1	Carob Peanut Clusters $1.99lb.
Fresh Texas Coffee Cake 16oz. $1.49	Candy Corn 98¢lb.
Fresh Decorated Cake 2-8" Layers $3.99	Orange Slices 59¢lb.
Fresh Danish Bear Claws Each 3/$1	Raspberry Ropes $1.19lb.

Figure A–6. Advertisements: Which items are identified as *on sale* for reduced prices? *(none)*

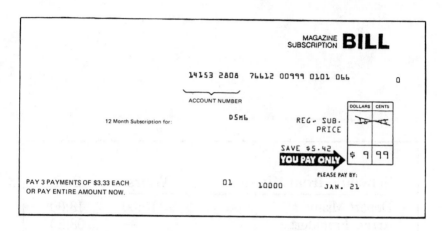

Figure A–7. Financial Statements: What is the smallest amount that can be paid toward this bill? *($3.33)*

```
000    PAYMENT RECEIVED  -  THANK YOU      12/28                Charges    Credits
100    PURGATORY SKI AREA DURANGO CO                                      10000
       INV#858                                                  4800
       CARD  73 - 9641 - 100 ---SUBTOTAL----->                 4800      10000



                                              PAGE  TOTAL      4800      10000
                                           ACCOUNT  TOTAL      4800      10000
```

Figure A–8. Financial Statements: How many items are charged to this account? *(one)*

Schedule from Miami	Thurs.	Sun.
Depart Miami	16:00	18:00
Arrive Frankfurt	—	08:50
Arrive Dusseldorf	06:50	10:30
Arrive Munich	09:15	—
from Germany	**Thurs.**	**Sun.**
Depart Munich	07:25	—
Depart Dusseldorf	09:50	09:40
Depart Frankfurt	—	11:10
Arrive Miami	13:50	15:40

Figure A–9. Schedules: If you wished to leave Munich on a Thursday, at what time would you depart? *(7:25 a.m.)*

ROUTE 1

Leave Transfer Point	Mulberry & Locus	Picacho & Melendres
6:15	6:25	6:35
6:45	6:55	7:05
7:15	7:25	7:35
7:45	7:55	8:05
8:15	8:25	8:35
8:45	8:55	9:05
9:15	9:25	9:35
9:45	9:55	10:05
10:15	10:25	10:35
10:45	10:55	11:05
11:15	11:25	11:35
11:45	11:55	12:05
12:15	12:25	12:35
12:45	12:55	1:05
1:15	1:25	1:35
1:45	1:55	2:05
2:15	2:25	2:35
2:45	2:55	3:05
3:15	3:25	3:35
3:45	3:55	4:05
4:15	4:25	4:35
4:45	4:55	5:05
5:15	5:25	5:35
5:45	5:55	6:05
6:15	6:25	6:35
6:45	6:55	7:05
7:15	7:25	7:35
7:45	7:55	8:05
8:15	8:25	8:35

Shaded areas DO NOT operate on Saturdays

Figure A-10. Schedules: On Saturday, what is the earliest time that one can catch a bus at Picacho and Melendres streets? *(8:35 a.m.)*

321

```
┌─────────────────────────────────────────────────────────────────┐
│ ☐ Please send me the new Catalog.                                 │
│    ☐ Enclosed is my check                                         │
│    ☐ Charge my $6 to   ☐ American Express   ☐ MasterCard   ☐ VISA │
│  Name (please print)                    Credit card number        │
│  _____    _____  │
│  Address                                Expiration date           │
│  _____    _____  │
│  City          State       Zip          Signature                │
│  _____    _____  │
│                                                                   │
│  Allow 4 weeks for delivery.                                      │
└─────────────────────────────────────────────────────────────────┘
```

Figure A–11.   Forms: In what ways can one pay for the catalog? *(check or credit card)*

```
┌─────────────────────────────────────────────┐
│        RENTAL FORM#  011720                   │
├─────────────────────────┬─────────────────────┤
│ DATE OUT                │ RETURN DATE         │
│                         │                     │
├─────────────────────────┴─────────────────────┤
│              CUSTOMER FILL IN                  │
│              USER INFORMATION                  │
│ NAME                                           │
│                                                │
│ ─────────────────────────────────────────────│
│ ADDRESS_____│
│                                                │
│ CITY _____│
│                                                │
│ STATE _____ZIP_____ │
│                                                │
│ DRIVERS LIC. _____│
│                                                │
│ CREDIT CARD _____             │
│                                    │  TYPE     │
│ HM PHONE _____   │           │
│                                    │  L  ☐     │
│ WK PHONE _____   │           │
│                                    │  A  ☐     │
│ SEX   │ WEIGHT │ HEIGHT │ AGE      │           │
│       │        │        │         │  S  ☐     │
├───────┴────────┴────────┴─────────┴───────────┤
│ WHAT DATE WILL YOU PICK                        │
│ THE EQUIPMENT UP?   .                          │
├────────────────────────────────────────────────┤
│ WHAT DATE WILL YOU                             │
│ RETURN THE EQUIPMENT?                          │
├────────────────────────────────────────────────┤
│ HOW MANY DAYS WILL YOU                         │
│ ACTUALLY USE THE EQUIPMENT?                    │
├────────────────────────────────────────────────┤
│ ARE YOU WITH A GROUP?  YES ☐  NO ☐             │
├────────────────────────────────────────────────┤
│ IF YES, WHAT IS THE NAME                       │
│ OF YOUR GROUP?                                 │
├────────────────────────────────────────────────┤
│        WHAT EQUIPMENT WILL YOU RENT?           │
│   SKIS ☐ SIZE_____        CAR RACK ☐          │
│   BOOTS ☐ SIZE_____                           │
│   POLES ☐ SIZE_____                           │
│   OTHER ☐ _____      │
└────────────────────────────────────────────────┘
```

Figure A-12.   Forms: What is a type of identification that is needed to rent ski equipment? *(driver's license or credit card)*

Figure A-13.   Road Signs: If you needed gas, for which sign would you look? *(gas pump)*

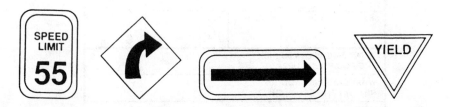

Figure A-14.   Road Signs: What would be the speed limit on a road along which all of these signs were located? *(55 miles per hour)*

Sardine Stuffed Eggs

12 hard-boiled eggs

12 sardines

2 Tbs. green onions, chopped

2 tsp. parsley, chopped

2 Tbs. butter

2 Tbs. sweet sherry

1 tsp. pepper

Cook and peel the 12 eggs. Cut them in half and remove the yolks. Chop the sardines. Add the chopped green onions and parsley. Melt the butter in a saucepan and add the sardine mixture, sherry, and pepper. Heat for a few minutes, stirring occasionally. Blend with the mashed egg yolks. Fill the egg whites with the mixture. Chill in the refrigerator for 30 minutes. Enjoy!

Figure A–15. Recipes: How many sardines would be needed if this recipe were doubled? *(24)*

High Altitude Cooking of Cake and Bread

At altitudes above 3500 feet, oven temperature should be increased by 25 degrees over the temperature that would be used at sea level. For example, cakes baked at 350 degrees at sea level should be baked at 375 degrees at all altitudes above 3500 feet.

In high altitudes, flour may become dry. In addition to increasing oven temperature, more liquid than that called for in the original recipes may be necessary.

Figure A-16. Recipes: If bread is baked at 400 degrees in low altitudes, what temperature would be used at altitudes above 3500 feet? *(425 degrees)*.

APPENDIX

B

Illustrations for Cued Reading Inventories

Figure B-1.   Cued reading inventory illustration: STOP

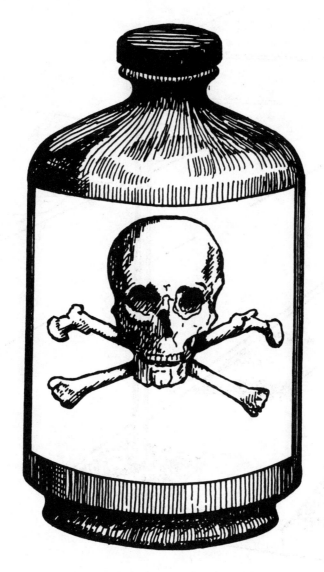

Figure B–2.   Cued reading inventory illustration: POISON

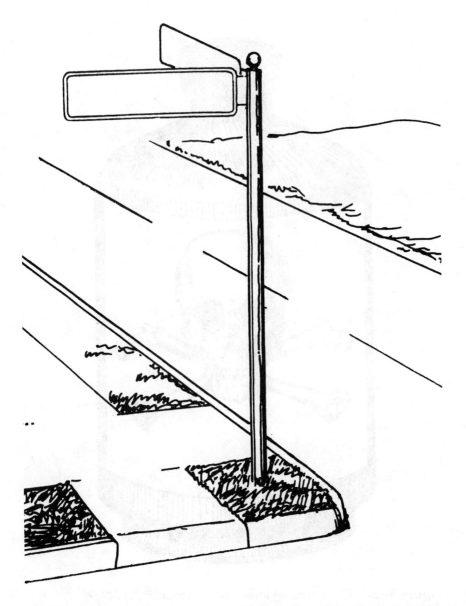

Figure B–3.   Cued reading inventory illustration: (NAME OF STREET)

Figure B–4. Cued reading inventory illustration: WOMEN

Figure B–5. Cued reading inventory illustration: MEN

Figure B–6.   Cued reading inventory illustration: ONE WAY

Figure B–7. Cued reading inventory illustration: HANDICAPPED

Figure B–8.   Cued reading inventory illustration: (TELEPHONE NUMBER)

Index